THOMAS HARDY AND HIS GOD

Thomas Hardy and His God

A Liturgy of Unbelief

Deborah L. Collins

*Lecturer, Department of English
University of California, Riverside*

St. Martin's Press   New York

© Deborah L. Collins 1990

All rights reserved. For information, write:
Scholarly and Reference Division,
St. Martin's Press, Inc., 175 Fifth Avenue,
New York, N.Y. 10010

First published in the United States of America in 1990

Printed in Hong Kong

ISBN 0-312-03673-6

Library of Congress Cataloging-in-Publication Data
Collins. Deborah L., 1951–
Thomas Hardy and his God: a liturgy of unbelief/ Deborah L. Collins.
p. cm.
Includes bibliographical references.
ISBN 0-312-03673-6
1. Hardy, Thomas, 1840–1928—Religion. 2. Belief and doubt in literature. 3. God in literature. I. Title.
PR4757. R4C65 1990
823'. 8—dc20 89-70306
CIP

For Gary and Lisa
with special thanks to
Ruth, Ed, Linda, Theresa and Angie

Contents

	Introduction	1
1.	The Complaining Door	15
2.	Nature, Darwin, and the Pattern in the Carpet	29
3.	The 'Great Adjustment': Evolutionary Meliorism in *The Dynasts*	56
4.	Freedom, Failure, and Fate: Reading the Web of Wessex	96
5.	Fascination and Forgiveness	122
6.	He Resolves to Say No More	146
	Notes and References	172
	Index	186

Introduction

> O God – if there is a God – save my
> Soul – if I have a soul.
> anonymous Victorian prayer

The second law of thermodynamics insists that as the universe continues to expand in space and time, so will disorder increase therein. The truth of this prediction is so simple and intuitive that man has always taken warning from its natural metaphors. Perhaps dreaming of an Eden wherein trimmed lawns and perennially blooming trees and gardens maintain themselves, early agrarians laboured under the back-breaking severity of this law in their daily struggle against strangling thistles, drought, flood, and voracious herbivores. Architects have long attempted to erect monuments embodying an ideal solution to the problem of encroaching entropy without sacrificing beauty to the ugly demands of utility. Philosophers have translated the law into abstract moral apothegms: Evil triumphs when good men do nothing, Edmund Burke has advised darkly. Scientists now hypothesise Grand Unification Theories in hopes of reconciling physics with itself, while taxonomists continue to classify chaos into genotypes and phenotypes and hierarchies of perfectly nested rings. The truth about Thomas Hardy, I shall argue in this book, is that as evolutionist, philosopher, humanitarian, and artist, he countered the law of increasing disorder by personalising it, scrutinising its formidable power, and bravely plotting its effects on the lives of ordinary men and women. Hardy's art emerges, as I will show that it must, as a polyphonic recapitulation and reinterpretation of his discovery that at the centre of man's growing despair and confusion is his inability to fathom the nature of God.

Hardy was not the first writer to establish this connection. At the outset of what he vowed would be his final series of lectures, Thomas Carlyle thundered at the crowd gathered to hear his discourse on *The Hero as Divinity* (1840) that 'a man's religion is the chief fact with regard to him'. He did not, of course, mean that a man's denominational preference is of any consequence, nor did he place much importance on the articles of faith he might endorse. Such professions are usually superficial expressions from a man's intellect, 'from the mere argumentative region of him', and rarely enlighten us to his degree of worth or worthlessness. A man's genuine religion, Carlyle argued, is essential and crucial to the man himself:

> But the thing a man does practically believe . . . the thing a man does practically lay to heart, and know for certain concerning his vital relations to this mysterious Universe, and his duty and destiny there, that is in all cases the primary thing for him, and creatively determines all the rest. That is his religion; or, it may be, his mere scepticism and no-religion: the manner it is in which he feels himself to be spiritually related to the Unseen World or No-World; and I say, if you tell me what that is, you tell me to a very great extent what the man is, what the kind of things he will do is.[1]

Born to a bricklayer and his wife in the remote backwater of Southern England less than a month after this lecture, Thomas Hardy demonstrated in life and in art that Carlyle's assertions were fundamentally correct. Hardy's spiritual relations to both the Unseen World and the No-World did indeed define what kind of man he would become and largely determined the kinds of things he would do. It is difficult to find in his canon a work – verse or fiction – which does not in some way address this 'chief fact' about Hardy; yet it is just as problematic to apprehend *what* it was he practically believed 'concerning his vital relations to this mysterious Universe'.

Because most critical readers have been taught to listen rhetorically to one persuasive voice at a time, it may well seem that, like Melville's confidence man, Hardy masked his true religious identity behind a number of guises. At the very least a superficial diagnosis might conclude that Hardy suffered from an embarrassment of riches in positing his views on the nature of the spiritual world. In a tentative voice, for instance, he aligns with Browning and Tennyson, the more optimistic of Victorian doubters, when he imagines in verse that earthly attempts at perfection will be redeemed in an afterlife in which his 'late irradiate soul' will 'Live on somewhere'.² Then in Arnoldian voice he rails against such 'Pippa Passes' dogmatism: 'The older one gets,' Hardy expostulates, 'the more deplorable seems the effect of that terrible, dogmatic ecclesiasticism – Christianity so called (but really Paulinism plus idolatry) – on morals and true religion: a dogma with which the real teaching of Christ has hardly anything in common.'³ A more reflective, Pater-like voice grants the possibility that men are condemned to mortality, but kindly and stoically, as though that fact was no tragedy, advises us to gather the best of each moment as it passes. Emulating the self-indulgent theme of Swinburne, Hardy grieves for those classical gods 'whom Christmas overthrew';⁴ and in a voice charged at once with courage and resignation, he casts his lot in favour of Mill's and Huxley's scientific humanism. If science reveals to man the sad, 'ghastly business' of how the universe operates, argues Hardy, it no less illuminates his desperate need for a rational worship of human ideals. As it stands, unfortunately:

> What is forced upon one . . . is the sad fact of the extent to which Theological lumber is still allowed to discredit religion, in spite of . . . devoted attempts . . . to shake it off. If the doctrines of the supernatural were quietly abandoned tomorrow by the Church, and 'reverence and love for an ethical ideal' alone retained, not one in ten thousand would object to the readjustment, while the enormous bulk of thinkers excluded by the old teaching would be brought into the fold, and our venerable old churches and cathedrals would become the centres of emotional life that they once were.⁵

Splintered into these many fragments, Hardy's canon may appear to be a logicless, senseless *discordia* of ideas and beliefs, and many readers have accused him of adding to the disorder in the universe. Michael Millgate, Hardy's definitive biographer, contends that like his hero in *A Laodicean* (1881), Hardy deliberately assumed an eclectic 'Laodiceanism' in his art which reflected in his personal 'reluctance to adopt absolute or even firm positions', his 'willingness to see virtue in all sides of a question', and pre-eminently in his 'insistence upon the provisionality of his opinions and the need to register them rather as a series of tentative impressions than as the systematic formulations of a philosopher'.⁶ Still, the majority of Hardy's contemporary critics were distressed at such curious diversity, for a poet without a creed, they argued, was like a scientist lacking a systematic philosophy: both were likely to limp about in confusion, disabled by their failure to commit themselves to one ideal. But for Hardy the days of creeds were 'as dead and done with as days of Pterodactyls'.⁷ To those who attempted to judge his writings against the articles of any pre-existing philosophy, he rather impatiently responded that his works of art were 'seemings, provisional impressions only, used for artistic purposes because they represent approximately the impressions of the age'.⁸ Until someone produced more plausible theories of the universe, Hardy would continue recording his 'unadjusted impressions' of life's phenomena as they occurred to him. Only in attending to the inconsistencies of the moment could one hope to discern a larger consistency in the whole of experience. Moreover, each man must develop his own philosophy according to his own peculiar experience.

But as an eminent, if not always admired, author Hardy continually formulated his private ideology in public, and, T. S. Eliot would later claim, at public expense. Although Hardy deeply believed in traditional Christian morality, he spoke at the same time with the tongue of a traditional heretic. The danger which Eliot recognised in Hardy's ambiguous art was that the public – largely uneducated and easily seduced – could not understand that writers who divest themselves of tradition and orthodoxy are only telling partial truths in their heresy. Speaking by his own admission as moralist rather than critic, Eliot accused Hardy of using his powerful position irresponsibly: 'He seems to me to have written as nearly for the sake of "self-expression" as a man well can; and the self which he had to express does not strike me as a particularly wholesome or edifying matter of communication.'⁹ Eliot's is gentle criticism, however. The brutal attacks Hardy received in his lifetime by those who failed to read beyond Jude's nihilism and Tess's sexuality, and who, not incidentally, failed miserably to hear the multiplicity of life-affirming voices present in the fiction as well, eventually forced the author into literary isolation.

Believing that he might escape further immolation, Hardy abandoned fiction for verse in 1896:

Perhaps I can express more fully in verse ideas and emotions which run counter to the inert crystallized opinion – hard as a rock – which the vast body of men have vested interests in supporting. To cry out in a passionate poem that . . . the Supreme Mover . . . the Prime Force . . . must be either limited in power, unknowing, or cruel – which is obvious enough, and has been for centuries – will cause them merely a shake of the head; but to put it in argumentative prose will make them sneer, or foam, and set all the literary contortionists jumping upon me, a harmless agnostic, as if I were a clamorous atheist, which in their crass illiteracy they seem to think is the same thing . . . . If Galileo had said in verse that the world moved, the Inquisition might have let him alone.[10]

Not so for Hardy. The world did not allow him to hypothesise with impunity simply because he had recast his medium of expression. The *discordia* of impressions recorded in his novels grew even more profuse in his poetry, and again the majority of common and critical readers listened primarily to the desperate voice. Hardy's critics demanded nothing short of a recantation of his provisional seemings and were enraged by his flat refusal to defer his bleak personal convictions to a more beneficial endorsement of optimism. The cost of his artistic intractability was exorbitant not only in terms of emotional distress but in professional validation as well: when the Poet Laureateship became vacant in 1913 and was awarded to the conservative Robert Bridges, Hardy mused in a letter to friend Edmund Gosse that his agnostic poem, 'God's Funeral', would have been singularly damning enough to crush his chances of filling the post.

Eliot's claim that Hardy wrote 'uncurbed by any institutional attachment or by submission to any objective beliefs' might be conceived as accurate if the standard of measurement is no more exacting than what Carlyle dismissed as the 'outworks of the man'. But the 'chief fact' regarding Hardy's internal, practical relation with the spiritual universe is only properly understood by considering that the catechism of his religion is the perpetual rehearsing of possible explanations for the nature and behaviour of the 'Prime Mover'. Such investigation necessarily produces conflicting evidence, and Hardy is regularly faulted for too often yoking together, rather than uniting, the heterogeneous strains of this liturgy. While I cannot defend Hardy on every count, I do believe that the majority of readers have failed to understand that in engaging Hardy we are also engaging a particularly convergent moment in history. The same is probably true to some extent for all authors and their literature, but Hardy's sense of the antinomy of his times is crucial to his art and his personal litany from which that art is drawn. If the voices narrating Hardy's fiction and verse are discordant, they are no more so than the spirit of the age into which he was born, the incongruent circumstances of his birth and childhood, and the irreconcilable public and private experiences of his life.

Even the most cursory observation of Victorian culture reveals the mid-nineteenth century to have been a time of transition and paradox in English history. Despite his command to 'Close thy Byron; Open thy Goethe', Carlyle had kept the Romantic spirit alive with his emphasis on transcendentalism and anti-materialism. At the same time, the rational outlook of the Age of Reason had resurfaced and gained new prominence under the utilitarian influence of the Benthamites and, in a more enlightened way, John Stuart Mill. In the clash of those ideologies, Edmund Burke's concept of a class-stratified society governed by *noblesse oblige* and Adam Smith's *laissez-faire* economics met head on. The casualties of that insoluble conflict were the masses of factory and displaced agricultural workers forced to accept starvation wages and squalid living conditions in return for establishing England as the world's wealthiest nation. While the retail value of British exports was quadrupling between 1842 and 1870, and the gross national income was well on its way to doubling between 1851 and 1881, Liverpool in the 1860s housed 66 000 labourers and their families for every square mile. By the dawning of the 1840s the flamboyant, dissolute self-indulgence of the Regency Period had begun to grate against the outward taboos of Victorian respectability. In response to this evolution of social consciousness occurred a shifting of literary paradigms as the 'silver fork' novels popular in the 1830s gave way to such angry protests as Charles Kingsley's *Alton Locke* and Elizabeth Gaskell's *Mary Barton*. The gap between the two nations of the rich and the poor, to borrow Disraeli's distinction, was widening and would continue to do so until the end of the 1860s when the Second Reform Bill enfranchised the manual labourer, doubling the electorate and reordering Great Britain's political structure to accommodate the common man.

The industrial revolution had incrementally separated past from present, but nothing set the ages in relief against each other more unequivocally than the construction of the railway. In 1860, after well over 7 000 miles of track had been etched through villages and across ancient landscapes, Thackeray was to brood over the implications of such progress, lamenting that the 'prae-railroad' existence once firm under his feet had been abruptly consigned to limbo: 'They have raised those railroad embankments up, and shut off the old world that was behind them. Climb up that bank on which the irons are laid, and look to the other side – it is gone.'[11] Passenger and mail coaches vanished, country inns, which for generations had functioned as vital community gathering places as well as refuelling stations, fell into decline and, within a few years, the provincialism which had sealed small, outlying counties inside their own cultures had virtually disappeared. In the space of a mere decade or two, a new nation had been literally sutured together out of fragments of the old, and, in some significant respects, at the latter's dear expense.

The advent of the railway was also responsible for the urbanisation of English life and as such was culpable, arguably, for one of civilisation's gravest blunders. By 1851 half the country's population had deserted the villages set against open fields and crowded into noisy, dirty cities in which factories and mills, slums and railway lines displaced trees and gardens, fashionable old neighbourhoods, artisans' shops, and, in increasing proportions, the irreplaceable architecture of man's history. Along with the explosion in urban habitation, especially in London and other large centres of industry and business, sprang up inner city rookeries in which flourished an expanse of poverty, filth, disease, drug abuse, child abuse and neglect, vice, and violent crime. The sinister cityscape depicted by Dickens in *Oliver Twist* loomed even more malignant by the mid-century when Melville's naive sailor, Redburn, discovered to his horror that this largely Christian society had conspired to ignore the wretched condition of thousands: 'Ah! what are our creeds, and how do we hope to be saved? . . . Surrounded as we are by the wants and woes of our fellowman, and yet given to follow our pleasures, regardless of their pains, are we not like people sitting up with a corpse, and making merry in the house of the dead?'[12]

Hardy's native Dorset, like most other pastoral counties distanced from the 'rusty-black' heart of the city, had only recently begun to recognise this urbanisation and sense the political and social upheavals of the era by the time Hardy was born in June 1840. Their agrarian lifestyle had not yet been irreparably disturbed; time still marked as it had been for generations by lambing season, shearing time, hay-making, harvest-gathering, and marketing of produce at the county exchange. Even as a boy, Hardy perceived that he had been born at a crucial moment of transition between old and new, 'just in time,' observes Millgate, 'to catch a last glimpse of that English rural life which . . . had existed largely undisturbed from medieval times'.[13] Juxtaposed in his memory were idylls of Dorchester, tranquil and prosaic, with its harvest home celebrations, cider-making, and country reels, against vivid recollections of his first railway journey to London, an enormous and impersonal metropolis where people whipped their animals in the streets and strangers cursed one another in passing. Hardy would later lament that the old traditional ballads and 'orally transmitted ditties of centuries' that he loved so well had been 'slain at a stroke by the London comic songs that were introduced' when the railway came to Dorchester in 1847.

Frank O'Connor observes that Hardy's vantage between staid tradition and progressive modern thought instilled in him a belief that 'when two cultures clash in this way, what happens at the time is not that the more sophisticated one triumphs, but that the less sophisticated takes refuge in the depths of the heart'.[14] Certainly O'Connor's statement is a valid one, yet I think it would be wrong to conclude that Hardy would have enthusiastically chosen to secure both feet in the past. The myth of an arcadian 'merrie old England' was just that – a myth – and for all his nostalgic affection for the church choir, maypoles, and mummers, Hardy might have agreed with Kingsley that picturesque country villages were 'generally the perennial hot-beds of fever and ague, of squalid penury, sottish profligacy, dull discontent too stale for words'.[15] If Hardy was a lover of tradition, he was ironically its harshest critic. One of John Holloway's most acute observations in his study of 'Hardy's Major Fiction', in fact, is that Hardy's novels about rural England reflect his 'gathering realization that the earlier way did not possess the inner resources upon which to make a real fight for its existence. The old order was not just a less powerful mode of life than the new, but ultimately helpless before it through inner defect'.[16]

The collision of past and present is perhaps the major theme in Hardy's life and art, but almost as significant is the convergence of life and death. Jemima Hand was allegedly four months pregnant with Hardy when she married his father, Thomas Hardy II, and assumed charge of his ancestral home at Higher Bockhampton. Jemima's delivery was extremely difficult, Hardy related in the 'biography' which he had largely composed himself, and the baby was laid aside as stillborn. Luckily, an attending nurse detected life and exclaimed, 'Dead! Stop a minute: he's alive enough, sure!'[17] Her words seem prophetic, if indeed they are true, for during his first months Hardy was just alive enough to be called alive at all. The story continues that the infant was so inactive and dull that his parents believed they had produced an idiot, whom they partly feared and partly hoped would not survive. In later years, thinking their little son asleep or incapable of understanding their hushed conversations, his parents now and again discussed the likelihood of his death. The child was, in fact, quite capable of comprehending the meaning of death and grew into adulthood acutely, perhaps neurotically, aware of his health and mortality. Hardy's collected letters are a veritable medical history recounting for friends chronic bouts with headache, toothache, influenza, and more serious maladies. Yet, despite his complaint that

> A world I did not wish to enter
> Took and poised me on my centre,
> Made me grimace, and foot, and prance,
> As cats on hot bricks have to dance
> Strange jigs to keep them from the floor,
> Till they sink down and feel no more,[18]

there flourished in Hardy a steady determination to survive, to postpone to the last possible moment necessity's epitaph.

However fragile his physical constitution might have been, there was obviously no defect in young Hardy's intellect. Even as a child he grappled with theological issues confounding to most grown-ups. Sheltered in his country home and surroundings – Thomas did not begin school until the age of eight when Jemima thought him strong enough to endure the strain – the precocious boy ruminated on what in *Jude the Obscure* (1896) he would later describe as 'the flaw in the terrestrial scheme' which allowed that what was 'good for God's birds was bad for God's gardener'.[19] His parents, themselves staunch High Church members as well as unsophisticated country folk, could find no answers to their son's questions and were frankly disturbed by his assessment that deemed Nature's logic a horrid paradox that 'sickened his sense of harmony'.[20] It was probably at this early juncture between childhood and adolescence that Hardy began his lifelong distrust of the 'Good-God' theory, for it was then that he recognised that to grow up in a world in which 'events did not rhyme quite as he had thought'[21] was to expose himself vulnerable to a Supreme Being whose sense of mercy he could not understand.

Judging his melancholic personality to be a sign of the boy's natural predisposition toward the spiritual world, Hardy's family members often laughed that 'Tommy would have to be a parson, being obviously no good for any practical pursuit'.[22] The thought of living in comfort while composing beautiful poetry in his ample spare time appealed to the Hardy who even so early on discovered that his doubt concerning the existence of God was insufficient cause for him to abandon his desire for a religious vocation. Services in the tiny Stinsford church where the Hardys attended regularly were rich in music and drama, engaging the boy's aesthetic sensibilities while bathing him in the dreamily muted light of stained glass. With its emphases on ritual and feeling, the Church would remain a synecdoche for Hardy's emotional nucleus even after his orthodoxy had faded into agnosticism, and he would retain his respect for daily Bible reading as an adjunct to 'Plain living and high thinking'. As late as 1865 Hardy scrutinised Newman's *Apologia* in hopes of being convinced that faith in the Unseen was worth the cultivating, but it was no use. Newman's style was charming and his logic sound, 'Only – and here comes the fatal catastrophe – there is no first link to his excellent chain of reasoning, and down you come headlong'.[23] But practical rather than religious obstacles forced Hardy to relinquish his hope for a country parish: his education, especially in Greek, was inadequate, and his financial resources limited. For Hardy, as later for Jude, there would be no Cambridge.

To the unfair criticism that Hardy was a philosophical writer who possessed no philosophy at all, I think it appropriate to respond that the critic has not freed himself from the effects of what Mikhail Bakhtin terms 'authoritative discourse', that privileged language which both establishes the writer as a sort of literary autocrat and disenfranchises the reader's prerogative to interpret it from the context of his own experience. Many otherwise perfectly self-determining readers are accustomed to reading (because authors are accustomed to writing) as though this authorial voice must pronounce the final truth about issues raised in the text. Heavy-handed eighteenth- and nineteenth-century novelists who lay claim to the Truth must certainly be included in the 'Who's Who' list of authorial offenders. Hardy's no-philosophy, on the other hand, his repeated disavowal of a single authorial voice is an excellent example of Bakhtin's concept of 'polyphony' – that multicentredness of human life which frees us from the danger of philosophical tunnel vision. For Bakhtin, as for Hardy, each of us enters the world at a specific time in a specific locale and is immediately rooted in the genetic and cultural world of our parents. Their ancestral traditions, religion, social status, and national identity are ours; thus, as Wayne Booth observes in his introduction to Bakhtin's *Problems of Dostoevsky's Poetics*, 'we come into consciousness speaking a language already permeated with many voices – a social, not a private language. From the beginning, we are "polyglot"'. Life's experiences may expand and enrich our social language, but to deny our multi-glossia is to 'maim ourselves arbitrarily to monologue'.[24] Easily deluded into believing that self-expression is the only rhetoric worth listening to, each of us to some extent alienates himself from all others in an infantile regression toward self-absorption. This is the anti-social crime committed by Michael Henchard in his inscription of a last testament which repudiates any wish but his own, committed by Jude Fawley in his neurotic preoccupation with Christminster, and even committed by Tess Durbeyfield in her unwillingness to admit to consciousness any voice other than that of her own condemning heart. The only unredeemable act in the Hardyan universe is that which maims the character to monologue while nullifying the polyphonic expression of the community encircling him; the only unredeemable act for Hardy as novelist and poet would have been that which falsely constrained him to propound one narrow philosophy.

Now I have said in so many words that Hardy was a human oxymoron, a man deeply aware and accepting of his own polyphony. He loved life, wishing heartily that he had never been born; loved tradition, thinking it largely stupid and crass; loved the Church, disbelieving that a merciful God had sanctified it. The paramount symbol of Hardy's polyphony is the handmade hymnal used by 'ecclesiastical bandsmen' who in years past had provided music in village churches until displaced by lone organists or harmonium players. In his preface to the 1896 edition of *Under the Greenwood Tree* (1872), Hardy affectionately describes the customs of these 'bygone instrumentalists' whom he admires for their great dedication to a task which promised small gratuity. Perhaps by trade a farmer, blacksmith, or cobbler, the musician worked in the evenings and on Sundays at his art, usually earning just enough to pay for fiddle strings and music paper. Each man ruled his own manuscript, bound it into a volume, and copied into it in his own hand religious melodies to be performed for church services and Christmas programmes. But the music book was not entirely a monological work, as Hardy shrewdly notes:

> It was customary to inscribe a few jigs, reels, hornpipes, and ballads in the same book, by beginning it at the other end, the insertions being continued from front and back till sacred and secular met together in the middle, often with bizarre effect . . . .[25]

The middle of the hymn-book is crucial ground in Hardy's world, for it is here – where in Bakhtin's conceptualisation the festive carnival world of profanity, laughter, and 'life turned inside out' edges against the official ecclesiastical hierarchy with its sombre emphases on 'religious, political, and moral values, norms, and prohibitions'[26] – that he lived every moment of his life and recorded his 'unadjusted impressions' in fiction, verse, and drama. The 'bizarre effect' of Hardy's deliberate enjambment of irreconcilable voices symbolises his art in its purest and highest form so that regarded as a whole, the canon no longer seems fragmented, but rather a fine example of what Coleridge perceives as 'multeity in unity'.

Bakhtin observes that it is difficult to widen one's conceptual horizon, primarily because 'what I see can never be what you see, if only . . . because I can see what is behind your head'.[27] Hardy wrote with a sense of his own ending and because he was always looking over his shoulder for death, he had a greater need than most Victorians to know the nature of the thing behind his head, to exact, as he wrote in 'In Tenebris II', 'a full look at the Worst'. The concussion of spheres in the mid-ground of the hymnal produced not a clattering of voices aimed at deconstructing one another to prove the citadel a house of cards, but instead created for Hardy a polyphony of consciousnesses exploring fictional possibilities for the nature of God and for the ending awaiting each man. He never intended that his fictions be taken as truths, nor did he think of them as hypotheses to be tested. Hardy invented his fictions for the same reason Hans Vaihinger believes all fictions are contrived:

> the mind is invention; under the compulsion of necessity, stimulated by the outer world, it discovers the store of contrivances hidden within itself. The organism finds itself in a world of contradictory sensations, it is exposed to the assaults of a hostile world, and in order to preserve itself is forced to seek every possible means of assistance.[28]

Is the upshot, then, that Hardy wrote to make himself feel a little better about the obscure ground behind his back? In part, yes. There have been less noble motivations for writing, and Nietzsche observes, besides, that the 'falseness of an opinion is not . . . any objection to it'. What matters in the end is 'how far the opinion is life-furthering, life-preserving, species-preserving'.[29] Hardy genuinely believed that his polyphony of 'as if's' might encourage men to practise a morality based not on supernatural edicts but on ordinary human concern for each other. If God should exist, then we have done the godly thing and need not fear damnation; if God happens not to exist or if purblind Doomsters alone command our fate, we have still done the godly thing and need not fear damnation.

Of all the authors in the great tradition, Thomas Hardy stands out as one of the most frequently and thoroughly criticised – often for good reason. At one point or another in his enormous canon, Hardy commits almost every possible literary indiscretion. His characters can be two-dimensional and his stories ineptly plotted; he may allow coincidence to intrude upon predictability a bit too unbelievably; his artistic integrity has been stretched to breaking more than once by his thick application of melodramatics and elevation of the trite; and certainly he is guilty from time to time of heaping before his readers platters of undigestible moralisation. Indeed, my first undergraduate impression of Hardy was so unfavourable that upon finishing *Tess of the D'Urbervilles'*, I flung it against my dorm room wall, cracking the book's cheap paper spine into halves. In the years since, I have discovered that my negative response was due much more to a personal misreading of the text than to any defect in its composition or philosophic content. I had failed to appreciate Thomas Hardy as an illustrator of transition and opposing paradigms, as a figure at once entirely Victorian and consummately modern. He is a philosopher of impressions tried and untried. No less is he Sidney's poet who, thrusting himself into the 'middest', plots the dimensions of past, present, and future, and divines from those epic constructs a 'pleasing analysis of all'. The only intelligent way to consider his art is as a *concordia discourse* in which his 'seemings', conveyed by a number of voices, represent fictions not only about the nature of God, but about human beginnings and middles and endings as they relate to the idea of God. In the following chapters I shall consider the genesis and nature of those fictions, the responses of Hardy's Wessex men and women to those voices and to the voices of their own hearts and intellects, and, finally, the embracing absence of voice which characterises both body and ending of his art.

1
The Complaining Door

I have been looking for God for 50 years, and I think that if he had existed I should have discovered him.[1]

The value of dialogic discourse in Bakhtin's concept of polyphony is not related to the theme each voice proffers, but to the socially significant fact that each voice is free to speak its mind. Because Bakhtin is not attempting to measure the proximity of any voice to reality, the validity of each consciousness is in his estimation equal to another. This is not the case, however, in Hardy's use of polyphonic impressions since all voices are not equal, the content of one or another appearing more privileged than others. The theme of this inaugural voice is that God does not exist, and the problem with it is that such a declaration is too simplistic to stand alone. It carries the ring of a half-truth or a poorly-reasoned theorem which may leave the reader wondering at the pointlessness of so dead-end an observation. For this reason, Hardy was right to object to the anatomising of one of his impressions apart from the rest, for they more properly belong in concordance; but we will do it anyway. At this point I feel Hardy glowering at me. I have not forgotten his lifelong contention that he had never attempted to create a 'coherent scientific theory of the universe'[2] in his imaginative writings, and I am not denying that any attempt (such as mine) to educe such consistency left him irate and defensive. My concern here is not how to reveal that grand, forbidden philosophy nor to fabricate what cannot be found; but an examination of the fragments of the various theories which influenced Hardy is essential to any understanding of his canon. If the *in vitro* exploration of this consciousness seems unsatisfactory, if issues surface which it appears to ignore, let the reader have faith that the corpus shall be reassembled in the following chapters and examined holistically.

The spring and summer of 1909 were bleak, painful seasons for Thomas Hardy, who at 69 had already outlived his wildest expectations for longevity. Accustomed to renting a house or flat in London each year during this peak interval of social and theatrical activity, he secluded himself at home in Dorchester, venturing out but little and steeping himself in sullen ruminations about the character of mankind. 'If all hearts were open and all desires known – as they would be if people showed their souls –' he complained bitterly in an August journal entry, 'how many gaspings, sighings, clenched fists, knotted brows, broad grins, and red eyes should we see in the market-place.'[3] And Hardy had sufficient cause to feel himself blighted. Within the last four years he had lost to the surgeon's knife four old friends and relations, and his sorrow was inestimably increased by the deaths of his longtime confidants and fellow-dissenters Algernon Charles Swinburne and George Meredith in April and May respectively, 'leaving a blank that nothing could fill'.[4] After both poets were refused burial in Westminster Abbey, an indignant Hardy scathingly suggested that a 'heathen annexe' should be built to accommodate England's great 'unbelieving' writers. Some time earlier he and Swinburne had joked about their reputations as atheists and had laughed off a newspaper slander which alleged that 'Swinburne planteth, & Hardy watereth; & Satan giveth the increase'.[5] But the frequency and intensity of similar attacks over the years had worn Hardy to a thin edge. Tired of the public eye which vigilantly monitored, evaluated, and, as often as not, denounced his art, he had given up novel-writing in favour of poetry. Contrary to his earlier expectation that such a move would spare him further critical hostility, however, Hardy discovered that Galileo might have been persecuted for his opinions even if he *had* presented them in verse, for his own poetic endeavours, especially those antithetic to the *zeitgeist*, were regularly and joyfully flayed.

It is fair to say that Hardy was an angry man whose fury smouldered ubiquitously throughout his writings, but it must also be said that he was equally sensitive to the suffering of his fellow man and compassionate in his treatment of their fears and sorrows. This first voice which emerges to sound the possibility that God does not exist is neither angry nor glib like the scorching voice of Swinburne, who found it in some way palli-

ative to mock and deny the idea of God's subsistence, even as
he felt it mocked and denied his own being:

> Is not this the great God of your sires, that
>   with souls and with bodies was fed?
> And the world was on flame with his fires?
>   O fools, he was God and is dead.
> He will not again hear the strong crying of
>   earth in his ears as before,
> And the fume of his multitudes dying shall
>   flatter his nostrils no more.
> By the spirit he ruled as his slave he is slain
>   who was mighty to slay,
> And the stone that is sealed on his grave he
>   shall rise not and roll not away.[6]

Hardy's first voice does concede that the usefulness of belief in God is dead, but its tone is more akin to Meredith's than to Swinburne's. Meredith's 'Dirge in Woods' traces the same conclusion that there is no God, no afterlife, yet its mood betrays no panic or outrage. Death, although resisted by all species, is a lovely stillness after the rush of life:

> A wind sways the pines,
>   And below
> Not a breath of wild air –
> Still as the mosses that glow
> On the flooring and over the lines
> Of the roots here and there.
> The pine-tree drops its dead;
> They are quiet, as under the sea.
> Overhead, overhead
> Rushes life in a race,
> As the clouds the clouds chase;
>   And we go,
> And we drop like the fruits of the tree,
>   Even we,
>   Even so.[7]

In a dignified voice similarly tinctured with regret and brave resolution, the poet in Hardy's 'A Sign-Seeker'[8] recounts his search for some portent to reassure him that, in Pippa's simplistic phrase, 'God's in his heaven – / All's right with the world'.[9] The speaker first scrutinises nature:

> I view the evening bonfires of the sun
>   On hills where morning rains have hissed;
>   The eyeless countenance of the mist
> Pallidly rising when the summer droughts are done.
>
> I have seen the lightning-blade, the leaping star,
>   The cauldrons of the sea in storm,
>   Have felt the earthquake's lifting arm,
> And trodden where abysmal fires and snow-cones are.
>
> I learn to prophesy the hid eclipse,
>   The coming of eccentric orbs;
>   To mete the dust the sky absorbs,
> To weigh the sun, and fix the hour each planet dips.

Next he studies men living, dying, and dead:

> I witness fellow earth-men surge and strive;
>   Assemblies meet, and throb, and part;
>   Death's sudden finger, sorrow's smart;
> – All the vast various moils that mean a world alive.
>
> In graveyard green, where his pale dust lies pent
>   To glimpse a phantom, parent, friend,
>   Wearing his smile, and 'Not the end!'
> Outbreathing softly: that were blest enlightenment.
>
> Or, when Earth's Frail lie bleeding of her Strong,
>   If some Recorder, as in Writ,
>   Near to the weary scene should flit
> And drop one plume as pledge that Heaven inscrolls the
>   wrong.

A few happier seekers examine the same phenomena, stand watch over the same graves, attend the same deathbeds, and yet are able to 'Read radiant hints of times to be – / Of heart to heart returning after dust to dust', but

> Such scope is not granted to lives like mine . . .
>   I have lain in dead men's beds, have walked

> The tombs of those with whom I had talked,
> Called many a gone and goodly one to shape a sign,
>
>   And panted for response. But none replies;
>   No warning loom, nor whisperings
>   To open out my limitings,
>   And Nescience mutely muses: When a man falls he lies.

Nescience, which reigned 'Before the birth of consciousness, / When all went well' and 'None suffered sickness, love, or loss',[10] was a humble yet ideal state of mind, and Hardy wished it were possible to 'Oust this awareness, this disease / Called sense'[11] which prevented his reversion to such an untroubled mentality. In fantasy he might gladly have returned to life in medieval times when 'the Church was supreme and unquestioned' and when existence before doubt and scepticism had arisen 'must have been very sweet and beautiful'.[12] And for that matter, his desire to have lived in the childhood of history is certainly parallel to his desire to return to a childlike belief in a God of good gifts and miracles, a God whom Hardy's High Church parents worshipped unquestioningly. But 'The Oxen',[13] a seemingly pastoral poem which is often presented as evidence that he nursed the hope of restored faith, reveals that Hardy never confused wishful thinking with perceived truth. Looking backward to his childhood, the speaker recalls being charmed by the story of oxen kneeling in their stalls each Christmas Eve, presumably like the nativital beasts attending Christ's birth. Normal curious youngsters, we think, would charge directly out to the stable to have a look for themselves, but these children are suspiciously composed. It is crucial to note that their experience is entirely imaginary:

>   We pictured the meek mild creatures where
>   They dwelt in their strawy pen,
>   Nor did it occur to one of us there
>   To doubt they were kneeling then.

As an adult, the speaker cannot mitigate the doubts that have collected over the years simply by calling to mind the sight of oxen kneeling mysteriously, miraculously, in the dark for one simple reason: he had not witnessed it as a boy. Either he is lying about the whole event, which seems difficult to believe, or his memory is accurate and, in retrospect, sadly short-sighted. For his uninquisitiveness as a child, he is left with an impression twice removed from reality by imagination and by time. Discovering his infant faith to be so nebulously grounded, he pretends to wish for a second chance to verify the miracle:

> So fair a fancy few would weave
>   In these years! Yet, I feel,
> If someone said on Christmas Eve,
>   'Come; see the oxen kneel
>
> 'In the lonely barton by yonder coomb
>   Our childhood used to know',
> I should go with him in the gloom,
>   Hoping it might be so.

But I suspect that he has no real intention of ever performing the oxen test, or he would have already done it. An enchanting tale, the Christmas Eve story is similar to so many other traditions which remain lovely, useless relics, powerless against modern scepticism.

Although this speaker does not visit the oxen, he – or another Hardyan narrator – does attend Cathedral services, not so much hoping to be persuaded as to be consoled for his inability to believe. Hardy's ambivalence, it must begin to be understood, is emotional rather than intellectual. Standing among the ranks of Christians in the poem, 'The Impercipient',[14] he feels conspicuously out of place since the faiths of his comrades are fantasies to him and their promised land a misty mirage. His mental dilemma is comparable to that of the knight in Swinburne's 'Laus Veneris', who cries in despair, 'Ah, God, that I were as all souls that be'.[15] It is not fair, Hardy's impercipient laments, that fate has consigned *his* soul to be unhappy, *his* eyes to be blind, while his brothers' hearts are eased with glimpses of heaven. What is radiant to them is vacant to him:

> I am like a gazer who should mark
>   An inland company
> Standing upfingered, with, 'Hark! hark!
>   The glorious distant sea!'

And feel, 'Alas, 'tis but yon dark
And wind-swept pine to me!'

The comrades' sympathies are not moved to Christian charity, however. They, not coincidentally like Hardy's critics, charge the speaker with preferring that 'blessed things' should not exist. He may be 'a bird deprived of wings', but he is so by self-mutilation and they have no compassion for his 'earthbound' plight.

It was up to Hardy, a man who 'past doubtings all, / waits in unhope',[16] to forgive and console himself and to construct his own liturgy of unbelief. In a journal entry written in 1907 he fashions a touching responsive reading of sorts for those unable to embrace Christian dogma, those genuinely grieved about that incapacity and yet profoundly concerned for the condition of man:

> We enter church, and we have to say, 'We have erred and strayed from Thy ways like lost sheep', when what we want to say is, 'Why are we made to err and stray like lost sheep?' Then we have to sing, 'My soul doth magnify the Lord', when what we want to sing is, 'O that my soul could find some Lord that it could magnify! Till it can, let us magnify good works, and develop all means of easing mortals' progress through a world not worthy of them.'
> Still, being present, we say the established words full of the historic sentiment only, mentally adding, 'How happy our ancestors were in repeating in all sincerity these articles of faith!' But we perceive that none of the congregation recognizes that we repeat the words from an antiquarian interest in them, and in a historic sense, and solely in order to keep a church of some sort afoot – a thing indispensable; so that we are pretending what is not true: that we are believers. This must not be; we must leave. And if we do, we reluctantly go to the door, and creep out as it creaks complainingly behind us.[17]

However much Hardy might have desired to believe in a God of miracles who might nurture man and reward him with heaven, it was in man's natural self-reliance that he placed his hope. He had read Bergson's *Creative Evolution* (1907) in which the French biologist maintained that human life is elementally different from the greater material world, thus allowing for the existence of a mystical God, but he rejected this theory as being old dualism disguised in new terminology. Hardy's comrades were wrong to accuse him of preferring that God did not exist, but in light of that overwhelming probability, he did indeed prefer that man should not confuse himself by clinging to theism. Hardy, as did Shelley and Coleridge before him, inclined instead toward a philosophical position of unity in multiplicity. All things, according to this epistemology parented by Spinozan monism, are composed of the same particles arranged in an infinite number of patterns controlled by the laws of motion-and-rest. Thus man's deviation from a maggot or a peach tree is only organisational and energetic rather than elemental. (It is not so giant a leap from here to the position accepted by modern biologists that the building block common to all life is the genetic molecule, DNA. The difference between a maggot, a peach tree, and a human gametocyte is, on the bottom line, the difference in sequence of nucleotides twisted together in a double helix.) For Spinoza, as for Democritus and Epicurus centuries before him, the human soul, too, is a variation of matter which is no more immortal than the flesh. Matter, more properly called 'substance', is infinite and composes everything from the lowest organic life form to the most abstract mental reasoning; therefore, the only God we can legitimately speak of is not the Christian father-figure, but that energy which is the infinite cause and essence of all substance. This is pantheistic determinism, and for embracing it even tentatively as he did any doctrine, Hardy was accused of resigning his humanity.

Hardy's philosophical bent may have been Spinozan, but his religious penchant appears to have resembled nothing less humanistic than Comte's positivism, an ideology which George Henry Lewes acclaimed as 'capable of embracing all the sciences, and with them all the problems of social life'. Science would eventually reveal man to himself just as it had already disclosed the laws of mathematics, physics, and biology; when that occurred, Hardy believed – at least, he believed early on – man would cease to delude himself that a power more supernatural than his own intelligence commanded his fate. For Hardy, as for Comte, the highest intellectual stage an individual can reach is that which allows him to discard the notion of a single God minding the universe, but such thought does not pre-empt his need to worship an ideal. Comte preached the gospel of religious humanism in which worship is most prudently dedicated to those men and women who have acted as noble examples for mankind, and George Eliot adapted this homage to include the ordinary citizen with whom she shared a 'deep human sympathy':

> There are few prophets in the world; few sublimely beautiful women; few heroes. I can't afford to give all my love and reverence to such rarities: I want a great deal of those feelings for my everyday fellow-men, especially for the few in the foreground of the great multitude, whose faces I know, whose hands I touch, for whom I have to make way with kindly courtesy.[18]

Hardy's deepest human sympathies were likewise reserved for those who plod on in work and love despite their awareness that the scriptures are not a gentleman's agreement with God and that good deeds may have no recompense either here or hereafter. In Hardy's version of Eliot's philosophy, it is 'Only a man harrowing clods / In a slow silent walk / With an old horse that stumbles and nods / Half asleep as they stalk' who is to be venerated for his earthy endurance. His kind, rather than dynasts and greedy potentates, will survive the 'Breaking of Nations',[19] and his immortality will be secured in the memories of those who worked beside him.

To the extent that shades of rational monism and positive humanism are discernible in Hardy, we can also conclude that his 'theory' of perception represents Humean idealism. Hardy's insistence that 'I have no philosophy – merely what I have often explained to be only a confused heap of impressions, like those of a bewildered child at a conjuring show',[20] is strikingly similar to Hume's assertion that the mind itself is nothing more metaphysical than a 'heap or collection of different perceptions',[21] which give the false impression of being purposely and perfectly united within a single identity. Because the only source of knowledge is that which is found in each man's capacity for personal sensation and reflection, Hume was thoroughly sceptical that any one truth or system of truths could ever be discovered to explain the nature of reality. The best man can do is to create composite pictures from his individual imaginings, all the while remembering that they are approximations, 'impressions of the age', as Hardy argues, rather than doctrines. For Hume, as later for Hardy, it is mandatory that man accepts the idea of God as being a derivative of his own perceptual process. At some early point in his development, man perceived a need to worship and rely upon a higher being than himself; he consequently fabricated the figure of God and finally agreed with fellow conspirators that their contrived imago constituted Truth. Public opinion might hold that a supernatural God truly exists independent of his creations, but this collective perception is nothing more than social subjectivity validated by the normal majority. The narrator in 'God's Funeral'[22] reflects disapprovingly on man's self-deceptive invention:

> Framing him jealous, fierce, at first,
> We gave him justice as the ages rolled,
> Will to bless those by circumstances accurst,
> And longsuffering, and mercies manifold.
>
> And, tricked by our own early dream
> And need of solace, we grew self-deceived,
> Our making soon our maker did we deem,
> And what we had imagined we believed.

The price of comforting self-dupery, he concludes, is man's treacherous betrayal of his own identity and autonomy.

The German idealist Ludwig Feuerbach branded this type of imagination a 'theogonic wish' in which man transcends his own nature by projecting his ideals onto a perfected double of himself. 'Consequently,' Feuerbach asserted in *The Essence of Christianity* (1841), 'the belief in God is nothing but the belief in human dignity, the belief in the absolute reality and significance of the human nature'.[23] While George Eliot was content to dispense Feuerbach's message that 'Man has his highest being, his God, in himself',[24] Hardy agreed in principle but approached it more cautiously in practice. It genuinely grieved him, on one hand, to think of publicly adding his voice to those who would willingly invalidate a generation's faith in God, for 'Since there is peace in that, why decry it? / Since there is comfort, why disdain?'[25] And yet, however painful it might be to face up to the probability that there is no God, it is more dangerous to believe in a God whose existence reflects man's inadequacy or unwillingness to solve his own problems. Such supernaturalism, John Stuart Mill had observed in *On Liberty* (1859), encourages 'passive obedience' to doctrine and lets man slip too easily off the hook in his social obligation to his community: in holding out 'the hope of heaven and the threat of hell, as the appointed and appropriate motives to a virtuous life', it inspires in 'human morality an essentially selfish character, by disconnecting each man's feelings of duty from the interests of his fellow creatures'.[26] The voice of God in Hardy's ironic poem, 'A Plaint to Man',[27] is actually the voice of man teaching himself this late lesson. When you first became flesh, the perception demands,

> Wherefore, O Man, did there come in you
> The unhappy need of creating me –
> A form like your own – for praying to?
>
> My virtue, power, utility,
> Within my maker must all abide,
> Since none in myself can ever be,
>
> One thin as a phasm on a lantern-slide
> Shown forth in the dark upon some dim sheet,
> And by none but its showman vivified.

The human representative whimpers that life can seem dreadfully hopeless unless one can 'conceive of a mercy-seat somewhere beyond earth', but God remains ruthless. Science is rapidly dispersing the shadows that used to frighten men, he retorts, and the perception of God will soon become too incongruent to survive the modern age. When that occurs, man will have to face the one truth 'that had best been faced in earlier years':

> The fact of life with dependence placed
> On the human heart's resource alone,
> In brotherhood bonded close and graced
>
> With loving-kindness fully blown,
> And visioned help unsought, unknown.

Hardy was not interested in constructing a Nietzschean superman, a self-sufficient aristocrat whose morality transcended good and evil, but he did agree with Nietzsche that man is impotent to emend himself until he puts to death the idea of God. Again, where Swinburne lambastes man's self-made deity,

> Thou art judged, O judge, and the sentence is
>   gone forth against thee, O God.
> Thy slave that slept is awake; thy slave but
>   slept for a span;
> Yea, man thy slave shall unmake thee, who
>   made thee lord over man,[28]

Hardy infuses the same sentiment with a gentler positivist voice. Among the attendants at 'God's Funeral' are those who grieve his loss, remembering

> How sweet it was in years far hied
> To start the wheels of day with trustful prayer,
> To lie down liegely at the eventide
> And feel a Blest assurance he was there!

and wondering

> ... who or what shall fill his place?
> Whither will wanderers turn distracted eyes
> For some fixed star to stimulate their pace
> Towards the goal of their enterprise?

And there are those who claim the requiem a mockery: 'Still he lives to us!' But there is also present a small composition of humanity's best, standing aloof from the mourners and gazing at 'A pale yet positive gleam', muted yet, but 'swelling somewhat' upon the horizon. The speaker, both 'dazed and puzzled 'twixt the gleam and gloom', cannot apprehend that the positive gleam is in fact the light of positivism rising for the first time above a universe freshly emancipated by the decease of God. Repudiation of 'visioned help' represented to Hardy an unequivocal act of faith in the power of brotherhood, in Mill's phrase, to 'produce the moral regeneration of mankind'.[29]

Still, Hardy was as much the reluctant departer from the

cathedral as he was the door that creaked complainingly behind him. Christianity, he argued again and again, was never intended to be systemised into a canon of doctrines which demand belief in the supernatural, and while Hardy admired the moral and altruistic teachings of Christ, he rejected the notion that he was suprahuman in any way. The consummate value of Christ's example lay in his very humanness; he, along with countless other 'Christs of unwrit names', Hardy insists in 'Unkept Good Fridays',[30] have suffered in a world 'not even worthy / To taunt their hopes and aims', trying to reveal the most moral way to live in a landscape devoid of divine intervention. Blake, Ruskin and Arnold had earlier complained that the present-day Church had dislocated its concern away from Christ's emphasis on brotherhood and toward a spiritless compliance with legalistic dogma, and Hardy was even more forthright in his plea that the Church should be modulated into an 'undogmatic, non-theological establishment for the promotion of that virtuous living on which all honest men are agreed'.[31] The beatitudes of this distillation of Christianity, positivism, and other humanistic philosophies would bless the poor in spirit and the humble and those who grieve, for they most profoundly understand their bond with others who suffer. The pure in heart, despite their persecution by man, nature, and fate, would be thanked for their perseverance; and those who teach mercy and peace would be honoured for disseminating man's most noble ideals. 'The Golden Rule', Hardy predicts in his diary, 'will ultimately be brought about . . . by the pain we see in others reacting on ourselves, as if we and they were a part of one body. Mankind, in fact, may be and possibly will be viewed as members of one corporeal frame.'[32]

To the congregation assembled in the gloomy cathedral in Thomson's 'The City of Dreadful Night', the priest of darkness delivers the tidings that there is no God: 'no fiend with names divine / Made us and tortures us; if we must pine, / It is to satiate no Being's gall'. Since life is nothing but random anguish and despair, he advises, 'End it when you will.'[33] Although the first of Hardy's voices bears the same intelligence regarding the non-existence of God, the counsel it offers is quite to the contrary: humanity freed from the perception of God is humanity freed to discover its own godliness. Swinburne only pretends to value the race in his proclamation, 'Glory to Man in the highest! for Man is the / Master of things',[34] for in practice he pledges little hope, faith, or encouragement toward man's enlightenment. By extreme contrast, Hardy's first consciousness finally and unconditionally agrees with Feuerbach's defence of his own belief: 'I deny only in order to affirm. I deny the fantastic projection of theology and religion in order to affirm the real essence of man'.[35]

2
Nature, Darwin, and the Pattern in the Carpet

> *As, in looking at a carpet, by following one colour a certain pattern is suggested, by following another, another; so in life the seer should watch the pattern among general things which his idiosyncrasy moves him to observe, and describe that alone. This is, quite accurately, a going to Nature; yet the result is no mere photograph, but purely the product of the writer's own mind.*[1]

Hardy's lifelong refusal to commit himself to a single theoretic position should not be interpreted as evidence of confusion or equivocation, for, it must be remembered, the times into which he was born and matured were dense and richly woven through with enormously divergent patterns in religious and philosophic thought. Sir Charles Lyell might never have published *Principles of Geology* in the diverse climate of 1833 had he foreseen that a score of rationalists hungry for scientific validation would appropriate its essential argument as proof of the incredibility of the Old Testament. His thesis, innocently enough, maintained that rather than a short series of cataclysmic events, natural forces such as erosion by wind and water, gradual land movement, and sedimentation were the causes of geological reformation of the earth's surface. In the process of these exceedingly slow alterations, many species had evolved and become extinct; one of these relatively new species was man, perhaps himself on his way to becoming a transmuted creature. While Lyell fought the hot backlash by insisting that his theories, like those of William Paley before him, supported the existence of God and provided 'clear proofs of a Creative Intelligence, and of His foresight, wisdom, and power', hardline creationists scowled and fumed and posited their own theories. (The formation of the earth, Philip Gosse asserted earnestly, was accomplished by one catastrophic act of God in which the planet suddenly sprang into full-blown lushness, cleverly giving the illusion that it had supported life for centuries.) The seeds of religious doubt sown – if inadvertently – by Lyell were nurtured during those decades by such German scholars as David Friedrich Strauss, author of *Das Leben Jesu* (1835), whose higher criticism concluded that the Bible was not the divinely inspired word of God, but rather a varied collection of histories, genealogies, laws, songs, biographies, and folk myths. Strauss, Coleridge, and other prominent higher critics insisted that the scripture remained a great work of literature rich in poetry, symbol, allegory, and spiritual significance – but only when stripped of the historical inaccuracies which imperilled its artistic authority.

Yet the 1830s and 1840s witnessed another faction of prominent Victorians labouring equally hard to renew England's literalist belief in God and Church. In July 1833, the same year in which Lyell published his controversial study, John Keble formally initiated the Oxford Movement with the delivery of his arch-conservative sermon on 'National Apostasy'. The Protestant Church of England, argued Keble and the other Tractarians, had become worldly, liberal, and unspiritual. By neglecting the rituals of baptism and communion, by failing to teach supernatural doctrine, by rejecting aesthetic symbolism, by substituting civil servants for priests and bishops, in short by divesting itself of holiness, the Anglican Church was deliberately and recklessly exposing Christianity to forces which would destroy religion altogether. The aim of the Oxford Movement, at least initially, was to resanctify the Church and re-establish it as infallible in its teaching of mystical dogma. With its sacerdotal caste, the Church was to be the ultimate authority in all matters concerning natural, human, and spiritual worlds; the spirit of the age, so defined by scientific enquiry in the search for truth, was to be denied in favour of blind acquiescence to dogma. To those radical thinkers such as Matthew Arnold who accused the Tractarians of placing sacrament above Christ by teaching old error instead of new truth, John Newman responded that Christ can only be fully known through the church and its ordinances; to inquire into the nature of the Unseen is treason against faith and inevitably ends in atheism.

Newman's conversion to Roman Catholicism all but ended the Oxford Movement in 1845, the same year in which an undistinguished young scientist named Charles Darwin completed his historic voyage aboard the *Beagle* and constructed two preliminary sketches of his theory of evolution by natural selection. Darwin's principle work would not be published for another fifteen years, but Darwinian evolution, we might say, was in the air despite the best efforts of natural theologians and zealous Church reformers. The concept of evolution was not new: Empedocles was an evolutionist in the fifth-century B.C., as were the good many after (and probably before) him who believed that the 'Great Architect' was engaged in a constant process of refining man into his own image. But Darwin's inference that Nature is a brainless machine grinding out change rather than a dark glass imperfectly – but certainly – reflecting God's existence provoked a mighty upheaval in Victorian thought. There were those happy enough to bid good riddance to a God whom they perceived as an omnipotent fiend, a God whose vindictive and petty character moved him to violate his own laws of order, and, most intolerably, a God who revealed his heartlessness in showy exhibitions of violence. Darwin's ideology also fitted chameleon-like into dogma embraced by humanitarians, socialists, and materialists, for, as Bernard Shaw was quick to point out, 'he had the luck to please everybody who had an axe to grind'. The delirium was soon to wear thin, however, as the implications of existence without God sank deep into the Victorian psyche. Man was suddenly untethered from his place in the universe, the universe likewise set adrift without purpose or principle in time. Humanity had not only fallen from grace but from guidance as well. The props were suspect, if not rotten. 'There is a hideous fatalism about it,' ruminated Shaw, 'a ghastly and damnable reduction of beauty and intelligence, of strength and purpose, of honor and aspiration.'[2]

As early as 1833 Tennyson, himself an amateur scientist, had begun to set the Victorian *angst* to verse in what, by 1850, would become his celebrated elegy, *In Memoriam*:[3]

> Are God and Nature then at strife,
>   That Nature lends such evil dreams?
>   So careful of the type she seems,
> So careless of the single life,
>
> That I, considering everywhere
>   Her secret meaning in her deeds,

> And finding that of fifty seeds
> She often brings but one to bear,
>
> I falter where I firmly trod,
> And falling with my weight of cares
> Upon the great world's altar-stairs
> That slope through darkness up to God,
>
> I stretch lame hands of faith, and grope,
> And gather dust and chaff, and call
> To what I feel is Lord of all,
> And faintly trust the larger hope.

Such re-examination of traditional beliefs, Tennyson implies, shakes a generation at its core because Nature, once a source of wonder and blessed reassurance, must now be feared as the thoughtless perpetrator of man's extermination. The dilemma seems all the more disheartening since in reaching toward God on behalf of all mankind, Tennyson ends up with nothing more reassuring or edifying than dirty hands. Nature is ferociously verbal; God is silent. Nature's message, spoken through bloody teeth and claws, geologic formations, and dinosaur remains, is unmistakable; God's reticence leaves man to trust nothing more concrete than his own feelings that He exists and cares for the 'single life'. Tennyson has no alternative but to conclude that life is frail and quite likely futile, but there can be no definitive answer nor redress until we are able to see – or *not* see – 'behind the veil.'

Due largely to his awareness of the prevalent mood of optimism at mid-century, however, Tennyson stopped short of proclaiming the equation which T. S. Eliot felt he truly believed: inasmuch as Nature reflects the essence of God, and Nature is a machine, God is the sightless, purposeless impetus behind every force in the universe. It would be Hardy in the next generation who would take up where Tennyson left off to trace this pattern in the carpet to its conclusion that God is no more than the machine which powers Nature. This conclusion, moreover, is the theme of Hardy's second voice. It emerges from the same philosophical battleground that inspired a despairing Tennyson to pen *In Memoriam*, but it even more distinctly represents the influence of full-blown Darwinism. Hardy's pre-adult readings ranged from Horace and Ovid to the Greek New Testament, *Pilgrim's Progress* to *Ecclesiastical Polity*, and Shakespeare to Newman. But during the same years that Hardy, then 19 or 20, was diligently studying and annotating his favourite passages from the Bible, *The Book of Common Prayer*, and Keble's *The Christian Year*, he was also devouring two newly-published controversial works: the classicist Benjamin Jowett's English version of higher criticism *Essays and Reviews* (1860), and Darwin's epoch-marking *The Origin of Species* (1859). These two texts flung the nineteenth century into an historically unprecedented religious crisis, radically transforming the 'soulscape' of the English-speaking world and leading John Ruskin to avow:

> The Middle Ages had their wars and agonies, but also intense delights. Their gold was dashed with blood; but ours is sprinkled with dust. Their life was inwoven with white and purple; ours is one seamless stuff of brown. Not that we are without apparent festivity, but festivity more or less forced, mistaken, embittered, incomplete – not of the heart . . . . The profoundest reason for this darkness of heart is, I believe, our want of faith. There never yet was a generation of men (savage or civilized) who, taken as a body, so wofully fulfilled the words, 'having no hope, and without God in the world,' as the present civilized European race.[4]

But for young Hardy, Nature was never the scene of consolation that it was for young Wordsworth. Nature's apparently random cruelty to one creature meant prosperity for another – this lesson had been impressed upon him as a child – and so for Hardy this darkness of heart had edged into his soulscape long before he had read books which affirmed it. He must have experienced an immediate sense of kinship with Darwin's assertion that 'there seems to be no more design in the variability of organic beings and in the action of natural selection, than in the course which the wind blows',[5] for his poetics were from the outset characterised by Darwinian themes and vocabulary. 'The Temporary the All',[6] the second poem in Hardy's first published collection of verse, is disguised as an ode to the poet's passing youth, but is actually a rather sly endorsement of Darwin's theory. 'Change and chancefulness in my flowering youthtime,' reflects the poet in dolorous sapphic metre, led him 'sun by sun' into making poor decisions about love, friendship, and even habitat. Intending someday to find a true friend, a 'wonder of women', and a more seemly hermitage, he squandered his life by accepting inferior substitutes which came along by chance. The poet foolishly looked to such pre-Darwinian constructs as pre-ordained fate and 'ripe time pending' to improve his lot, all the while deluding himself that 'Life is roomy yet, and the odds unbounded'. Hardy's *double entendre* works brilliantly here because the odds are unbounded for the species; for the individual, however, the temporary is the all. Comparisons such as 'flowering youthtime' and 'ripe time pending' represent the speaker's early symbiosis with Nature, but the end of the poem as it converges with the end of his life reveals his unavoidable divergence from Nature's power to renew itself. Man dies in his 'onward earth-track – / Never transcended!' while Nature continues to flower in infinite variation.

This second of Hardy's voices repudiates Lyell's and Paley's thesis that Nature's capacity to regenerate itself in infinite variety is testimony to God's creative genius and grace. The same voice, observes Joseph Warren Beach, underlies all Hardy's speculation regarding the universe and culminates in his belief that 'Nothing remains of purposiveness but the vague aesthetic recognition of unity and pattern in things. Conscious design, providence, harmony, benevolence have all evaporated from the concept of nature'.[7] Beach argues convincingly, in fact, that Hardy's approach to Dame Nature so turns the tables on traditional poetic convention that for the first time we find reversed the Romantics' procedure of searching field, flock and tree for answers to their questions regarding the universe. In 'Nature's Questioning'[8] Hardy represents field, flock and tree as weary, bewildered creatures seeking wisdom from the poet, and, it seems to me, he freely anthropomorphises Nature in his attempt to project the Victorians' existential dilemma onto a landscape which is at once familiar and inscrutable:

> When I look forth at dawning, pool,
>   Field, flock, and lonely tree,
>   All seem to gaze at me
> Like chastened children sitting silent in a school;
>
> Their faces dulled, constrained, and worn,
>   As though the master's ways

Through the long teaching days
Had cowed them till their early zest was overborne.

Upon them stirs in lippings mere
  (As if once clear in call,
  But now scarce breathed at all),
'We wonder, ever wonder, why we find us here!'

All Nature's beings look to the poet, himself a highly-evolved 'thinking reed', for answers to their simple inquiry: 'Why are we here?' They are exhausted from endlessly regenerating for no other purpose than to continue their orbit through the seasons. Unable to respond, the speaker listens to the solutions they propose:

'Has some vast Imbecility,
  Mighty to build and blend,
  But impotent to tend,
Framed us in jest, and left us now to hazardry?

'Or come we of an Automaton
  Unconscious of our pains? . . .
  Or are we live remains
Of Godhead dying downwards, brain and eye now gone?

'Or is it that some high Plan betides,
  As yet not understood,
  Of Evil stormed by Good,
We the Forlorn Hope over which Achievement strides?'

These creatures are more astute than the poet, for they possess the forethought and hindsight necessary to consider all the possibilities. Perhaps their existence is the result of a grand practical joke in which the earth was framed for the entertainment it provided God and will eventually return to nebulae when the sport wears off. Perhaps, as the voice of this chapter suggests, man and Nature are products of a stupefied machine; or it may be that pantheism has become pandemonium as both God and Nature wind down together. The final possibility, that God moves in mysterious ways according to a higher plan, is the most hopeful and the least likely, as their cowed, constrained faces attest. The most feasible of their various theories is the Darwinian one because it posits no personality to be reckoned with, no malign prankster, no terminally ill benefactor. 'Urgence . . . unconscious formative activity',[9] as Hardy would later define the 'obvious process' of evolution, is the automaton which accounts for Nature's existence and perpetuation, but the speaker in this poem has not yet perceived this. His conclusion – tentative, at best – is pervaded by a Tennysonian echo that life on earth is painful and that decay and rebirth are kindred stages in the struggle:

> Thus things around. No answer I . . .
>   Meanwhile the winds, and rains,
>   And Earth's old glooms and pains
> Are still the same, and Life and Death are neighbours nigh.

The Ethics of Ambiguity, Simone de Beauvoir's treatise on existential freedom, is essentially an exploration of this conclusion that 'Life and Death are neighbours nigh'. The aim of life is, in fact, death, she observes, and 'man knows and thinks this tragic ambivalence which the animal and the plant merely undergo'.[10] The poet in 'Nature's Questioning' becomes temporarily paralysed by the weight of this ambiguity, but the birds in 'The Bullfinches'[11] are able to continue singing precisely *because* they lack the consciousness to comprehend what man knows and thinks:

> Brother Bulleys, let us sing
> From the dawn till evening! –
> For we know not that we go not
> When today's pale pinions fold
> Where they be that sang of old.

The narrating bird has been to Blackmoor Vale, the setting of Hardy's *The Woodlanders* (1887), and has overheard the green-gowned faeries discussing 'queenly Nature's ways, / means, and moods'. The fays are probably nothing more bewitched than a group of woodlanders discussing the mechanics of evolution:

> All we creatures, nigh and far,
> (Said they there), the Mother's are;
> Yet she never shows endeavour

> To protect from warrings wild
> Bird or beast she calls her child.
>
> Busy in her handsome house
> Known as Space, she falls a-drowse;
> Yet, in seeming, works on dreaming,
> While beneath her groping hands
> Fiends make havoc in her bands.
>
> How her hussif'ry succeeds
> She unknows or she unheeds,
> All things making for Death's taking!

Understanding nothing of what he has overheard, the finch merely mocks the linguistic sounds made by the faeries and incorporates that repetition into his song. He cannot be discouraged to find that Mother Nature is no more conscious of her product than of its welfare because he, in turn, is equally oblivious to that intelligence. Unlike Nature's children in 'Nature's Questioning', these creatures carol instinctively in the face of rote annihilation:

> Come then, brethren, let us sing,
> From the dawn till evening! –
> For we know not that we go not
> When the day's pale pinions fold
> Where those be that sang of old.

But for such nineteenth-century agnostics as Darwin and Hardy, it was impossible to sing as 'unweetingly'. For all his wishful thinking, Hardy could not delude himself into believing that a higher intelligence surveys and supervises the world; despite his early eagerness to believe in God, neither could Darwin. Like young Hardy, he loved all things natural and aspired to become a country clergyman who could spend his time collecting and cataloguing plant specimens. The academic rigours of Cambridge, however, were a 'waste of time' for the impatient young man who rarely attended class and passed his BA examination only because he had carefully studied Paley's *Natural Theology* and, convinced of its accuracy, could extemporise on its arguments at length. His intention of becoming a minister 'died a natural death' when owing to a rather Hardyan coincidence,¹² Darwin joined the HMS *Beagle* as ship's naturalist. Experiencing for the first time the exotic beauty of the tropics, Darwin found his senses over-powered and his conviction of the existence of God and the immortality of the soul fortified. A journal entry from those years asserts emphatically that 'whilst standing in the midst of the grandeur of a Brazilian forest, it is not possible to give an adequate idea of the higher feelings of wonder, admiration, and devotion which fill and elevate the mind'. Even as late as the drafting of *The Origin of Species*, Darwin defended himself as a theist because not only did he feel the presence of God in natural scenes, but he believed that the existence of God was a logical deduction:

> This follows from the extreme difficulty or rather impossibility of conceiving this immense and wonderful universe, including man with his capacity of looking far backwards and far into futurity, as the result of blind chance or necessity. When thus reflecting I feel compelled to look to a First Cause having an intelligent mind in some degree analogous to that of man; and I deserve to be called a Theist.¹³

Admitting later that religious orthodoxy had never been strongly cultivated in him, Darwin retracted these early sentiments in his autobiography. Nature's 'grand scenes' had piqued his emotional excitement, he explained, and had confused 'what is often called the sense of sublimity' for profession of faith in God. What he had formerly conceived as a rational construct became a ridiculous improbability when, by the light of the cold English sun, Darwin reasoned that man can hardly trust his own reasoning:

> can the mind of man, which has, as I fully believe, been developed from a mind as low as that possessed by the lowest animal, be trusted when it draws such grand conclusions? May not these be the result of the connection between cause and effect which strikes us as a necessary one, but probably depends merely on inherited experience? Nor must we overlook the probability of the constant inculcation in a belief in God on the minds of children producing so strong and perhaps an inherited effect on their brains not yet fully developed, that it would be as difficult for them to throw off

their belief in God, as for a monkey to throw off its instinctive fear and hatred of a snake.[14]

Darwin would eventually accept the title 'agnostic', but contradictory voices similar to those posited by Hardy continued to be heard in his own speculations. He did not want to conceive of God as an impersonal machine, an 'Eternal Urger, pressing change on change', as Hardy would later describe it in his epic drama, *The Dynasts* (p. 118), and yet there seemed no honest alternative. 'My theology is a simple muddle', Darwin confessed to fellow botanist Sir Joseph Hooker, 'I cannot look at the universe as the result of blind chance, yet I can see no evidence of beneficent design, or indeed of design of any kind, in the details.'[15]

Because Darwin was a scientist whose emotions and appreciation for art, poetry, and music had atrophied through the years – 'My mind seems to have become a kind of machine for grinding general laws out of large collections of fact,' he confessed rather regretfully in his autobiography[16] – he was more able than Hardy to detachedly accept Nature/God as an evolution machine. Despite his insistence that 'the mystery of the beginning of all things is insoluble by us',[17] Darwin remained convinced that the machine operated according to laws of modification of offspring and adaptation to the environment. As a consequence, the process is both generative in its constant creation of new species and new adaptive strategies in old ones, and destructive in its rote elimination of those species unable to survive environmental and epigenetic change. The indifference of Nature was not, for Darwin, the indifference of a God who from time to time rears up in percipience to observe that his operation of the universe is cruel and who uncaringly sinks again into unconsciousness despite man's cries of 'Unfair!'; it was, rather, the indifference of necessity, the force which powers life – impossible to anthropomorphise, absurd to take personally.

Critics delighted in charging Hardy with postulating a 'malignant and fiendish God', but he countered that he 'never held any views of the sort, merely surmising an indifferent and unconscious force at the back of things'.[18] While Hardy argued passionately that 'neither Chance nor Purpose governs the universe, but Necessity',[19] he accepted this hypothesis with a depth of emotional ambivalence not present in Darwin. As early as 1938 literary historian Ernest Baker recognised that 'by accepting the scientific attitude he [Hardy] rationalized his acute apprehension of mankind's tragic plight; but it was only with the intellect that he accepted it, something deeper was always in conflict with the rationalization'.[20] In Bakhtin's later terminology it may be argued that this 'something deeper' is the issue which causes Hardy's second voice to fragment into polyphonic discourse with itself. Emerging from this split are three subconsciousnesses representing the author's divergent attitudes toward evolution: the first reflects Hardy's cynicism and anger, the second reveals his melioristic inclination, and the third, which will be considered in the next chapter, suggests a hopeful solution to the problem of God's indifference.

Unlike Hardy's cynical persona, George Meredith found evolution a comforting ideology to believe in because he liked to think that its continual process of adaptation and refinement had enabled man to advance his capacity to act creatively, intelligently, and even to some extent, freely. Although man shares many characteristics with brute creatures and is obliged to respect the inhabitants of the enchanted woods of Westermain, he alone is rational and far-sighted enough to use the earth's resources for the betterment of the planet. In observing human behaviour – particularly in its most significant social context – Meredith fancied that he was beholding creative evolution in progress. His obligation, he believed, was to document in art the steady advance of that glorious process. Thus it is that Meredith's themes are most often centered around the personal development of highly self-conscious characters whose successes and failures along the upward evolutionary track are chronicled for their didactic impact on the reader. Hardy's angry sub-voice, on the other hand, is disparaging of evolution because wherever Hardy looks, to borrow again from Baker's analysis, he sees '"Crass Casualty" thwarting man's best endeavours, and what the scientist [Darwin] described as natural selection eliminating with blind indifference both the fit and unfit to survive'.[21] If a man imagines himself elect among species or a free agent in a Meredithian history, he is deluded by egoistic fantasies of free will and personal refinement dreamed up by those yearning to escape the absolutely inescapable. In contrast to Meredith's optimistic fantasising, Hardy grimly employs mixed metaphors to speculate upon the disposition of this evolution machine which divests man of his liberty. It may be that it operates *'like a knitter drowsed, / whose fingers play in skilled unmindfulness'*, or perhaps it functions as nothing more than a collection of electrical circuits:

> These are the Prime Volitions, – fibrils, veins,
> Will-tissues, nerves, and pulses of the Cause,
> That heave throughout the Earth's compositure.
> Their sum is like the lobule of a Brain
> Evolving always that it wots not of;
> A Brain whose whole connotes the Everywhere,
> And whose procedure may but be discerned
> By phantom eyes like ours; the while unguessed
> Of those it stirs, who (even as ye do) dream
> Their motions free, their orderings supreme;
> Each life apart from each, with power to mete
> Its own day's measures; balanced, self complete;
> Though they subsist but atoms of the One
> Labouring through all, divisible from none.[22]
>
> The Dynasts

Having recently discovered man's percipience to be the bastard child of evolution, nineteenth-century thinkers could not, as their ancestors had done, relax in smug assurance that a perfectly ordered hierarchy of being placed man in an elevated niche nearer Divinity than Nature because they now understood that nothing divided the species but man's rational sensibilities. If the idea of the evolution of man's consciousness inspired in Meredith a hopeful prospect of brilliant, genteel refinement of the race, it inspired Hardy's angry voice, which found no evidence that man could or would use such a unique power to profit the race, to blast evolution for allowing this gratuitous modification to occur. Humanity would be infinitely happier were it not precocious enough to discern the webbed anatomy of the Immanent Will superimposed across its history. Such a vision reduces man's historical achievements and failures to a one-dimensional stimulus-response timeline and leaves the individual to contemplate – without hope – the veil even as he is pushed mechanically toward it. Hardy's indignation over this injustice erupts consistently throughout his notebooks:

> Law [of evolution] has produced in man a child who cannot but constantly reproach its parent for doing much and yet not all, and constantly say to such parent that it would have been better never to have begun doing than to have overdone so indecisively; that is, than to have created so far beyond all apparent first intention (on the emotional side) without mending matters by a second intention and execution, to eliminate the evils of the blunder of overdoing. The emotions have no place in a world of defect, and it is a cruel injustice that they should have developed in it . . . .[23]

> A woeful fact – that the human race is too extremely developed for its corporeal conditions, the nerves being evolved to an activity abnormal in such an environment. Even the higher animals are in excess in this respect. It may be questioned if Nature, or what we call Nature, so far back as when she crossed the line from invertebrates to vertebrates, did not exceed her mission. This planet does not supply the material for happiness to higher existences. Other planets may, though one can hardly see how.[24]

While it is unlikely that Hardy would have traded places with an invertebrate, there is a suggestion in his poetry, consistent with his anti-vivisectionist sympathies, that animals might be all the nearer to Divinity because they lack the emotional cognition Nature has witlessly evolved in man. The infant bird 'Blinded ere yet a-wing', is cruelly treated 'with God's consent' in the same way that Browning's Porphyria is strangled by her lover as God allegedly looks on in mute complicity. The narrator of 'The Blinded Bird'[25] is a human whose rational sensibilities cause him to evaluate the creature's dilemma in terms of mortal happiness: This bird is blind. How can it fly? Why should it sing? How can it avenge its tormentors? A man would shake his fist at the gods and rail against their fiendishness, but the bird, 'resenting not such wrong', is reconciled with its 'Eternal dark . . . lot', knowing neither that it is dark nor eternal. Its zestful singing teaches the poet that true Divinity may be the unconscious acceptance of fate:

> Who hath charity? This bird.
> Who suffereth long and is kind,

> Is not provoked, though blind
> And alive ensepulchred?
> Who hopeth, endureth all things?
> Who thinketh no evil, but sings?
> Who is divine? This bird.

Of course this recognition does not solve man's problem, for he can scarcely evolve 'Back to hours when mind was mud', as Meredith frames it. Man is flatly stuck in his undivine lot, supremely conscious that it is dark and eternal, and, unlike the forgiving bird, unable to overlook the trespasses committed against him. Had the bird been human, it might well have been the narrator of 'Hap',[26] Hardy's first important commentary on Nature's savage apathy and man's unfortunate awareness of it. The sonnet begins with the if/then model of deductive reasoning that works well in man's rational arts of mathematics and science:

> If but some vengeful god would call to me
> From up the sky, and laugh: 'Thou suffering thing,
> Know that thy sorrow is my ecstasy,
> That thy love's loss is my hate's profiting!'
>
> Then would I bear it, clench myself, and die,
> Steeled by the sense of ire unmerited;
> Half-eased in that a Powerfuller than I
> Had willed and meted me the tears I shed.

If a Caliban-like god had chosen the speaker as his cosmic scapegoat, then the strength of his indignation would empower him to bear any degree of torture. Justice would ironically be served by the poet's sacrifice which reveals the gods to be unjust. Theoretically, the gods might as easily mete out prosperity; other men, profiting from this one's unfortunate example, could develop strategies to appease the deities or at least defend themselves against future 'ire unmerited'.

But not so. At the sonnet's volta, traditionally that moment when the problem presented in the preceding verses is solved with a witty twist, the poet dashes his exact, consoling if/then proposition against the rocks. He is not the prototype of Camus' absurdly happy Sisyphus who 'knows himself to be the master of his days' because he has scorned the gods by embracing his fate as his own free choice. The poet here is doubly imprisoned by a rational mind within a random universe:

> But not so. How arrives it joy lies slain,
> And why unblooms the best hope ever sown?
> – Crass Casualty obstructs the sun and rain,
> And dicing Time for gladness casts a moan . . . .
> These purblind Doomsters had as readily strown
> Blisses about my pilgrimage as pain.

When the Nature machine produced in man the ability to recognise design, it accordingly extinguished his ability to understand irrational events and processes. To evil intent, this speaker could respond with action, even if that action is to clench himself heroically in death; to 'Crass Casualty', to the sentient belief that his fate is determined not by design but by dice, he can respond only with anger, frustration, despair, and paralysis.

According to this angry voice, Tess is Hardy's most striking and distressing example of the individual trapped between Nature's hap and her own evolved consciousness. (Tess's case will be re-examined in Chapter 5 by an opposing voice which insists that she is victimised by her own unwillingness to exercise intelligent, self-accepting freewill.) The most eloquently written advocation of this popular old view is offered by Dorothy Van Ghent, who argues that 'the dilemma of Tess is the dilemma of moral consciousness in its intractable earthy mixture; schematically simplified, the signifying form of the Tess-universe is the tragic ineffectuality of such consciousness in an antagonistic earth where events shape themselves by accident rather than by moral design'.[27] Animated by an innocently sensual passion for life, the archetypal dairy-maid is on one hand Nature made flesh in its most luxuriant aspect. Likening her to ripe strawberries, rose blossoms, and a 'thyme-scented morning in May', a smitten narrator reflects that even after three years of mental anguish, 'some spirit within her rose automatically as the sap in the twigs. It was unexpended youth, surging up anew after its temporary check, and bringing with it hope, and the invincible instinct towards self-delight'.[28] Tess's nature – as Nature – is irrepressible as the blinded bird's, but unlike the bird she is regrettably convinced that 'purblind Doomsters' will conspire to 'unbloom' her 'best hope ever sown'. As instinct moves Tess to sing, intellect abruptly ends her chant because she cannot honestly voice sentiments such as, 'bless ye the Lord, praise Him and magnify Him for ever'. When Nature seduces her with its midsummer dawns and green scapes, experience leads her to believe that although other worlds may be 'splendid and sound', hers is 'a blighted one'. And if the healthy propulsion toward survival prompts Tess to escape after the murder of Alec, it should come as no surprise that rational thought sabotages her flight because, after all, 'It is as it should be . . . . This happiness could not have lasted'.

Tess accepts her fate with the resolution of Sisyphus and her sacrifice does ultimately prove the gods unjust, but what most grieved this cynical sub-consciousness and earned Hardy the reputation of being a pessimist was that the courage and integrity of this 'pure woman' won her absolutely nothing. Hardy would disagree with Irving Howe that she is 'human life stretched and racked, yet forever springing back to renewal',[29] for the whole dark point of the novel is that even Tess, exemplar of the finest of both Nature and culture, reaches a point where her emotional energy plays out. The sheer magnitude of her misfortune may stun the reader, but Tess had lived too comfortably with the spectre of her own death ever since the night when the family horse impaled itself on the spiked shaft of a mailcart. Like the 'knitter drowsed in skilled unmindfulness', she had slept while her wagon travelled mechanically down the road; the fatal collision was senseless and unfair, an economic disaster for the Durbeyfields and a foreshadowing of future calamity for Tess, but most significantly it was accomplished by an indifferent, accidental toss of the dice. In horror Tess reads in the pool of Prince's blood the truth about the inconsequentiality of her own existence. Van Ghent explains:

> the iridescence of the coagulating blood is, in its incongruity with the dark human trouble, a note of the same indifferent cosmic chemistry that has brought about the accident; and the smallness of the hole in Prince's chest, that looked 'scarcely large enough to have let out all that had animated him,' is the minor remark of that irony by which Tess's great cruel trial appears as a vanishing incidental in the blind waste of time and space and biological repetition.[30]

As Tess despairingly clasps her hand over the puncture in the horse's breast, she begins to grasp an awareness that as victims of the same Circumstance, she is as helpless to save Prince as she will be to save herself. What happiness she might achieve will be shadowed always by a certainty that the greater configuration of her life will unfold as a series of mishaps until death arrives at the reigns of a sleeping driver.

On behalf of Tess – as well as Jude, Henchard, and other characters who consistently misapprehend their human condition – Hardy insistently begs the Prime Mover to explain what it means 'By crowning Death the King of the Firmament', and forcing man's awareness of his mortality. The speaker in 'New Year's Eve'[31] demands to know why God has finished another year, 'strewn the leaf upon the sod, / Sealed up the worm within the clod, / And let the last sun down,' and why the futile process will begin again the next day. There are ninety-nine good reasons why nothing should exist at all, he complains, so:

> . . . why shaped you us, 'who in
>   This tabernacle groan' –
> If ever a joy he found herein,
> Such joy no man had wished to win
>   If he had ever known!

The answer comes, as it must if it is to come at all in words, from the poet's own interpretation of God's silence:

> Then he: 'My labours – logicless –
>   You may explain; not I:
> Sense-sealed have I wrought, without a guess
> That I evolved a Consciousness
>   To ask for reasons why.
>
> 'Strange that ephemeral creatures who
>   By my own ordering are,
> Should see the shortness of my view,
> Use ethic tests I never knew,
>   Or made provision for!'

It may appear shameful to man that Nature works in 'fore-thoughtless modes' and has no purpose in ordering a world in which beings more conscious and moral than itself are regularly doomed, and we may, like the speaker in 'Hap', wish to discover a vengeful presence at the back of things in the hope that in time we may persuade it to become merciful. But as Albert J. Guerard contends, the 'seeming vindictiveness' of Nature 'is a figment of our atavistic imagination appalled by the unregenerate nature of things'.[32] A fine illustration of Guerard's point is presented in Hardy's early novel, *A Pair of Blue Eyes* (1873), in which an obsessed suitor discovers that Nature's apathy is not to be taken personally, even as it hurls a man into the teeth of his own mortality. As he clings to the Cliff without a Name, Henry Knight begins to fancy that the wind lashing at his coat and the rain piercing 'into his flesh like cold needles' are antagonistic agents of Nature sent purposely to pry loose his hold and dash him into the sea below. Spitted to the rock, he moreover finds himself face-to-face with the fossil of a crustacean whose 'eyes, dead and turned to stone, were even now regarding him' as if to authenticate his welcome to the realm of evolutionary extinction. But at the instant when Knight gives up hope for his life, help arrives and he realises, maintains Guerard, that his 'nihilism is induced not by the momentary illusion of cosmic hostility embodied in the lashing rain, but by the lonelier sense of a total and timeless indifference'. Hardy's storms may destroy crops and his natural coincidences devastate lives the length and breadth of Wessex, but 'they are incapable of calculated malice. Their "malice" lies in their very lack of calculation and purpose'.[33]

This nihilistic sub-voice flares up in angry bonfires here and there along Hardy's artistic terrain, and yet it is oftentimes subdued by a steadier voice – Hardy's second sub-voice – which articulates a less desperate message. These two voices converge in the centreground of another hymnal – Egdon Heath, itself a symbol of transition between night and day, man and Nature, life and death, past and present, intent and aimlessness. It is at once a real plot of earth to be traversed in heat and torrent by Clym and Eustacia and the others in their passage to real places like Mistover or the Quiet Woman, and it is a metaphor for the wild predictability of both process and product of evolution. In its 'lonely face, suggesting tragical possibilities', and in its primitive 'antique brown dress', man sees reflected his own solitary image and finds himself resartored in earth's simplest clothing. There is no deceiving the ancient heath, for it recognises man as its own creation and knows, without knowing, his destiny. And there is no fooling man, not even Eustacia and Wildeve, that he is superior to the wasteland or separate from it in any way because it is 'a place perfectly in accord with man's nature – neither ghastly, hateful, nor ugly: neither commonplace, unmeaning, nor tame; but, like man, slighted and enduring . . . '.[34]

Theologian Nathan A. Scott is only partially correct, however, when he writes that 'believing a barren waste to be the appropriate image of what life in the modern world is like, Hardy makes this obscure isolated country of Egdon Heath . . . to be the type . . . of man'.[35] True: man is frail and his attachment to life evanescent, but, the more optimistic voice reminds us, the source of life is omnipotent and eternal. This voice heartily disagrees with de Beauvoir that the moment between past and present, indeed the singular moment man truly exists, is nothing. On the contrary, that moment is *everything* because the primal, instinctual throb of the heath beats in it. It was the heath that invested in Tess the robust vitality for which we admire her, and it was the heath that collected so many inanimate particles into a virile young Jude and propelled him to explore life; their purposes may have seemed futile, but that does not matter so much as the fact that the sensation of life itself was good. Who places a stethoscope to his breast and, listening to the sound of life, loathes his heart because it will one day cease to beat? 'Close to the body of things', D. H. Lawrence reflects of the heath, 'there can be heard the stir that makes us and destroys us', but we do not condemn it for giving what we know it will inevitably take back:

> The Heath heaved with raw instinct. Egdon, whose dark soil was strong and crude and organic as the body of a beast. Out of the body of this crude earth are born Eustacia, Wildeve, Mistress Yeobright, Clym, and all the others. They are one year's accidental crop. What matters if some are drowned or dead, and others preaching or married: what matter, any more than the withering heath, the reddening berries, the seedy furze, and the dead fern of one autumn of Egdon? The Heath persists. Its body is strong and fecund, it will bear

many more crops beside this. Here is the sombre, latent power that will go on producing, no matter what happens to the product. Here is the deep, black source from whence all these little contents of lives are drawn. And the contents of the small lives are spilled and wasted. There is savage satisfaction in it: for so much more remains to come, such a black, powerful fecundity is working there that what does it matter?

Three people die and are taken back into the Heath; they mingle their strong earth again with its powerful soil, having been broken off at their stem. It is very good.[36]

F. R. Leavis commends Hardy for 'the integrity with which he accepted the conclusion, enforced, he believed, by science that nature is indifferent to human values . . . the completeness of his recognition . . . and . . . the purity and adequacy of his response'.[37] Leavis's early observation that Hardy was 'betrayed into no heroic postures' extends even to the present sub-voice which asks not that man be content with his natural terminal status, but that he accept it, cease to analyse it, and refocus his attention to joys evident in temporal life. It is standard in Hardy criticism, notes Harold Orel, to quote letters and journal entries which iterate his distrust of blind Nature and blame it for endowing man with a consciousness that alienates him from the rest of creation – and to leave it at that. But Orel rightly moves beyond that point to consider the persona of 'Hardy the naturalist' whose many 'close-up observations' of the elements are 'filled with wonder that the world is so various'.[38] This sense of wonder duplicates, I believe, the spiritual essence of wonder which Carlyle advanced as the basis of worship and reverence, without which 'man's mind become[s] an Arithmetical Mill',[39] a machine geared to selfishly calculate the equation of its own mortality. Beach's charge that Hardy sounds the 'death-knell of the old nature poetry' is an accurate observation since Shelley's skylark and Wordsworth's cheery linnet do seem to have been exchanged for a darkling thrush in 'blast-beruffled plume'. I find little implication, however, that in this conversion the exquisite beauty of Nature has lost its power to awe and comfort Hardy simply because its complexities are not purposely ordained.

There are more overtly optimistic poems in Hardy's canon than 'The Darkling Thrush', and yet very often the hopeful spirit investing them overpowers the ordinary language of their narrative. Such is the case in 'Before and After Summer'[40] when the poet, half-frozen by February's 'wintry scourgings', compares himself with a muted bird perched in the pine tree outside his window. For both man and beast, 'those happy suns' of May and June are long gone, but their shared mood is one of anticipation: 'Looking forward to Spring / One puts up with anything'. Though less subtly, spring is also a source of wonder in 'The Year's Awakening'[41] in which the speaker asks bird and crocus root how they know that warm weather is approaching. Neither can intelligently trace the sun's 'pilgrim track' along 'the belting Zodiac' nor discern that 'light has won a fraction's strength, / And day put on some moments' length'; yet both are equipped with a wonderful timing mechanism that responds in rote to the rote changing of seasons. Like the trees in 'A Backward Spring', they have no capacity to 'ruminate on or remember / What happened . . . in mid-December', but that is as it should be. It is man, not birds or roots, who needs to recall in dark moments the promise of lighter ones. Relying on hope and human memory, we read irony in the icy 'Earth's apparelling', and, as intended, we contrast Hardy's poetic images of sky wrapped in a 'clammy shroud' with our own recollection of summer's warm congeniality.

Witness, too, the wonder of regeneration as Hardy presents it in the third phase of *Tess*. Just as the 'Maiden No More' has rallied from her cruel encounter with Alec, spring evolves again out of winter:

> The season developed and matured. Another year's instalment of flowers, leaves, nightingales, thrushes, finches, and such ephemeral creatures, took up their positions where only a year ago others had stood in their place when these were nothing more than germs and inorganic particles. Rays from the sunrise drew forth the buds and stretched them into long stalks, lifted up sap in noiseless streams, opened petals, and sucked out scents in invisible jets and breathings.[42]

Of course it has been rather fervently argued that Hardy's diction in this passage, particularly his use of terms like 'instalment', 'germs', and 'inorganic particles', forces a mechanistic reading of the natural process. And a similarly superficial reading of 'Proud Songsters'[43] echoes this misinterpretation:

Nature, Darwin, and the Pattern in the Carpet 51

> The thrushes sing as the sun is going,
> And the finches whistle in ones and pairs,
> And as it gets dark loud nightingales
>   In bushes
> Pipe, as they can when April wears,
>   As if all Time were theirs.
>
> These are brand-new birds of twelve-months' growing,
> Which a year ago, or less than twain,
> No finches were, nor nightingales,
>   Nor thrushes
> But only particles of grain,
>   And earth, and air, and rain.

Admittedly, regarding these passages from a purely empirical perspective, one might be persuaded that Hardy viewed Nature as a mass-production factory. But a truer reading, one properly tinctured with Carlyle's Wonder, reveals Hardy's ingenious use of atomic imagery to completely transform the atom. Flowers that seemed to have breathed autonomously and birds formerly reduced to their 'basic, dull constituents', Tom Paulin contends, are strangely brought to life:

> The mystery of their being, which the chemical equation seems about to completely account for, becomes suddenly uppermost with all the force of a last-moment surprise. They're only particles of grain – already the idea of growth is starting to surface here – they're earth and they're air – the list is becoming just slightly too long to have the decisive force of a simple, negative reduction. And then the word 'rain' suddenly and so aptly completes the rhyme that the question of what their exact basic constituents are is left open at the very moment when it should have been neatly answered and summed up. The mechanism is suddenly refreshed and transformed.[44]

Even the creeping undergrowth in the woods of Blackmoor Vale assumes a kindlier visage, I think, when we compare its

> mats of starry moss . . . interspersed tracts of leaves . . . trunks with spreading roots whose mossed rinds made them

like hands wearing green gloves; elbowed old elms and ashes with great forks, in which stood pools of water that overflowed on rainy days and ran down their stems in green cascades

and its incessant process of 'unfulfilled intention' by which

the leaf was deformed, the curve was crippled, the taper was interrupted; the lichen ate the vigour of the stalk, and the ivy slowly strangled to death the promising sapling[45]

with Darwin's final thoughts in *The Origin of Species*:

It is interesting to contemplate a tangled bank, clothed with many plants of many kinds, with birds singing on the bushes, with various insects flitting about, and with worms crawling through the damp earth, and to reflect that these elaborately constructed forms, so different from each other, and dependent upon each other in so complex a manner, have all been produced by laws acting around us . . . . Thus, from the war of nature, from famine and death, the most exalted object which we are capable of conceiving, namely, the production of the higher animals, directly follows.[46]

What to human sensibilities resembles trench warfare is actually a variant face of evolution's creativity in motion. Despite its decay – or perhaps arguably because of it – the undergrowth is animated with the same 'untameable, Ishmaelitish' beauty shared by Egdon Heath and celebrated by Darwin. The woodlanders living near the Vale do not find the copse oppressive or menacing, for they perceive their natural bond with the place and regard the dark tangle of ancient forest as a living, fortifying presence among them. Analysing the woods in terms of their composition or decomposition is as absurd as reducing a nightingale to particles of grain, earth, air, and water.

Darwin's conclusion that there is

grandeur in this view of life, with its several powers, having been originally breathed by the Creator into a few forms or into one; and that, whilst this planet has gone cycling on according to the fixed law of gravity, from so simple a beginning endless forms most beautiful and most wonderful have been, and are being evolved[47]

is echoed by Mill in his *Autobiography*:

> The intensest feeling of the beauty of a cloud lighted by the setting sun, is no hindrance to my knowing that the cloud is vapour of water, subject to all the laws of vapours in a state of suspension; and I am just as likely to allow for, and act on, these physical laws whenever there is occasion to do so, as if I had been incapable of perceiving any distinction between beauty and ugliness.[48]

Both are determined to delight in the beauty of Nature's handiwork, even though it is an accidental by-product of universal laws. The 'Creator', Darwin's term for the mysterious – but not divine – reaction which began all things, is indifferent to its offspring, and yet Hardy declares along with Darwin and Mill that man with his mixed-blessing consciousness must not be indifferent to the wonders of earth. After all, Hardy observes pensively, all creatures are inherently possessed of a mighty determination to endure and enjoy:

> We see it in all nature, from the leaf on the tree to the titled lady at the ball. It is achieved . . . under superhuman difficulties. Like pent-up water it will find a chink of possibility somewhere. Even the most oppressed of men and animals find it, so that out of a thousand there is hardly one who has not a sun of some sort for his soul.[49]

Consciously and wilfully, Hardy resolves to treasure field, flock, and tree, to gather inspiration from his fellowman, and to seize the day in whatever condition Crass Casualty tosses it to him:

> Let me enjoy the earth no less
> Because the all-enacting Might
> That fashioned forth its loveliness
> Had other aims than my delight.[50]

Suspecting, as he had for years, that death was at hand, Hardy concluded his fifth volume of verse with the reflective, melancholy 'Afterwards'.⁵¹ Elegiac in tone and content, the poem was included under the heading, 'Finale', and was intended to disclose those things for which the private man, rather than the famous author, most wanted to be remembered. The public Hardy might have been expected to rage more fiercely against the dying of the light or even to hurl himself into an Etna of his own making when, like Arnold's Empedocles, he grew sick to death of thinking; but at this moment the introspective personal figure found some comfort in the thought of being remembered as nothing more ennobled than a good man 'who used to notice such things' as the 'wind-warped upland thorn' and 'May's glad green leaves like wings, / Delicate-filmed as new-spun silk'. Neighbours who had watched him feed and protect the birds and hares that ravaged his garden would recall his wish that 'such innocent creatures should come to no harm' and would grieve to think that even though he could do little to safeguard them in life, 'now he is gone' and can do nothing. He was a man, they might remind one another, who had an eye for the mysteries of Nature and who, though he can no longer hear church bells in a 'crossing breeze', used to appreciate such things. Unlike Empedocles who, 'dead to life and joy', reads into everything his own deadness, this happier sub-voice reads into all things its own vitality.

It would be misleading, however, to conclude on such a cheerful note, for the pattern in the carpet yet reveals God to exist only as 'rapt Determiner', 'Prime Mover', 'Immanent Will'. Hardy's contemplation of the beautiful and yet harrowingly sublime process of evolution places him – in a uniquely Victorian way – squarely in the Romantic dilemma. Once an innocent who believed in kneeling oxen, he must now as mature observer of God's indifference submit himself in a wrenching epistrophe to the fact of his own mechanism. Hardy emerges from this crucible as a man determined to sustain wonder and courage against the imminence of chaos. If he is bitterly disappointed in Nature's automaton, he is no less willing to bask forever in the beauty of its resplendent by-products:

Why not sempiternal
Thou and I? Our vernal
   Brightness keeping,
   Time outleaping;
Passed the hodiernal!⁵²

3
The 'Great Adjustment': Evolutionary Meliorism in *The Dynasts*

> *The old theologies may or may not have worked for good in their time. But they will not bear stretching further in epic or dramatic art. The Greeks used up theirs; the Jews used up theirs; the Christians have used up theirs. So that one must make an independent plunge, embodying the real, if only temporary, thought of the age. But I expect that I shall catch it hot and strong for attempting it!*[1]

Many a bourgeois sensibility was offended by Hardy's ruminations concerning the nature of God. While it might seem unlikely that he could further alienate the reading population, the speculations offered by his third voice achieved just that. At least fifty modern meanings attach to the word 'God', this voice suggests, and it is therefore deceptive to 'call any force above or under the sky by the name of "God" – and so pass as orthodox cheaply, and fill the pocket'.[2] Never one to economise by filling his pocket with ersatz happy endings, Hardy argues that the only reasonable translation of the term for and concept of 'God' is 'the *Cause of Things*, whatever that cause may be'.[3] His implication that all modern thinkers are necessarily 'atheists in the ancient and exploded sense'[4] caused his critics to bristle at such audacity. G. K. Chesterton counter-accused Hardy of being a disillusioned, depressed, blasphemous 'village atheist' who invented the First Cause in order to 'give it a piece of his mind';[5] Carl Van Doren concurred that 'Whatever Mr. Hardy's conceptions, he demands some responsible deity upon whom he can lay the blame for the crass casualties which he encounters'.[6]

No amount of outcry or public indignation, however, quieted the voice of this chapter which unequivocally denies the antiquated notion of God as an old gentleman who guides his children with a stern but kindly hand. Yet it is in this voice that Hardy modifies his tentative theorising to posit his best hope thus far for humankind: Nature is at *present* a Darwinian evolution machine, an immanent force both creative and destructive, yet entirely unmindful of either consequence of its governance. The hope as Hardy advances it is that perhaps someday – perhaps even over billions of years – this absolute power will become conscious of its own motivation. Precedence has already been established in the form of man's percipience, and just as man has evolved a rational morality, so will the First Cause develop the capacity to recognise and evaluate its own conduct. When the 'drowsed knitter' awakens, Hardy maintains in this voice, it will revise its cruel rubric to make amends for the suffering it has unknowingly caused its creations. Moreover, since life at present is but an atomic fragment of humanity's evolving history, man must look forward in thought and action toward the fulfillment of time when Nature becomes rational. In 'Fragment'[7] a dark gallery of catacombs entombs the bodies of men neither dead nor alive who wait sempiternally for the 'Ultimate Cause' to heed the miserable conditions of life on earth. 'It is clear he must know someday', they agree among themselves while waiting obediently 'for him to see us before we are clay'. A stranger, surely an agnostic, prowling through the crypt demands of the faithful a reason why they are so sure God will ever achieve enough consciousness to concern himself with their affairs. Their response reflects the same logic Hardy uses to construct his third voice:

> Since he made us humble pioneers
> Of himself in consciousness of Life's tears,
> It needs no mighty prophecy
> To tell what he could mindlessly show
> His creatures, he himself will know.
> By some still close-cowled mystery
> We have reached feeling faster than he,
> But he will overtake us anon,
>   If the world goes on.

But man is hardly off the hook, for lingering patiently in the half-dark is not the most difficult thing he is called to do. In the meantime he must prepare for the 'Great Adjustment', as Hardy liked to think of it, by proving himself a worthy model for the Ultimate Cause to emulate. 'Loving-kindness', ironically a term borrowed from Swinburne, would be the ethic which encouraged man to set aside enmities and work as one brotherhood to improve the race and protect the environment; hopefully, the same ethic would be adopted by the Immanent Will in its eventual dealings with humanity. Devoid of any such metaphysical construct as an Immanent Will, T. H. Huxley's 1893 Romanes lecture on 'Evolution and Ethics' had already attempted to convince a disheartened generation that the cosmic struggle for existence could and should become subordinate to human virtue and intelligence. Perhaps as a longtime admirer of Huxley, Hardy modelled his concept of loving-kindness on the scientist's vision of the survival of the most ethical. This course of conduct, Huxley advised, is exactly opposite that which guarantees survival of the fittest:

> In place of ruthless self-assertion it demands self-restraint; in place of thrusting aside, or treading down, all competitors, it requires that the individual shall not merely respect, but shall help his fellows; its influence is directed, not so much to the survival of the fittest, as to the fitting of as many as possible to survive. It repudiates the gladiatorial theory of existence. It demands that each man who enters into the enjoyment of the advantages of a polity shall be mindful of his debt to those who have laboriously constructed it; and shall take heed that no act of his weakens the fabric in which he has been permitted to live. Laws and moral precepts are directed to the end of curbing the cosmic process and reminding the individual of his duty to the community, to the protection and influence of which he owes, if not existence itself, at least the life of something better than a brutal savage.[8]

Hardy's unique philosophical position reflects his personal coalescence of evolution theory with ethical meliorism and projects his hope that the improvement of the race and the awakening of the Immanent Will, though it be as gradual a process as the weathering away of a mountain range, will result in the enlightenment of life on earth.

This voice of evolutionary meliorism demands that since man

The 'Great Adjustment'

has preceded the Creator in evolving consciousness and developing the aptitude to discern good from evil, he must assume responsibility for teaching it likewise to value human ideals and ethics. The poet in 'God's Education'[9] thus chides the Creator for retracting from a young woman its gifts of beauty, health, and 'sprightliness of spirit'. Straining to understand what he perceives as robbery, he inquires:

> Why do you serve her so?
> Do you, for some glad day,
> Hoard these her sweets – ?

The Creator's response merely accentuates its obvious indifference:

> He said, 'O no,
> They charm not me; I bid Time throw
> Them carelessly away.'

Angered by such insouciance, the poet accepts his tutorial duty and volunteers a lesson which for the moment, at least, inspires the Creator to muse upon the ethic of loving-kindness:

> Said I: 'We call that cruelty –
> We, your poor mortal kind.'
> He mused. 'The thought is new to me.
> Forsooth, though I men's master be,
> Theirs is the teaching mind!'

Imagine the result, contends Hardy, if each of us were to take upon ourselves the enlightenment of the Immanent Will, if each generation were to practise even the most negligible amount of compassion greater than the last. If the globe does not prematurely self-destruct through ecological exhaustion or catastrophic war, then the millions of acts of loving-kindness compounded over billions of years should serve man well against the Great Adjustment. That man is competent to actualise this trust, Hardy had no doubt – at least not in this voice: after watching hours of patient labour conducted by men and women in the streets of London, he observed affectionately, 'Yes, man has done more with his materials than God has done with his'.

As early as 1907 in a letter to his longtime friend Edward Wright, Hardy boldly assumed credit for conceiving the ideas expounded by this melioristic voice. Discussing his invention of the term 'Immanent Will' and its role in *The Dynasts* (1908), Hardy confided:

> In a dramatic epic – which I may perhaps assume *The Dynasts* to be – some philosophy of Life was necessary, and I went on using that which I had denoted in my previous volumes of verse (and to some extent prose) as being a generalized form of what the thinking world had gradually come to adopt, myself included. That the Unconscious Will of the Universe is growing aware of itself I believe I may claim as my own idea solely – at which I arrived by reflecting that what has already taken place in a fraction of the whole (i.e. so much of the world has become conscious) is likely to take place in the mass – that is, the Universe – the whole Will becomes conscious thereby: and ultimately, it is to be hoped, sympathetic.[10]

In subsequent correspondence with Edward Clodd in 1908 and eugenist Caleb Saleeby in 1914, Hardy defended his right to claim those notions as his own:

> The assumption of unconsciousness in the driving force is, of course, not new. But I think the view of the unconscious force as gradually becoming conscious: i.e. that consciousness is creeping further & further back towards the origin of force had never (so far as I know) been advanced before *The Dynasts* appeared.[11]

Scholars have since challenged Hardy's contention and disputed his claim that the only philosophers who genuinely influenced his art were Darwin, Huxley, Spencer, Comte, Hume, and Mill. While the tenets of those thinkers are undoubtedly manifest in Hardy's poetry and fiction, they argue, it is the philosophy of Arthur Schopenhauer and the theories of Eduard Von Hartmann which seem to have been most radically adopted by Hardy in his construction of the character and qualities of the Immanent Will. His first recorded memorandum regarding the scheme of *The Dynasts* appeared in a journal entry on 27 March 1880, but the disposition of the Will – not as yet named – was quite skeletal: 'Action mostly automatic; reflex movement, etc. Not the result of what is called motive, though always ostensibly so, even to the actors' own consciousness'.[12] It was not until he had read Schopenhauer's *The World as Will and Idea* (1818) in the late 1880s that Hardy began to imagine the First Cause in terms of a willing force. By 1907, therefore, he could confess in the same letter to Wright:

> I quite agree with you in holding that the word 'Will' does not perfectly fit the idea to be conveyed – a vague thrusting or urging internal force in no predetermined direction. But it has become accepted in philosophy for want of a better, and is hardly likely to be supplanted by another, unless a highly appropriate one could be found, which I doubt.[13]

In his definitive study of *The Dynasts*, J. O. Bailey contends that Hardy embraced and modified Schopenhauer's concept of the Will and progressed from there to adopt Von Hartmann's theory of the unconscious nature of that immanent force. Hardy finished reading Von Hartmann's *Philosophy of the Unconscious* (1869) by the late 1890s, the same years in which he was planning and drafting the epic drama. It is Bailey's speculation that 'Hardy read the *Philosophy of the Unconscious* as thoughtfully as he had read *The Origin of Species* many years before. To him, for he was no professional scientist or philosopher, Von Hartmann's interpretation and criticism of the sciences and philosophies of his time may have seemed wholly valid', and it is likely that he 'reviewed or referred to it [*Philosophy of the Unconscious*] from time to time all during his composition of *The Dynasts*'. The final design of the epic, Bailey emphatically concludes, 'reflects, from the Fore Scene to the last line, the influence of Von Hartmann'.[14]

Since authorial intent can never be posthumously established, a resolution to the debate can only be approximated. I offer the following hypothesis. Hardy was indeed greatly influenced by Schopenhauer and Von Hartmann in so far as their theories regarding the universe added dimension to and provided a more adequate terminology for his own speculations. But his assertion that he was the first to suggest that the Will may become conscious and benevolent cannot be disputed on the basis of any pre-existing philosophies expounded by Schopenhauer or Von Hartmann, for neither supposed that event likely to occur. A brief discussion of their hypotheses and an examination of Hardy's rather renegade recapitulation may illuminate the manner in which he integrated all three in creating *The Dynasts*.

The World as Will and Idea, labelled by one historian as Schopenhauer's 'great anthology of woe', appeared in 1818 in the aftermath of Waterloo. The French Revolution had been a catastrophic failure, Napoleon lingered near death in his exile on St Helena, Europe lay in ashes, poverty, and economic ruin, and England's farmers and industrial workers had not even begun to recover their disastrous losses incurred by the fall in the price of grain. Her charred landscape punctuated by the graves of millions of her finest and strongest, Europe's prevalent mood was one of relentless despair. 'I thank God', mused Goethe, surveying the wasteland, 'that I am not young in so thoroughly finished a world'. But Schopenhauer *was* a young man in this exhausted world, and the misery in his own life found the age companionate. In *The World as Will and Idea*, he outlined his philosophy of the evil and essentially worthless nature of life, although to be fair we must at least perfunctorily acknowledge that pessimism was only one aspect of his complex theory.

It was not Schopenhauer's reserved optimism which attracted Hardy to his ideas, however. *The World as Will and Idea* begins with Schopenhauer's maxim 'The world is my idea', a statement meant to echo and endorse Kant's position that we can only know the external world through our sensations and ideas, and that the nature of the world of objects is peculiar to each consciousness which perceives it. But Schopenhauer was not satisfied with solipsism, nor did he accept Kant's belief that the reality behind the world of appearances, the 'thing in itself', is unknowable. Claiming that he had solved the riddles of the Sphinx, Schopenhauer proposed that reality was, in fact, knowable to any human being capable of introspection. All objects in the universe, even man's corporeal form, are expressions of the ultimate force of being, that power which is the essence of the will to live. In order for this Will to achieve gratification, it created the visible world, the world of phenomena, to obtain what it desires. The German novelist Thomas Mann describes the Will as 'something independent of knowledge . . . entirely original and absolute, a blind urge, a fundamental, uncaused, utterly unmotivated impulse'. Its purpose is not to evaluate the quality of its products; its sole desire is to will life. Mann demonstrates how the Will translates itself into roots and insects and granite and flesh:

> The will, then, this 'in-itself-ness' of things, existing outside of time, space and causality, blind and causeless, greedily, wildly, ruthlessly demanded life, demanded objectivication; and this objectivication occurred in such a way that its original unity became a multiplicity . . . thus dispersing itself into the myriad parts of the phenomenal world existing in time and space; but at the same time it remained in full strength in each single and smallest of those parts. The world, then, was the product and the expression of the will, the objectivication of the will in space and time.[15]

Every individual can know this Will because each of us possesses it undiluted in our bodies and in our ideas. The systems and organs of the body are inseparable from the Will which produced them, Schopenhauer insisted, and act as visible expressions of its desires:

> Teeth, throat and bowels are objectified hunger; the organs of generation are objectified sexual desire . . . . The whole nervous system constitutes the antennae of the will, which it stretches within and without . . . . As the human body generally corresponds to the human will generally, so the individual bodily structure corresponds to the individually modified will, the character of the individual.[16]

Man's ideas about himself and others form his character or intellect, itself symbolic of the Will's need for a rational guide to help its master discover the most effective means of wish-gratification. The relationship between the Will and the intellect, which Freud would later term the 'id' and the 'ego', was for Schopenhauer similar to that of 'the strong blind man who carries on his shoulders the lame man who can see'. An example extracted from the most ordinary experience should clarify this principle: you believe, if you share basic ideological similarities with the majority of your countrymen, that you are acting for the benefit of humanity by establishing a solid home, procreating children, training them to become fine citizens, and modelling for them virtues of hard work and righteous living. But in fact, children are the accidental result of your very own sexual instincts demanding fulfilment, which is in turn the Will's very own propensity to continue manufacturing life. The society which you imagine yourself preserving and defending is itself an artifact of your intellect, which is in turn an objectification of the Will. Simply stated, 'the will alone is'.[17] In the same way, the will to eat develops the digestive tract, and, crowning the hierarchy, the will to know – and consequently to rationalise what it perceives about its true motives – develops the brain and the intellect. 'Men are only apparently drawn from in front', Schopenhauer maintained, for 'in reality they are pushed from behind'. This kinship between the Will and the intellect is a premise which Mann finds humiliating, deplorable, and comic – though not untrue:

> It puts in a nutshell the whole tendency and capacity of mankind to delude itself and imagine that its will receives its direction and content from its mind, whereas our philosopher asserts the direct opposite, and relegates the intellect – aside from its duty of shedding a little light on the immediate surroundings of the will and aiding it to achieve the higher stages of its struggles for life – to a position as mere mouthpiece of the will: to justify it, to provide it with 'moral' motivations and in short to rationalize our instincts.[18]

These ideas appealed tremendously to Hardy, who had had the advantage of reading *The Origin of Species* in 1859 and of pondering the process of evolution, writing about it, brooding over it, for thirty years before discovering the much earlier published *The World as Will and Idea*. Fortunately, as Pierre d'Exideuil has asserted, 'between Schopenhauer and Hardy . . . stands Darwin, the channel whereby meliorism, the idea of the greatest possible enriching and perfecting of life, reaches the poet of *The Dynasts* . . . . Life, therefore, may become its own aim, whereas Schopenhauer stopped short with the denial of any final aim'.[19] Thus Hardy's theory of evolutionary meliorism both embraces Schopenhauer's concept of the will and forges beyond it. Where Schopenhauer asserted that

The 'Great Adjustment'

it is not the individual, but only the species that Nature cares for, and for the preservation of which she so earnestly strives . . . . The individual, on the contrary, neither has nor can have any value for Nature . . . and hence it is not only exposed to destruction in a thousand ways by the most insignificant accident, but originally destined for it, and conducted towards it by Nature herself from the moment it has served its end of maintaining the species,[20]

Hardy's third voice revises the message to assign future value to every individual member of every species. At *present* Nature remains absolutely indifferent, but eventually she will awaken and patiently mend.

While Schopenhauer's influence is frequently alluded to in Hardy criticism, Von Hartmann's quirky synthesis of optimism, pessimism, rationalism, mysticism, materialism, and idealism is generally ignored except in those essays specifically examining his contribution to *The Dynasts*. In his formidable three-volume *Philosophy of the Unconscious*, he embraced Schopenhauer's position that the impelling force behind reality is the Will and that it operates in every bit of matter in the universe; but in other ways he viewed the characteristics of that Will quite differently. Where Schopenhauer spoke of the Will as a blind, unmotivated urge toward life, Von Hartmann conceived of the Will as unconscious energy whose *very definite* goal is to evolve consciousness in all its creations. Von Hartmann took issue with Darwin's theory of natural selection because it made no sense according to law of mathematical probability to conclude that man's intellect and brilliantly constructed body – not to mention the intricate structures and functions of plants and animals – were generated by purely accidental haps of nature. (I think the philosopher mistook Darwin's idea of cumulative natural selection for the evolutionary equivalent of spontaneous generation, but in so doing took his place among fine Victorian company.) For Von Hartmann every act of the Will, even though it remains unconscious, presupposes a purpose. The vocal mechanisms of humans, for instance, were evolved with the intent of allowing expression and communication; what began as primitive grunts and cries became speech, from which sprang a linguistic *tour de force* including logic, philosophy, and culture. In its incessant propulsion to rationalise all things, the Will presupposed the need for the physical components necessary for articulation and deliberately evolved them over millions of years.

Von Hartmann's heavy-handed emphasis on teleology in Nature may have put Hardy off somewhat since the latter was extremely pro-Darwin, but he was intrigued by the philosopher's contention that the Will's ultimate purpose was to fashion all things conscious. Having always believed consciousness to be an exquisite gift and at the same time a sentence of doom, Hardy must have imagined himself a kindred spirit with Von Hartmann who believed the same. If the Will were successfully to develop consciousness in all matter, as Von Hartmann contended, then the world of objects would in the process become entirely rational – and the Will itself would be nullified. The problem (or the ideal solution, if you sympathise with Von Hartmann's logic) is that once consummate Reason seizes possession of the universe, it has no choice but to recognise that life is both self-defeating and evil in the illusion of hope that it promises but cannot deliver. Since rational totalitarianism would have already pre-empted unconscious instinct, without which the species would experience no urge to reproduce or even survive from one moment to the next, all life would voluntarily extinguish itself. Life may be good, Von Hartmann was willing to grant, but absence of life is better:

> We have seen that in the existing world everything is arranged in the wisest and best manner, and that it may be looked upon as the best of all possible worlds, but that nevertheless it is thoroughly wretched, and worse than none at all.[21]

> ... we who perceive in Nature and history only a single grand and marvellous process of development, we believe in a final victory of the ever more radiantly shining reason over the unreason of blind volition; we believe in a goal of the process that brings us release from the torment of existence, and to whose induction and acceleration we too may contribute our mite in the service of reason.[22]

The wisest application of consciousness, claimed the philosopher in terms again prefiguring twentieth-century Freudian ideology, would be one which eliminated the Will – ironically the same cruel instinct for life which mothered consciousness in the first place – and consequently annihilated the planet. Not until total obliteration of all matter and thought is achieved can peace and homeostasis prevail.

Meliorism was impossible in Von Hartmann's philosophy for the simple reason that consciousness, at least thus far, has been misused by man for selfish, greedy purposes. Man has no place to turn for guidance, furthermore, because 'the will can never become conscious' and therefore has no rational power to reveal man's foolishness to himself. In *The Dynasts* Hardy inverts Von Hartmann's theory and reassigns emerging consciousness to the Immanent Will – his own revised version of Schopenhauer's and Von Hartmann's Will – rather than to the objective world. And rather than imagining that the Immanent Will might awaken to Reason and consequently destroy the earth in an ambiguous gesture of furious generosity, Hardy formulates a genuinely optimistic ending. So it is that when Hardy claimed never before to have met with 'the idea of the unconscious will becoming conscious with the flux of time',[23] he was not, as some have suggested, simply an ageing man suffering natural lapses in memory. Hardy had instead rather astutely extracted ideas from his own speculations and those of Schopenhauer, Von Hartmann, and Darwin, as well as a polyphony of other philosophers, to originate the voice of evolutionary meliorism.

Early Victorian optimism had ebbed considerably by the end of the century. Hardy's guardedly optimistic voice seemed but a frail cry in the wilderness to those who embraced it and a new form of blasphemy to those who condemned him as an atheistic agitator. He made no attempt to restore his countrymen's faith in a Christian persona of God, nor did he allow any provision for life after death; the hope he advanced in an admittedly tremulous voice was that if mankind does his duty for the next several aeons, future man's short stay upon earth could be much less painful than it is now. The last poem included in *Poems of the Past and Present* (1902) foreshadows the plot of the then unpublished *The Dynasts* by describing the character of the Prime Mover and revealing the manner in which it will redeem its creation. 'Long have I framed weak phantasies of Thee, / O Willer masked and dumb!' begins the poet in 'Agnostoi Theoi'.[24] He has observed the numb reverie in which the one 'who makest Life become' eternally labours, and he wonders whether any consciousness at all informs the Will as it creates and destroys. After lengthy pondering the poet migrates from agnosticism to a theism of sorts. As the title suggests, he determines to believe that God will eventually loosen his automatic bonds and remedy man's ills:

> Perhaps Thy ancient rote-restricted ways
>   Thy ripening rule transcends;
>   That listless effort tends
> To grow percipient with advance of days,
>   And with percipience mends.

This awakening – which Hardy significantly terms 'Thy ripening rule' for its vivid image of the process of evolution – will come about imperceptibly at evolutionary pace as the Prime Mover now and again recognises moments of its own abominable behaviour:

> For, in unwonted purlieus, far and nigh,
>   At whiles or short or long,
>   May be discerned a wrong
> Dying as of self-slaughter; whereat I
>   Would raise my voice in song.

Knowing that he will be long dead before redress even begins, the poet finds solace and hope in the thought that the Mover is presently capable of tossing uncomfortably in its sleep.

Classical mythology and ancient religious documents such as the Bible reveal this omnipotent force to have been at one time an active participant in affairs on earth. It, he or she, depending upon its ritual function in a given culture, intervened in miraculous ways to provide for man's needs, avenged deserving victims of their adversaries, annihilated entire cities to illustrate a point, and even occasionally smote the 'good guys' for no apparent reason. But in his complex examination of post-medieval literature, J. Hillis Miller concludes that over the centuries man has become aware of God's gradual disappearance from the human world. By the nineteenth century, English authors such as De Quincey, Carlyle, Browning, Arnold, Clough, Hopkins, and Emily Brontë had begun to rethink the ethics of a world in which the Word may have at one time been flesh, but at present no longer dwells among us. The index of such a loss, as these writers demonstrate all too wrenchingly, is man's increasing sense of the disconnection which characterises his relationships with other men and nature and himself. If there exists a way to reharmonise the broken world, he is either incapable of perceiving it or powerless to mobilise his psychic and emotional energies toward achieving it. God may still be present but uncommunicative or it may be that he has moved on to another cosmos; in any case, he no longer functions as that centripetal Might which has formerly secured man in his rightful position in the world. As a result, Miller theorises from a deconstructivist vantage,

> the nineteenth and twentieth centuries seem to many writers a time when God is no more present and not yet again present, and can only be experienced negatively, as a terrifying absence. In this time of the no longer and not yet, man is 'Wandering between two worlds, one dead, / The other powerless to be born.'[25]

Browning, Arnold, and the others are designated by Miller as 'romantics' in the sense that they find the absence of God so intolerable that in desperation they reach into the void to take 'the enormous risk of attempting to create in that vacancy a new fabric of connection between man and the divine power'. For Browning, poetry could be engaged as a medium through which to re-establish the connection because it allows any man to admit that he knows nothing about God and permits him voluntarily to 'step out of the circle of his own perfection', which may shield him – but surely suffocates him as it did Andrea del Sarto. Arnold, on the contrary, condemns the creation of poetry at present, for it only magnifies our loss of the music of the spheres and further obscures what little light we have left. While we must not relinquish hope for brighter times, as Miller summarizes Arnold's position, we must, like the Scholar-Gipsy, 'hover in the void, in one direction waiting for the lightning to strike, the dawn to come, and in the other direction sternly and implacably criticizing all present cultural forms as false'.[26]

While Hardy did not believe in God *per se*, he perfectly matches Miller's more fundamental criterion of a romantic artist who is a 'maker or discoverer of the radically new, rather than the imitator of what is already known'.[27] In the absence of a universe with God inhabiting it, nurturing it, guiding it, Hardy attempts in poetry and dramatic verse to harmonise man, Nature and the ultimate Will through his radically new philosophy of evolutionary meliorism. In varying degrees of intensity, the entire Victorian culture felt the anguish of God's disappearance, and Hardy's third voice, in plainer poetry than that of Browning or Arnold, anticipates a way to call both man's and Mover's attention to the insufferable breach between them. In the octet of his sonnet 'The Sleep-Worker',[28] Hardy demands of Mother Nature when she will awaken and reconcile the antagonistic forces that waste humanity:

> When wilt thou wake, O Mother, wake and see –
> As one who, held in trance, has laboured long
> By vacant rote and prepossession strong –
> The coils that thou hast wrought unwittingly;
>
> Wherein have place, unrealized by thee,
> Fair growths, foul cankers, right enmeshed with wrong,
> Strange orchestras of victim-shriek and song,
> And curious blends of ache and ecstasy?

The Sleep-Worker ignores the question, but the poet, undaunted by silence he has likely heard before, reframes his inquiry in the sestet. He cannot know when the Great Adjustment might occur, but the more significant issue is what will happen when it does:

> Should that morn come, and show thy opened eyes
> All that Life's palpitating tissues feel,
> How wilt thou bear thyself in thy surprise?
>
> Wilt thou destroy, in one wild shock of shame,
> Thy whole high heaving firmamental frame,
> Or patiently adjust, amend, and heal?

Had Von Hartmann supposed that the Will could become conscious, he would surely have concluded that it would destroy the earth in one wild shock of sanity; Hardy presupposes a more forgiving force at the back of things.

Years before his third voice materialised, Hardy's observation

The 'Great Adjustment' 71

of human relationships had led him to judge that 'Love lives on propinquity, but dies of contact'.[29] Within a few days after recording that journal entry in 1888, he began work on what would become *Tess of the D'Urbervilles* (1891), but the sentiment remained with him and resurfaced frequently in the poetry of his later years. Most often it reverberates throughout arch-realistic love verses like 'At Waking'[30] in which a young man averts his eyes in repulsion as dawn reveals his lover to be 'but a sample / Of earth's poor average kind', and wails that 'the prize I drew / Is a blank to me!' Echoes of love dying of too-intimate contact are also distinctly heard in 'God-Forgotten',[31] one of Hardy's strongest melioristic statements. The ingenious premise is that the speaker is elected by the 'sons of Earth' to seek audience with God to demand some response to their cries for help:

> I towered far, and lo! I stood within
> The presence of the Lord Most High,
> Sent thither by the sons of Earth, to win
> Some answer to their cry.

God is puzzled by his visitor's story and frankly admits that he cannot recall creating any such planet. As observers of this vignette, we can easily imagine God shaking his head, frowning, pinching his beard, mentally reviewing the vast catalogue of his designs, drawing a blank:

> – 'The Earth, sayest thou? The Human race?
> By Me created? Sad its lot?
> Nay: I have no remembrance of such place:
> Such world I fashioned not.' –

'O, Lord,' the messenger timidly reminds him, 'forgive me when I say / Thou spakest the word that made it all.' God mutters to himself a moment, perhaps folds his arms and gazes again into space. At length he recollects:

> 'The Earth of men – let me bethink me. . . . Yea!
> I dimly do recall
>
> 'Some tiny sphere I built long back
> (Mid millions of such shapes of mine)

> So named. . . . It perished, surely – not a wrack
>   Remaining, or a sign?
>
> 'It lost my interest from the first,
>   My aims therefor succeeding ill;
> Haply it died of doing as it durst?'

Obviously no fond memories surface with God's recollection of earth and man; no father-figure leafs dotingly through the pictorial album of his children's historical development. It is almost as though he cared most for earth while its creatures were yet proximate ideas in his brain, but lost interest in humanity's welfare even before it toddled a first step. In time vanished love, contact, and memory altogether.

Such is not the case, it becomes clear, as God continues. He is shocked to learn that earth still exists, exclaiming that life there must be very dark, indeed, since he has heard NOTHING of its troubles until now. 'Of its own act the threads were snapt whereby, / Its plaints had reached mine ear,' God lectures testily, explaining his withdrawal from the world. The poor speaker must quiver as he faces God and accepts the reproof intended for all humanity:

> 'It used to ask for gifts of good
>   Till came its severance, self-entailed,
> When sudden silence on that side ensued,
>   And has till now prevailed.
>
> 'All other orbs have kept in touch;
>   Their voicings reach me speedily:
> Thy people took upon them overmuch
>   In sundering them from me!'

God's anger flares as he talks, and his speech charges with indignation. He turns aside from the trembling reprobate to resume his tirade to himself. Earth is foolish and pompous to think it can get along without him, the Almighty, the One who daily frames perfect spheres with merely a word. Why should he heed the tardy whimpering of this tainted ball when it repaid his love with rejection? Mankind's gratitude and affection for him died as its own self-importance increased; there began the intolerable separation. Lay it at man's feet.

And yet here is man contritely appealing for help after aeons of pointless torment. His wrath dissipating, God turns back to the messenger:

> 'But sayest it is by pangs distraught,
> And strife, and silent suffering? –
> Sore grieved am I that injury should be wrought
> Even on so poor a thing!'

Inclining toward the earthling like a minister shaking his finger at a wayward congregation, God prepares to make his most important point. This is the message he wants disseminated among all men, and it is the very crux of evolutionary meliorism:

> 'Thou shouldst have learnt that *Not to Mend*
> For Me could mean but *Not to Know*:
> Hence, Messengers! and straightway put an end
> To what men undergo.' . . .

The Immanent Will, call it God or Sleep-Worker or any of Hardy's epithets, is in the process of awakening from its historical unconsciousness. Perhaps man's self-absorption is culpable for breaking the bond between himself and God, as this poem suggests, or perhaps the Immanent Will has been tending other worlds while leaving this one subject to the random misconduct of Nature. Or it may be that God's disappearance is figurative and symbolic rather than literal, that the Word was never flesh except in man's ancient fantasies, that we are homesick for a place we have never been. In any case, this voice maintains, this force will one day know and mend the wounds inflicted during its absence.

The first allusion to what would emerge as Hardy's *magnum opus* appeared in an 1888 diary entry in which he recorded his sketchy idea for *The Dynasts*: 'A Homeric Ballad, in which Napoleon is a sort of Achilles, to be written. Mode for a historical drama. Action mostly automatic; reflex movement, etc. Not the result of what is called motive, though always ostensibly so, even to the actors' own consciousness. Apply an enlargement of these theories to, say, "The Hundred Days"!'[32] Working against the time constraint of his imagined impending death – although he outlived its publication by twenty years – the poet was enormously relieved when the epic-drama, written in three parts, nineteen acts, one hundred and thirty scenes, and encompassing action occurring over ten years, was completed in 1908. The grains for this grand epic were sown inadvertently by Hardy's relatives. His grandfather had been one of the 'Bang-up locals', a profoundly patriotic (if somewhat skittish) band of Dorset farmers and artisans armed and ready to fight the French should they invade from the south. Other family members who had lived during Napoleon's conquests had raised the boy on their stories and songs as matter-of-factly as they passed an ancestral cot or tea-kettle from one generation to the next, so it is no surprise that Wessex scenes crop up from time to time in Parts I and III as Hardy steals an affectionate peek at his familiar rustics. Some real, some artistically designed, they track the war and prepare to defend their little countryside from 'ol' Boney', whom they believe eats rashers of baby every morning for breakfast. Hardy's fascination with the French Emperor was further stimulated by the fact that an early namesake, Thomas Masterman Hardy, had served as Nelson's flag-captain aboard the HMS *Victory* at Trafalgar and had brought momentary fame to an otherwise undistinguished family.

By 1885, almost thirty years before publication of Part First, Hardy had begun researching the Napoleonic era and reviewing the British Museum's collection of newspapers, drawings, and other memoirs of the period. His visits to Waterloo and Napoleon's tomb, although infrequent, were extremely profound encounters with a history which Hardy felt flowed through him like a stream. Even as late as 1917, he still observed the anniversaries of Waterloo and Quatre Bas and recounted with glee the evening in 1903 when John Tussaud, proprietor of Madame Tussaud's famous waxworks, allowed him to touch the museum's Napoleonic relics and wear the *Petit Caporal's* infamous bicorne hat. An admiring, if rather bewildered T. E. Lawrence (of Arabia) mused in 1923 that 'Napoleon is a real man to him, and the country of Dorsetshire echoes that name everywhere in Hardy's ears. He lives in his period, and thinks of it as the great war'.[33] Continental authors had written prolifically about Napoleon's career, but except for Hardy's own few Napoleonic ballads included in *Wessex Poems* (1898) and his novel,

The Trumpet Major (1880), which recounted his grandparents' experiences during a threatened invasion, little had been published which duly credited English 'influence and action throughout the struggle'. In adopting the Napoleonic 'Clash of Peoples artificially brought about some hundred years ago' as the structure and content of his epic drama, Hardy could at once expose the ineptitude of the British dynasts and vindicate the heroic war efforts of England's ordinary men, women, and even animals. Hardy claimed 'tolerable fidelity' to facts and dates and assured readers that, whenever possible, every attempt had been made to paraphrase actual dialogue and to describe characters, events, scenery, and relics in as much accurate detail as research into an era past could permit.

But facts and dates were actually of minor concern to Hardy, for he never pretended to be an historian, and despite its subtitle, 'An Epic-Drama', *The Dynasts* was never intended to be performed on stage. From the outset he conceived of it as an Elizabethan verse drama which would employ a hierarchy of plots sustained by the commentary and action of an immense cast of principals, common soldiers, rustics, and chorus figures. It should be read in much the same way we would read any other work of fiction, except that we must adjust our expectations toward the broadly cinematic spectacle and away from the tightly confined narrative of the traditional novel. Hardy envisioned *The Dynasts* as a magnificent, living illustration of cosmic complexity, and he chose the Napoleonic wars as his landscape because their arena was sufficiently colossal to display history in both macroscopic and microscopic views. All factions of earth's population are represented as if on a giant screen: flowers, snails, and moles crushed by men marching to war; nameless soldiers left dead on foreign battlefields; intermediate officers torn between command and conscience; dynasts tossing off arbitrary decisions which will alter history for the next millennium. Stretched like a map over the shifting scenes is the preternatural figure of the Immanent Will whose rote designs are bared now and again throughout the drama. In his 1903 Preface to Part First, Hardy forewarns the mental spectator about to read on that he must be willing to maintain poetic faith not only in the unusual panoramic structure of the play but in the contents as well. His rationale for invoking Coleridge's 'willing suspension of disbelief' is his conviction that the public would otherwise misapprehend his use of Spirits in the work and forfeit to that ignorance the deeper message intended. Hardy was right, of course.

The play begins with a Forescene occurring in the Overworld, a plane high above earth on which are assembled a number of Spirits, Choruses, Shades, Rumours, Messengers, and Recording Angels. The preface has already introduced this controversial cast and explained their presence:

> It was thought proper to introduce, as supernatural spectators of the terrestrial action, certain impersonated abstractions, or Intelligences, called Spirits . . . . The wide prevalence of the Monistic theory of the Universe forbade, in this twentieth century, the importation of Divine personages from any antique Mythology as ready-made sources or channels of Causation, even in verse, and excluded the celestial machinery of, say, *Paradise Lost*, as peremptorily as that of the *Iliad* or the *Eddas* . . . . These phantasmal Intelligences are divided into groups, of which one only, that of the Pities, approximates to 'the Universal Sympathy of human nature – the spectator idealised' of the Greek Chorus; it is impressionable and inconsistent in its views, which sway hither and thither as wrought on by events. Another group approximates to the passionless Insight of the Ages. The remainder are eclectically chosen auxiliaries whose signification may be readily discerned.[34]

Most of the dialogue between these Intelligences occurs between Spirit of the Years, the oldest and most rational spirit who must repeatedly demonstrate the unconscious nature of the Immanent Will, and Spirit of the Pities, the youngest phantom who cannot comprehend a Creator entirely lacking conscience and sympathy. Spirit Sinister enjoys contemplating the suffering caused by the Immanent Will's sleeping machinations; Spirit Ironic finds the whole situation laughable and entertaining. All the phantoms with their diverse personalities and opinions represent Hardy's polyphony of voices embodied in metaphysical beings. If the personas of Spirits Ironic and Sinister are factored out, for instance, what remains is a recitation of Hardy's gloomier voices as they declare in 'Thoughts from Sophocles':[35]

Who would here sojourn for an outstretched spell
His senseless promptings, to the thinking gaze,
Since pain comes nigh and nigher with lengthening days,
And nothing shows that joy will ever upwell.

Death is the remedy that cures at call
The doubtful jousts of black and white assays.
What are song, laughter, what the footed maze,
Beside the good of knowing no birth at all?

And in the constant exchange between Years and Pities can be heard the familiar debate between Hardy's mind, logical and resolute in its unequivocal profession of Darwinism, and his empathic heart which reluctantly abjures Christianity and cleaves to the thread of evolutionary meliorism. Pities, John Galsworthy affectionately wrote to Hardy, is 'a kind of excrescence, a pearl as it were, on the oyster of life', and since existence has become so diseased, 'the pearls thereof are the most beautiful thing we know; and have become more precious than the oyster'.[36] In carnival-like disorder, if Bakhtin's term can be invoked to describe the industry of supernatural beings, the several consciences argue among themselves, reassure each other, upstage, ridicule, defend, and enlighten one another within a conceptual framework Hardy could achieve only in epic expanse.

From this lofty perspective earth is introduced at the close of the Forescene, and it becomes apparent that most of the action will take place there among its troubled inhabitants. Hardy had conceived of 'The human race to be shown as one great network or tissue which quivers in every part when one point is shaken, like a spider's web if touched',[37] and his stage directions begin accordingly with a wide-angled pan of Europe's topography, narrowing as the imaginary camera lens zooms close enough to distinguish general behaviours of people:

> The nether sky opens, and Europe is disclosed as a prone and emaciated figure, the Alps shaping like a backbone, and the branching mountain-chains like ribs, the peninsular plateau of Spain forming a head. Broad and lengthy lowlands stretch from the north of France across Russia like a grey-green garment hemmed by the Ural mountains and the glistening Arctic Ocean.

The point of view then sinks downwards through space, and draws near to the surface of the perturbed countries, where the peoples, distressed by events which they did not cause, are seen writhing, crawling, heaving, and vibrating in their various cities and nationalities.³⁸

Superimposed over the corpse-like earth and its swarms of people is the eerily transparent shape of the Immanent Will, revealing to the Spirits the manner in which all matter and energy are *'fibrils, veins, Will-tissues, and pulses'* of the splendid process of evolution.

The action of Part First begins *in medias res* in England, March 1805, where rumours that Napoleon is planning to invade London have stirred the population to prepare for war. The House of Commons is divided over the situation – Fox and Sheridan demanding a strong, unified army, Pitt concerned that a display of power might aggravate the despot's bluffing into blood-and-guts war. The plot develops slowly over the ensuing six acts as Napoleon crowns himself King of Lombardy and sets in motion his scheme to conquer Europe and Britain. His plan to decoy Nelson into the West Indies while French troops penetrate the English Channel is thwarted when his naval commander, Admiral Villeneuve, flees to Cadiz rather than follow orders. Snipers from the mizzen-tops of Villeneuve's ships kill a number of officers aboard H.M.S. *Victory*, among them the heroic Nelson. The British win the battle at Cape Trafalgar despite their loss, and an indefatigable Napoleon turns back to invade unsuspecting Austria. Within three days after the initial clash at Ulm, Austria surrenders to France; from there Napoleon sweeps east to massacre the Russian forces at Austerlitz. An uneasy armistice is agreed upon by France and Russia, the terms requiring Russian soldiers to stay on their own soil and the government to sever all relations with England, including closing Russian seaports to British vessels. After all, Napoleon propagandises, it is in Europe's best interest that Austria and Russia should align with France in order to destroy

> False-featured England, who, to aggrandize
> Her name, her influence, and her revenues,
> Schemes to impropriate the whole world's trade,
> And starves and bleeds the folk of other lands.³⁹

The 'Great Adjustment'   79

Pitt, meanwhile, has received news of Austerlitz and realises in horror that England stands alone against France and, partially thanks to his short vision, is largely unprepared to resist her attack. He has been ill for some time, but takes to his deathbed soon after in January 1806. 'My Country!' he moans just before sinking into a final stupor, 'How I leave my country!' Pities urges Years to whisper some word of comfort to the tortured man, but it declines. Time and again it has attempted to warn Pitt about this national disaster, but the minister could never fathom the intelligence. '*Now I would leave him to pass out in peace*', Years sighs solemnly, '*And seek the silence unperturbedly.*' Sinister sneers that '*Even ITS official Spirit can show ruth / At man's fag end, when his destruction's sure!*' But Years interjects the last word of Part First by soberly reminding all present that they, too, are temporary emanations of the Will: '*It suits us ill to cavil each with each. / I might retort. I only say to thee / ITS slaves we are: ITS slaves must ever be!*'[40]

Part Second encompasses the events between Pitt's death in 1806 and the invasion of Russia in 1812, a period sometimes referred to as Napoleon's seven fat years. The Corsican tyrant cannot make a wrong move, it appears, for every confrontation ends in his wresting greater glory for France. He conquers the Prussians on the field of Jena and in the aftermath catches a first prophetic glimpse of the King's beautiful daughter, Archduchess Maria Louisa. In a tearful scene in Josephine's boudoir, he has already informed his wife that her inability to produce an heir endangers the future of his dynasty. Manipulatively appealing to her compassion and patriotism, Napoleon begs his wife to agree to divorce for the sake of their beloved country:

> selfish 'tis in my good Josephine
> To blind her vision to the weal of France,
> And this great Empire's solidarity.
> The grandeur of your sacrifice would gild
> Your life's whole shape.[41]

Defeated by her husband's cruelly persuasive tactics, Josephine agrees.

The British win several bloody battles in Spain, while at home King George's insane paroxysms grow more frequent and turbulent. Neither leeches nor opium restrain him for long, and it is obvious, sadly for the country, that his gambling, womanising, self-aggrandising son will soon take the throne. As George III retires into feeble obscurity, Napoleon's new wife, Maria Louisa, delivers his first legitimate heir. Their union has produced not only a son, but, ironically, the seeds of Napoleon's downfall: before marrying the Hapsburg Archduchess, he had promised to wed Anne Romanov, sister of Tsar Alexander, in order to secure relations with Russia. Shrewdly calculating that he could seize the entire Ottoman Empire rather than divide it with Russia, Napoleon breaks the engagement. Part Second ends as Russia gears for retribution in the east, and in the west the Prince of Wales receives word that he is officially Prince Regent of England. Drawing into a royal stance, he decrees that his reign will be easy and comfortable if Napoleon falls to Russia. His only regret is that the glory of battle will be over. 'I was born for war,' exclaims the *enfant terrible* who has seen little active duty, 'it is my destiny!'

War truly is Napoleon's destiny, however, and Part Third chronicles the lost battles and failing luck which stem his years of success. The action proper begins at midsummer 1812 on the bank of the Niemen River as the Imperial columns of the French army make ready to invade Russia; from there they plan to conquer India and impound her English settlements. This final instalment of the drama is structured upon the theme of fate and the workings of the Immanent Will therein, and Napoleon foreshadows his doom in Act I, Scene I by falling from his horse as it stumbles over an embankment. Following a joyless victory at Borodino, the exhausted French troops march toward Moscow – which they discover is deserted and in flames. Inside the empty Kremlin, which begins to smoulder and crackle as he confers with his officers, Napoleon is forced to admit that the Muscovites have outsmarted him. Retreat is imperative, he cries, 'Or we shall let this Moscow be our tomb'.

Winter has advanced as the French trudge like caterpillars along the road from Smolensko to Lithuania. Snowstorms and winds are merciless, Hardy no less merciless in his description of freezing, starving soldiers. Tattered like skeletons and unable to bind together their gaping boots, they hover around small fires and eat rashers of dead horse seasoned with gunpowder for salt. Noses and ears are frostbitten, pus oozes from swollen eyes, ice crystals suspended from frozen beards clink together

The 'Great Adjustment' 81

as the men hobble from fire to fire. In the midst of the gloom enters a straggler who whispers an electrifying message: Napoleon has deserted to Paris. As the news circulates throughout the encampment, some men sob like children, others rage in impotent despair, and some few commit suicide. Wellington's forces together with allied Spanish and Portuguese companies, in the meantime, have trounced the French on the Plain of Vittoria and again in the Pyrenees. They advance north toward Paris as Russia, Prussia, and Austria make their way west across the frozen landscape. Napoleon is detained in Paris as he tries to escape and grudgingly signs abdication papers to the new Bourbon government; lying in wait along the old city walls of Avignon, French *misérables* hurl stones at the coach dispatching him to exile and weep for the 'Ogre of Corsica' to return their fathers, sons, and husbands murdered in war. Confident that his star has not yet set, Napoleon escapes within the year from his imprisonment on the island of Elba, reassembles a miniature army, and confronts the allied forces at Waterloo in June 1815. The remnants of France's *Grand Armée* are slaughtered in great bloody streams, and on every side banks of corpses lie with faces contorted and lips blackened by smoke and cartridge-biting. Napoleon attempts a rally, but at long last convinced that his regime has ended, gallops into the dark woods of Bosu. The moon sinks, blotting out the final scene, as Napoleon soliloquises on his inevitable damnation by future historians:

> So, as it is, a miss-mark they will dub me;
> And yet – I found the crown of France in the mire,
> And with the point of my prevailing sword
> I picked it up! But for all this and this
> I shall be nothing . . . .[42]

Predictably, Pities feels sorry for the man whose *'loaded heart / Bears weight enough for one bruised, blistered while'*,[43] but Napoleon cannot play innocent. Often he had heard the promptings of the Spirits foretelling his doom and had even felt the web of the Immanent Will etched across his mind and body; yet clearly he did not expect to take the tragic fall of other dynasts before him. His immodest aim was to become the apotheosis of heroes:

> To shoulder Christ from out the topmost niche
> In human fame, as once I fondly felt,
> Was not for me. I came too late in time
> To assume the prophet or the demi-god,
> A part past playing now. My only course
> To make good showance to posterity
> Was to implant my line upon the throne.
> And how shape that, if now extinction nears?

One ambiguous consolation remains:

> Great men are meteors that consume themselves
> To light the earth. This is my burnt-out hour.[44]

There can be little doubt that as he finalised the scheme for *The Dynasts*, Hardy kept in mind a passage from *The World as Will and Idea* in which Schopenhauer imagines an 'earth-Spirit' introducing man to the machinations of the Will in history:

> Suppose we were allowed for once a clearer glance into the kingdom of the possible, and over the whole chain of causes and effects; if the earth-spirit appeared and showed us in a picture all the greatest men, enlighteners of the world, and heroes, that chance destroyed before they were ripe for their work; then the great events that would have changed the history of the world and brought in periods of the highest culture and enlightenment, but which the blindest chance, the most insignificant accident hindered at the outset; lastly, the splendid powers of great men, that would have enriched whole ages of the world, but which, either misled by error or passion, or compelled by necessity, they squandered uselessly on unworthy or unfruitful objects, or even wasted in play. If we saw all this, we would shudder and lament at the thought of the lost treasures of whole periods of the world. But the earth-spirit would smile and say, 'The source from which the individuals and their powers proceed is inexhaustible and unending as time and space; for, like these forms of all phenomena, they also are only phenomena, visibility of the will. No finite measure can exhaust that infinite source; therefore an undiminished eternity is always open for the future for the return of any event or work that was nipped

The 'Great Adjustment' 83

in the bud. In this world of phenomena true loss is just as little possible as true gain. The will alone is . . . .'[45]

This portrayal of the Will is reminiscent of D. H. Lawrence's description of the infinite, vital fecundity of Egdon Heath as it consumes one generation to sustain the next. Hardy's Immanent Will, similar to the immanent energy in Schopenhauer's theory, is autonomous, unconscious, aimless, and indestructible, its strange and mysterious patterns the underpinning of human will.

The first line in *The Dynasts* is uttered by Shade of Earth as it asks, 'What of the Immanent Will and Its designs?' Hardy is not usually so direct, but this is the first of three seminal issues treated in the drama, and its immediate introduction provides opportunity for immediate definition. Years answers the question with a summary of the Will's uncanny nature:

> IT *works unconsciously, heretofore,*
> *Eternal artistries in Circumstance,*
> *Whose patterns, wrought by rapt aesthetic rote,*
> *Seem in themselves Its single listless aim,*
> *And not their consequence.*[46]

Chorus of the Pities, heard as aerial music, is incensed. It refuses to believe that the Immanent Will remains unconscious after so long:

> *Still thus? Still thus?*
> *Ever unconscious!*
> *An automatic sense*
> *Unweeting why or whence?*
> *Be, then, the inevitable, as of old,*
> *Although that so it be we dare not hold!*

Believe whatever you like, Years retorts, but understand that

> *You cannot swerve the pulsion of the Byss,*
> *Which thinking on, yet weighing not Its thought,*
> *Unchecks Its clock-like laws.*

Pities is stubborn as only the heart can be. In the face of all history as evidence to the contrary, it debates the issue until in exasperation Years offers to prove that the Immanent Will operates like a sleeping knitter. A war among great dynasties is shaping on the planet below and will serve as excellent illustration that all actions, even man's most brilliantly conceived endeavours, are but involuntary spasms in the knitter's dream:

> *Methinks too much assurance thrills your note*
> *On secrets in my locker, gentle sprites;*
> *But it may serve. – Our thought being now reflexed*
> *To forces operant on this English isle,*
> *Behoves it us to enter scene by scene,*
> *And watch the spectacle of Europe's moves*
> *In her embroil, as they were self-ordained*
> *According to the naive and liberal creed*
> *Of our great-hearted young Compassionates,*
> *Forgetting the Prime Mover of the gear,*
> *As puppet-watchers him who pulls the strings –*
> *So may ye judge Earth's jackaclocks to be*
> *Not fugled by one Will, but function-free.*[47]

Schopenhauer's phrase, 'The will alone is' is thereafter echoed and amplified in almost every scene. Even as Villeneuve agonises over his decision to 'fail the Emperor; / But shame the navy less', Years shows him to be acting out a doom which was prescribed before he was born; no less are Napoleon's military accomplishments the consequence of the Will's willing. He, like King George, Tsar Alexander, and all other dynasts, is

> *Moved like a figure on a lantern-slide.*
> *Which, much amazing uninitiate eyes,*
> *The all-compelling crystal pane but drags*
> *Whither the showman wills.*[48]

Spirit Ironic enjoys watching humans galvanised helplessly into combat because 'War makes rattling good history', but Hardy makes it clear that the Immanent Will twitches its creations with absolute impunity. After Nelson's stirring death scene, Pities wails that Sophocles visioned it too well in his observation that the gods shame themselves by grossly mistreating their own creations. 'Why make Life debtor when it did not buy?' it demands.

Years is quick to defend the Will by explaining that it functions on a metaphysical level above conscious intent. It metes life and death purposely but aimlessly, and any being's capacity to comprehend that fact is a tragic accident of evolution:

> Nay, blame not! For what judgment can ye blame? –
> In that immense unweeting Mind is shown
> One far above forethinking; processive,
> Yet superconscious; a Clairvoyancy
> That knows not what It knows, yet works therewith. –
> The cognizance ye mourn, Life's doom to feel,
> If I report it meetly, came unmeant,
> Emerging with blind gropes from impercipience
> By listless sequence – luckless, tragic Chance,
> In your more human tongue.[49]

You may object, as have a good many before you, that Hardy cannot have it both ways. The Will must either predetermine all events or operate as the blind motivation behind accidentalism. Hardy must have anticipated such rebuttal, but Years' speech was almost certainly drawn from the following excerpt from Von Hartmann's *Philosophy of the Unconscious* in an attempt to explain how the Will could be both purposive and designless. In the same way that a mirror can never reflect its own image, the Immanent Will produces patterns it cannot see:

> this unconscious intelligence is anything but blind, rather far-seeing, nay, even clairvoyant, although this seeing can never be aware of its own vision, but only of the world, and without the mirrors of the individual consciousnesses can also not see the seeing eye. Of this unconscious clairvoyant intelligence we have come to perceive that in its infallible purposive activity, embracing out of time all ends and means in one, and always including necessary data within its ken, it infinitely transcends the halting, stilted gait of the discursive reflection of consciousness, ever limited to a single point, dependent on sense-perception, memory, and inspirations of the Unconscious. We shall thus be compelled to designate this intelligence, which is superior to all consciousness, at once unconscious and super-conscious.[50]

In his construction of the Immanent Will, Hardy surely adopted Von Hartmann's conclusion that action which is both purposive and unmotivated must also be considered instinctive. Each time the Will is superimposed over man's behaviour, it is likened to a brain, a living organism which instinctively manipulates activity without conscious awareness of its unplanned goal – but with determination to continue producing flux in matter. The Will is a Mind, then, asleep, dreaming, unable to control what it dreams because those emanations rise from its unconscious impulses to create at any expense.

Assuming that man's intelligence is the result of the Will's purposive movement toward an unplanned goal, Hardy is indeed able to have it both ways. Even though Spirit Ironic taunts that *'things to be were shaped and set / 'Ere mortals and this planet met'*,[51] Hardy counters:

> The will of a man is . . . neither
> wholly free nor wholly unfree. When
> swayed by the Universal will (as he
> mostly must be as a subservient part
> of it) he is not individually free; but
> whenever it happens that all the rest of
> the Great Will is in equilibrium the
> minute portion called one person's will
> is free, just as a performer's fingers
> will go on playing the pianoforte of
> themselves when he talks or thinks of
> something else & the head does not
> rule them.[52]

If the bad news is that history is a predetermined web woven by an automaton, the good news is that along with man's accidental evolution of consciousness has come the possibility for freewill. This is the second issue addressed in *The Dynasts*, and it is exceedingly more profound than Hardy's earlier observations, couched in so many fantastic metaphors, that the Immanent Will works by rote.

Hardy may have penned more insults about consciousness than any other author, but he quite valued freewill as the flip side of the coin. In a letter to Galsworthy, who had just finished reading *The Dynasts* straight through, he remarked on the seeming absurdity of the notion: 'If we could get ouside the Universe and look back at it, Free Will as commonly understood would appear impossible; while by going inside one's individual self and looking at it, its difficulties appear less formidable . . . .'[53] While Hardy was not about to ensnarl himself in the old debate between St Augustine's doctrine of predeterminism and Kant's counter-notion of noumenal freewill, he did insist adamantly that man's sole hope for freedom from Necessity is to probe himself internally and apply his intelligence toward making visioned choices about those things which he allows to happen and prudent responses to those coincidental haps which threaten his endurance. Energy expended 'hoping, or feeling vext, / Tugged by a force above or under / Like some fantocine', Hardy chides in 'He wonders About Himself',[54] is precious energy wasted. The appropriate attitude is that which accepts at least a fractional degree of responsibility for life's turns and asks how a man can employ his freewill to make things better:

> Part is mine of the general Will,
> Cannot my share in the sum of sources
> Bend a digit in the poise of forces,
> And a fair desire fulfil?

Napoleon, Nelson, and Villeneuve are among the few characters in *The Dynasts* who command Hardy's admiration because they, like him, discern in themselves both the twitchings of the Immanent Will and the stirrings of their own individuality. King George, Pitt, Emperor Francis, Tsar Alexander, Josephine, and Maria Louisa fail their race – even though they initiate less bloodshed than Napoleon – by submitting puppet-like to the Mind's control. Stopping their ears to the warnings of the celestial Intelligences, they are in reality electing to silence the voices of their own intellects. For Hardy, as I shall argue in the following chapter, such action is irresponsible and negligent. It mortgages the sole merit to be found in consciousness and, in modern psychodynamic terms, both passively and aggressively insures that a man will not use his freewill to benefit another.

Napoleon's application of his own intellect fell far short of the mark of excellence, and for all his fascination and obsession with the historical figure, Hardy did not condone his behaviour. But whereas Nelson and Villeneuve exercised their volition by choosing to die – one a hero, one a suicide – at their own time, Napoleon rejected such Von Hartmann-like rationality in his violent mobilisation of freewill in defiance of *'the ordered potencies, / Nerves, sinews, trajects, eddies, ducts of It / The Eternal Urger, pressing change on change'*. When all is going well for the French, Napoleon uses the Immanent Will as his endorsement to continue brutalising his fellowman. After slaughtering the Austrian forces, the opportunist wins the heart of Maria Louisa by pleading innocence in the bloody affair. I deserve your pity, he pleads gravely, for

> Some force within me, baffling mine intent,
> Harries me onward, whether I will or no.
> My star, my star is what's to blame – not I.
> It is unswervable![55]

The same strategy comes in handy when his luck runs out in Spain and Russia. 'History makes use of me to weave her web', he sulks, and later complains – while incinerating documents in his haste to flee Paris – that God's sky has tumbled him from the sublime to the ridiculous. Now that all is lost, he rationalises his involvement in a war of fate's contrivance:

> I had no wish to fight, nor Alexander [the Tsar],
> But circumstances impaled us each on each;
> The Genius who outshapes my destinies
> Did all the rest! Had I but hit success,
> Imperial splendour would have worn a crown
> Unmatched in long-scrolled time![56]

Hundreds of thousands have died by Napoleon's hand, and he is haunted in sleep by spectres of rotting corpses gazing at him reproachfully from battlefields and burial mounds. Yet there is no contrition in the tyrant's final speech, for his greatest regret if he could not implant his line upon the throne is that he was not killed in battle:

> Did not my clouded soul incline to match
> Those of the corpses yonder . . . ?
> If but a Kremlin cannon-shot had met me

My greatness would have stood: I should have scored
A vast repute, scarce paralleled in time.[57]

There are moments in the drama when Napoleon actually suffers involuntary neuromotor seizures as Hardy reminds the reader that his will is shared in unequal balance with that of the Prime Mover. And Years rarely misses a chance to demonstrate that men such as Napoleon who

> wade across the world
> To make an epoch, bless, confuse, appall,
> Are in the elemental ages' chart
> Like meanest insects on obscurest leaves
> But incidents and grooves of Earth's unfolding;
> Or as the brazen rod that stirs the fire
> Because it must.[58]

But these promptings are not intended to discount Napoleon's hand in his own destiny. They are instead shrewdly designed by Hardy to reveal how immanently powerful is the determination of one individual who sets his intellect, his freewill to the test.

If Schopenhauer found in Napoleon a 'magnificent and bloody apparition of the Will made flesh', Hardy also imagined him in some ways suprahuman and imposed the Napoleonic wars over the map of earth just as Years displayed the Immanent Will's network of currents and lobules atop that. Yet for Hardy, Napoleon embodied much more than convenient scaffolding upon which to pin *The Dynasts*. The magnitude of Napoleon's energy, his cunning and his endurance in the face of inevitable defeat were exemplary traits which Hardy exalted in all his fiction, prose, and verse. Had the Corsican not deployed his consciousness like a weapon against his fellow man in a greedy quest for power, his meteoric vitality might have been utilised to enlighten the same continent he so thoroughly desecrated. His contribution to humanity was ironically bifurcated: great vision, malevolent intent.

Both Napoleon and the Immanent Will share the same need to be infused with human sympathy. Pities argues that just as *'men gained cognition with the flux of time'*, so can the Inadvertant Mind develop the same percipience:

> Yet It may wake and understand
> 'Ere Earth unshape, know all things, and
> With knowledge use a painless hand,
>   A painless hand![59]

In this way, the world can be altered for the good and history can discharge a wiser plan than the original intent of Nature to eternally ravage its creations, '*Mangle its types, re-knead the clay / In some more palpitating way*'.[60] To model our behaviour on Nature's conduct, Hardy warned, 'can only bring disaster to humanity',[61] for the sole way to keep pain to a minimum is to practise loving-kindness.

The noble ambassador of loving-kindness is Spirit of the Pities, whom Harold Orel observes is 'more sensitive to the needs of ailing man than to the demands of the Immanent Will . . . . He commemorates the defeated, the fallen, the unhappy everywhere. He is less concerned with heroism than with men's reactions to the numbing pressure of everyday circumstance'.[62] Pities is a juvenile sprite, who, as any adolescent, exasperates its elders by self-righteously questioning their belief in established tradition. Over the ages Years has grown prosaic about the Immanent Will's unthinking mistreatment of man, but Pities demands respect for earth's common labourers. '*They are shapes that bleed, mere mannikins or no*', it insists hotly, and should not be dismissed as insects. If no-one else takes note of pain and injustice, Pities champions the sufferer. As King George succumbs to insanity, it moans:

> Something within me aches to pray
> To some Great Heart, to take away
> This evil day, this evil day!

Chorus Ironic taunts the hysterical spirit like an older brother badgering his little sister:

> Ha ha! That's good. Thou'lt pray to It: –
> But where do Its compassions sit?
> Yea, where abides the heart of it?
>
> Is it where sky-fires flame and flit,
> Or solar craters spew and spit,

The 'Great Adjustment' 91

> *Or ultra-stellar night-webs knit?*
> *What is Its shape? Man's counterfeit?*
> *That turns in some far sphere unlit*
> *The Wheel which drives the Infinite?*

But Pities will not be hushed nor discouraged:

> *Mock on, mock on! Yet I'll go pray*
> *To some Great Heart, who haply may*
> *Charm mortal miseries away!*[63]

We miss Hardy's point if we fail to see that the Great Heart is the heart of human pity which, until the Immanent Will awakens, is our lone charm against mortal misery.

At the end of Part Third, a group of Ironic phantoms sings a chorus recapitulating all that can be known, it assumes, about the Unknowable:

> *Of Its doings if It knew,*
> *What it does It would not do!*
>
> *Since It knows not, what far sense*
> *Speeds Its spinning in the immense?*
>
> *None; a fixed foresightless dream*
> *Is Its whole philosopheme.*
>
> *Just so; an unconscious planning,*
> *Like a potter raptly panning!*
>
> *Are then Love and Light Its aim –*
> *Good Its glory, Bad its blame?*
>
> *Nay; to alter evermore*
> *Things from what they were before.*[64]

A remarkable transformation has occurred, however, for the irony in the speech of Spirit Ironic is that it sounds as deluded and naive at the end of the play as young Pities did at the beginning. The voice of Hardy's evolutionary meliorism peals the last word in the Afterscene, its resonance even swaying Years' superannuated belief in scientific determinism. After a semi-chorus of the Pities chants a prophetic song about the

'Wellwisher, the kindly Might', who deserves adoration because it has awakened and tenderly remedied man's poor blighted planet, Spirit of the Pities offers a closing benediction:

> But – a stirring thrills the air
> Like to sounds of joyance there
>   That the rages
>   Of the ages
> Shall be cancelled, and deliverance offered from the darts that were,
> Consciousness the Will informing, till It fashion all things fair![65]

The young sprite's affirmation that the Immanent Will can 'Its blindness break . . . Its heart awake' and restore a real or imagined broken connection with man is the third and cardinal lesson taught in *The Dynasts*. In this inverted Feuerbachian philosophy, the rousing Will defines its character according to the morality it perceives in its creatures. Man's responsibility in the Great Adjustment process is to demonstrate the type of unselfish loving-kindness personated in Pities by using his intellect and freewill to harmonise humanity rather than – as did Napoleon – to divide it. 'As the Will is immanent in man', concludes Bailey, 'so is man within It . . . . It needs man's help to redeem Itself from mechanism'.[66]

For Von Hartmann, history is the working out of a secret plan that makes sense to those keen enough to interpret the upheavals and declines which mark its course. Hardy, too, conceives of history as readable, but only to those who correlate its movements with evidence of man's intervention:

> History is rather a stream than a tree. There is nothing organic in its shape, nothing systematic in its development. It flows on like a thunderstorm-rill by a road side; now a straw turns it this way, now a tiny barrier of sand that. The offhand decision of some commonplace mind high in office at a critical moment influences the course of events for a hundred years.[67]

Particularly here in *The Dynasts*, Hardy's third voice calls for evolutionary meliorism to replace the unsystematic flow of history. As both man and Will progress in a Romantic spiral toward self-education, the mood of history will become less darkened by determinism and more enlightened by compassion bred of intellect and empathy. It is at this point, Lionel Stevenson suggests, that the poetic creed of Hardy 'joins hands with Meredith's creed of the "sighting brain"', which, for survival's sake, must be cultivated in all human beings. 'If the race unites to seek humanitarian ends, clearly recognising the non-existence of supernatural aids and post-mortem rewards, and frankly confronting the prevalence of pain and sorrow', Stevenson astutely interprets Hardy's meliorism, 'the course of evolution will become synonymous with genuine progress.'[68]

No doubt Hardy expected *The Dynasts* to earn unfavourable reviews among certain critics. Max Beerbohm quipped that *The Dynasts'* overblown epic scale reduced historical figures and events to the size of marionettes and facetiously proposed that it be adapted into a puppet show. No more complimentary was A. B. Walkley, who used the play to declare as inaccessible the entire closet-drama genre. Book sales in England and America were pitifully lacking, for as Hardy had suspected, few were those who exercised their ability to willingly suspend a modicum of disbelief: Hardy's Spirits were ridiculed and his Immanent Will attacked as unconvincing but dangerous, its author a vulpine heretic bent on undermining the *zeitgeist*'s confidence in the nexus between God and material progress. Like his poetic persona in 'Xenophanes, the Monist of Colophon',[69] who undertook it to plumb the depths of the 'Great Dumb', Hardy was generally censured for his precocious ideas:

> Three thousand years hence,
> Men who hazard a clue
> To this riddle immense,
> And still treat it as new,
> Will be scowled at, like you,
> O Xenophanes!

Once again Hardy was cast in the position of defending his work against the large number of 'narrowly Philistine' critics who were too puzzled by the inventive ideas illustrated in *The Dynasts* to review them fairly in their public commentary:

> I suppose I have handicapped myself by expressing, both in this drama and previous verse, philosophies and feelings as yet not well established or formally adopted into the general teaching; and by thus over-stepping the standard boundary set up for the thought of the age by proctors of opinion, I have thrown back my chance of acceptance in poetry by many years. The very fact of my having tried to spread over art the latest illumination of the time has darkened counsel in respect of me . . . . If, instead of the machinery I adopted, I had constructed a theory of a world directed by fairies, nobody would have objected, and the critics would probably have said, 'What a charming fancy of Mr Hardy's!'[70]

One cannot help wondering whether Hardy truly believed in the case of evolutionary meliorism he so passionately argued in *The Dynasts*. Most modern reviewers think not, although earlier critics like Hardy's rather doting biographer, Edmund Blunden, allege that he 'based his *Dynasts* in a First Cause other than that of the churches, meaning this with all his might if ever he meant anything'.[71] On one hand I fear that had he lived today in this age of molecular biology when any schoolchild can open a copy of an astounding science text such as Richard Dawkins' *The Blind Watchmaker* to find charted before him the computerised evolution of biomorphs strung up in genetic space, Hardy might have been embarrassed to present so naive a notion as meliorism in any form. But I can also imagine Hardy delightedly investigating our Neo-Darwinian understanding of DNA, mutation, and epigenetic embryology. He might well conclude, along with Dawkins, that – given the essentially non-random nature of cumulative natural selection – the evolution of intelligence is practically inevitable. If consciousness arises, as Dawkins suggests, 'when the brain's simulation of the world becomes so complete that it must include a model of itself',[72] is it not then possible that the Immanent Will just *might* gain percipience by first observing man's example and from there assuming its own self-awareness? Perhaps not, but the point is that Hardy's extended metaphorical demonstration of how life on earth could be revolutionised by loving-kindness is in no way negated by scientific advances which make that hope appear all the more improbable. In the end we are begging the question in a dispute that cannot be settled. Whenever pinned down

Hardy fell back on his disclaimer that because he lived in 'a world where nothing bears out in practice what it promises incipiently, I have troubled myself very little about theories . . . . I am content with tentativeness from day to day'.[73] In the last years of his long life, Hardy's tentativeness assumed a fourth voice – perhaps best described as a brooding absence of voice – which at once incorporated and superseded these first three; it shall be the subject of the final chapter.

4
Freedom, Failure, and Fate: Reading the Web of Wessex

> There was a glorious time
> At an epoch of my prime;
> Mornings beryl-bespread,
> And evenings golden-red;
> Nothing gray:
> And in my heart I said,
> 'However this chanced to be,
> It is too full for me,
> Too rare, too rapturous, rash,
> Its spell must close with a crash
> Some day!'
>
> The radiance went on
> Anon and yet anon,
> And sweetness fell around
> Like manna on the ground.
> 'I've no claim,'
> Said I, 'to be thus crowned:
> I am not worthy this: –
> Must it not go amiss? –
> Well . . . let the end foreseen
> Come duly! – I am serene.'
> – And it came.[1]

Almost from infancy, it seems, Hardy sensed a discrepancy between the voices of heart and mind in an unnatural division which at best bruised his perception that life might be worth the living and at worst nullified his desire to proceed with the futile process of growing up. The melancholy effects of stained glass and hymns rich in ancient poesy moved the child to weeping during services at Stinsford Church; but at home, lying on his back in the sun while contemplating his own uselessness and trying to reason out cosmic ambiguity, his intellect detached him from religious doctrine and the emotional theatrics ritually inspired in him. Most of Hardy's adult impressions of the mind are embedded in poetry where hugely varied rhyme schemes, metrics, and verse forms provide contexts for his equally varied polyphonic trying out of fictions regarding the nature and ultimate intent of God. While we can certainly discover ample emotion in his verse and intellectual voicings in his fiction, it is in the novels that Hardy preponderantly listens to the heart. If he declares in poetry that consciousness is a great source of man's suffering, he also demonstrates in fiction that maladies of the heart just as severely compromise man's well-being. Any proper assessment of human ills must include diagnostic evaluation of both intellect and heart, and a remedy must address the balance between them. The aim of this chapter and the following chapter is to examine the voice of the heart both in and out of equilibrium with the intellect as Hardy articulates it through his Wessex characters.

Like Darwin, Hardy was a natural observer of the earth and its occupants, and while strange new sights may have earned his momentary attention, his greater fascination attached always to the consistency of pattern detectable in the most ordinary events and objects. The human face, to use a concrete example, represented much more to him than a plain or attractive configuration of brow, nose, and lips marked, or happily unmarked, by scars or lines. The almost supernatural quality of the face was for him its quiet symbolism of man's heredity, the evidence of his genetic kinship with thousands of ancestors unseen and unknown. It rather astonished Hardy to think that the countenance peering back at him from his looking glass was not entirely his own:

> I am the family face;
> Flesh perishes, I live on,
> Projecting trait and trace
> Through time to times anon,
> And leaping from place to place
> Over oblivion.

To meet oblivion behind the veil was a dread which haunted a good many Victorians, but here in 'Heredity'[2] Hardy mocks its power to frighten the family face. The incline of the chin and the tint of the eye are genetic testimonial to the fact that something about man is transcendent, immortal, and itself oblivious. Hardy can finally claim his image as an intensely personal connection with an unending repetition of faces past and faces yet to come:

> The years-heired feature that can
> In curve and voice and eye
> Despise the human span
> Of durance – that is I;
> The eternal thing in man,
> That heeds no call to die.

Just as there are no truly original faces left in the world since matter repeats itself through genetic permutation, so are there no new events or human behaviours to be acted out. J. Hillis Miller has examined Hardy's static and illusionary sense of time in which no response invokes a proper beginning or end, and insists that the crucial point of Hardy's spatial perspective is that every act exists before it is performed and is continually duplicated afterward within experience:

> A nonprogressive, spatialized view of time means that the significance of any particular event lies not in its particularity but in the way it doubles in essential outline other examples of the same pattern of experience. Any one example refers to another such which is anterior to it, and that one is to be interpreted by way of another more anterior still in an endless interpretive process of deferred meaning.[3]

In the Wessex novels, I believe, Hardy frames moments of this 'endless interpretive process of deferred meaning' by examining to the point of ruthless scrutiny the usually dark patterns of human behaviour. What he discovers almost invariably is that despite noble intentions, men and women are consistently and enormously self-destructive at heart. Henchard's hounding himself to death is repeated in Tess's readiness to be violated by anyone; Clym's desperate pursuit of identity is protracted and mirrored in Jude's suicide; Bathsheba's longing for passion is tragically re-enacted in Eustacia's desire 'to be loved to madness'; even Egdon Heath's loneliness and utter indifference is reflected in the cityscape of Christminster.

Of course many of Hardy's readers – contemporary and modern – have thought him guilty of weighting the scales against his characters to ensure their defeat. Not only is he an atheist and pessimist, they have clamoured, but he is a naturalist as well; the only tragic problem inherent in his work is the author's perverse pleasure in watching his puppets fragment even as their examples fragmented the Victorian value scheme. 'He gathered up all the data he could find that encouraged his pessimism', David Daiches unfairly complains, 'and threw them magnificently and carelessly at the face of Heaven and his public. He heard the Victorian foundations creaking and mistook the sound for the ironic laughter of the gods.'[4] Such a claim is offensive, though not atypical of Hardy's detractors, and Hardy vehemently defended himself against a similar insinuation that he was a naturalist in the tradition of Zola. Never was his intention to expose man's atavistic disposition in a world wherein we are each dependent solely upon our survival instincts, nor did he orchestrate the grim, contrapuntal fugue of human behaviour which his characters play out in fiction.

That Hardy was a shrewd observer of life's repetitions rather than an inventor of them is apparent in his treatment of pattern in tradition and coincidence. Maypole dances, sheep-shearing suppers, autumnal bonfires, Guy Fawkes festivities at Halloween, Yuletime carolling and mumming, country weddings and funeral wakes, christenings, baptisms, and hangings were all events which, pragmatic considerations aside, lent a feeling of order and stability to the agricultural peasants of Wessex. Most of the memorable scenes in Hardy's novels occur as they do because they are in some way appended to the seasonal celebrations of the community. Hardy employed the repetitive cycle of tradition in his fiction to show that regardless of whatever unexpected circumstances occurred between one May Day and the next, another spring would follow, and another and another, until a succession of Maypoles had balanced unpredictability against staid ritual. Not a single angry critic accused Hardy of inventing these traditions or decried his reliance on such picturesque repetition; but hordes became apoplectic over his demonstration that coincidental happenings influence life no less in recognisable patterns. Hardy purposely set accidentalism against the background of folk ritual in order to demonstrate that designless, specifically Darwinian, happenings have evolved a human context in which the odds for survival can be calculated and adaptive strategies implemented. If coincidences appear demonically instigated, it is because society, thrown off centre, assigns them a negative value based on their power to disrupt ordinary routine. Likewise, if readers insist on attributing naturalist values to Hardy's use of natural accidentalism, it is because they, too, are uncomfortable with what appears to be 'Crass Casualty'.

Angry indictments of 'Naturalist!' notwithstanding, Hardy persisted in his reliance on the repetition of coincidence for reasons both realistic and anti-realistic. Reflecting on his writing in 1890, he mused that 'Art is a disproportioning – (i.e., distorting, throwing out of proportion) – of realities to show more clearly the features that matter in those realities, which if merely copied or reported inventorially, might possibly be observed, but would more probably be overlooked'.[5] Art, as the Romantics had envisioned it, was the only medium imaginative enough and free enough from social and political ideology to teach man to himself, and Hardy used its symbolic capacity to attempt just that. He approached the real, Frederick Karl suggests, not head-on as did Thackeray and George Eliot, but off-centre like Conrad and Lawrence:

> his reliance on cosmic irony and the chance occurrences of implausible events bolstered his way of working; for a dependence on chance enabled him to touch his subject, as it were, from the side and gave substance to his oblique attacks upon complacency, deviation, and immoderation. Chance, in effect, was his weapon to strike through surface reality to areas where the poetry of man offers resistance to the drab starkness of a malevolent universe.[6]

While this is reality focused microscopically on the oddities of life, it is also what Albert J. Guerard terms Hardy's 'anti-realism', which superficially surveys the everyday world while idiosyncratically penetrating beyond it into the metaphysical realm of 'macabre ironies, visible absurdities, and unseen hostilities'.[7]

Take the case of the misplaced letter in Tess of the D'Urbervilles (1891), which, according to my reading, demonstrates very well Hardy's anti-realistic realism. Ever braced for impending calamity, Tess tries to avert one by writing a four-paged confessional to her fiancé, informing him of her erstwhile liaison with another man. In thrusting the letter beneath Angel's door two or three nights before the wedding, she accidentally conceals it under his carpet as well. The realistic sceptic may be put off by the improbability of such a stroke of bad luck at so decisive a moment in the pair's relationship, while the analyst may interpret it psychodynamically, citing as the culprit Tess's unconscious desire to sweep her old identity under the rug. But the imaginative realist who admits the inclusive nature of possibility must affirm that coincidences – even life-altering ones – can happen to anyone at any moment. From the anti-realist perspective, however, the incident reveals much more than the chanciness of the universe, for it is in Tess's response to her failed effort that we witness Hardy 'strike through surface reality' to pinpoint those features that really matter. In her conscience Tess knows that there is still time to disclose her secret, yet she destroys the letter and acquiesces to Angel's request that she save any small talk about her 'faults and blunders' for some 'dull time' after their marriage. No ingénue to cosmic blight, Tess surely apprehends that her tractability can only postpone the inescapable ordeal, but at this instant 'Her one desire, so long resisted, to make herself his, to call him her lord, her own – then, if necessary, die – had at last lifted her up from her plodding reflective pathway'. She prepares for the wedding 'in a mental cloud of many-coloured idealities, which eclipsed all sinister contingencies by its brightness'.[8]

Still there is a deeper 'macabre irony' which Hardy's treatment of the accident implies. Although Tess should have known better than to trust her 'appetite for joy', it is extremely probable that the incident of the misplaced letter has no effect at all upon the outcome of the story. Angel's reaction to Tess's past would have been irrationally excessive regardless of the informing circumstance. Whether he had listened to an oral confession or read a note, whether it had come before the wedding or after would have made no difference in his capacity to forgive. The coincidence is merely a 'visible absurdity'; the only thing that matters is Tess's sin. And even though she might not have been left in so exposed a position, Tess would have agonised just as profoundly over her lover's reaction had he noticed the envelope wedged between floor and carpet.

Hardy allows Tess the comfort of being fatalistic about the events of her life in the same way that he permits Henchard to believe that his downfall is 'the scheme of some sinister intelligence bent on punishing him'. But Hardy was not himself a fatalist, nor was he purely a determinist who viewed the individual as a figure entirely helpless against the great battery of evolutional forces with which he must deal. In truth, Hardy's determinism extended no further than the point at which man's small fraction of freewill begins; this miniscule share invalidates the determinist equation because, as *The Dynasts* clearly illustrates, even the most insignificant exercise of freewill is itself freeing. Darwinism may yet be countered by individualism, 'change and chancefulness' by adaptability. The problem with most of Hardy's characters is that they pity themselves as victims of fate or purblind Doomsters or natural oppression and they do not recognise their own self-immolation, the self-destructive propensity they bear at heart, their bankruptcy of freewill enlightened by intellect; in short, they have not had the advantage of reading a Hardy novel and therefore have little light to see the gloomy patterns emerging as he reads the great web of humanity. Henchard, Clym, Tess, Jude and the others are forced by heredity and natural instinct in one direction and just as violently wrenched by tradition, society, and law in the opposite; yet no cruel author harries them to insanity and death as Zola does poor Therese Raquin because in Hardy's case the author loves his meek human models and, through them, flesh and blood prototypes.

Hardy did not write novels for his characters, however, and insisted that he did not conceive them for moral instruction for anyone. Miller suggests that Hardy declined to organise his perceptions into doctrine and refused to advise people how to live because he, like Dickens, feared 'the guilt involved in becoming the value-giving center of his world'.[9] I imagine it likely that the foremost reason Hardy refused to offer more than 'impressions' of the tragic consequences of certain behaviours is that he was essentially a man who did not meddle in other people's affairs nor accept responsibility for their gains or losses. The most he could do for any reader was to afford him a brief encounter with realistic anti-realism, whereupon the reader could extract, if he was not as 'narrowly Philistine' as many of Hardy's critics, a personal impression of coping strategies superior to those used by a handful of ignorant characters. Responsibility always accompanies enlightenment, and Hardy shows in novel after novel, if sometimes too obliquely, how it is possible to survive the world of random events and natural determinism if heart and intellect are united and balanced.

More than natural laws of cause and effect and certainly more than any accidental misfortune it is the voice of the heart which undermines individual will among Hardy's Wessex figures. All represent the Victorian Christian in varying degrees of belief, and, although they are also rustics at scattered levels of sophistication, each has experienced terrible alienation resulting from God's withdrawal from the world and man's depletion of lovingkindness for those around him. Each feels incomplete since, to borrow Feuerbach's phraseology, 'God is his alter ego, his other lost half; God is the complement of himself; in God he is first a perfect man'.[10] I do not mean that every Wessex inhabitant paces about in a vacuum, scientifically pondering man's existential rootlessness like Beckett's disembodied 'Unnamable' consciousness. None, not even Sue Bridehead, is as intellectually cosmopolitan as that. However, in differing ways each character responds to God's inscrutability and human indifference by internalizing that abandonment deep within his heart, accepting it as his own fault, resolving to make recompense for his culpability, and promising to feel worthless until the debt is paid or miraculously pardoned. For the Wessex folk, as for the nonfiction Victorian population, systematised religion had failed to make good its troth of salvation so that they must improvise the means for their own redemption in a way that will both edify God if he is within earshot and restore a connection with their more immediate fellow man. Their quest, simply, is to restore the hearth. This is the healthy ambition of an essentially healthy collection of individuals who have no morbid, conscious desire to self-destruct. They seek salvation and integration because intellectually, instinctively, emotionally, they understand the nature of healing.

What Hardy's characters do not understand is how to

implement the strategies they know to be redemptive. Without having read Feuerbach's dictum that love is divine and the only true religion we can practise or Carlyle's beatitude that 'Blessed is he who has found his work',[11] these country men and women comprehend that love and labour are the keys to the kingdom. The 'chief fact' regarding them, sadly and ironically, turns out to be their chief failing: almost universally they misapply work and intimacy under the misdirection of hearts hellbent on self-destruction.

In recent days of debate over critical theory, when there is no gold-standard method by which to interpret a literary text, one may feel – as I do – some reluctance to emphasise the author's autobiographical inclusions in that text for fear of alienating a host of other critics either formalist, Marxist, feminist, psychoanalytic, structuralist, or post-structuralist. And yet, unlike Dickens or Trollope or Thackeray, Hardy wrote primarily about distinct personalities and rustic types he had known in youth and even staged their histories against the backdrop of Wessex, fictional in name but almost perfectly correlated with his native Dorset in topography. I submit this disclaimer before beginning discussion of Gabriel Oak, shepherd-protagonist in *Far From the Madding Crowd* (1874), because he is the healthiest of Hardy's major characters and, not coincidentally, he appears early in a career which would soon lose its pastoral vision.

Although it is unfair to allege that Hardy penned *Far From the Madding Crowd* in a pre-marital haze, it is significant that it was the first of his principal novels and was written during his four-year engagement to Emma Lavinia Gifford. Each of the novel's prominent characters, isolated as they are from the community's vital mainstream, projects Hardy's own struggle with loneliness and rejection, and I think it not unjust to conclude that as an unmarried man still living with his parents at the age of thirty-four, Hardy knew both loneliness and passion's power to end it. Rumours that he was a notorious lover of beautiful ladies are largely true, but his first meeting with Emma at her brother-in-law's rectory in St Juliot, Cornwall, left the bachelor unprecedentedly smitten. Emma was a vivacious country charmer, to be sure, and Hardy was instantly beguiled by her coy yet sexually seductive façade. The passionate urgency of their courtship was made all the more intense by the fact that Hardy's visits to St Juliot were occasioned by his commission to restore the local church and were necessarily infrequent. Had Emma lived up the lane from him in Higher Bockhampton, he might have discovered that the Lyonesse maid who sparked 'magic' in his eyes was not the intellectually free-thinking, physically active girl she pretended to be, nor would she ever become the moon goddess to his Endymion. Perhaps there is even truth in the whispered conjecture that, just as Arabella would deceive Jude some twenty-five years later, Emma conspired to catch her beau with a pregnancy which was announced mistaken only after he had committed himself to marry her.

In such a pre-marital pre-consciousness, Hardy composed *Far From the Madding Crowd* and cast in fiction the kind of 'intensely humane man' he most admired and probably hoped to emulate. Oak is an unassuming person who, like his creator, 'had just reached the time of life at which "young" is ceasing to be the prefix of "man" in speaking of one', and, like Hardy but for his blinding fascination with Emma, was

> at the brightest period of masculine growth, for his intellect and his emotions were clearly separated: he had passed the time during which the influence of youth indiscriminately mingles them in the character of impulse, and he had not yet arrived at the stage wherein they become united again, in the character of prejudice, by the influence of a wife and family.[12]

Even in his religious convictions, he is Hardy, disarmed of his anger towards the Church and pastoralised, perhaps, but no less poised in the middle of the hymn-book:

> on working days he was a young man of sound judgement, easy motions, proper dress, and general good character. On Sundays he was a man of misty views, rather given to postponing, and hampered by his best clothes and umbrella: upon the whole, one who felt himself to occupy that vast middle space of Laodicean neutrality which lay between the Communion people of the parish and the drunken section . . . .[13]

Oak is not 'churchy', as Hardy once described himself, but he does bear his author's reverential appreciation for natural scenes and creatures. If Oak regards sky, field, and flock as 'superlatively beautiful' useful instruments and arts, it is because Hardy was a man who noticed such things before him. The shepherd carries his grandfather's silver pocketwatch, but prefers to tell time more accurately by reading the sun's position in the sky and the stars' arrangement along the meridian. 'A common pulse' throbs through the twinkling constellations, he reflects with awe, and through the humming of windswept grasses, the bleating of lambs, through all human shapes, even his own. 'Introspective far beyond his neighbours', Oak, of all the Wessex characters, is the one who best understands that his salvation depends upon love and work undertaken in the proper spirit of the heart. He is always aware that he has 'no great claim on the world's room' and no God-given right to happiness; he is a realist from beginning to end. A long ancestry of sheep-farmers has produced in Gabriel a willingness to work hard and enjoy his industry without expecting recompense exceeding the labour itself. His moral code is personal, honest, self-respecting rather than self-despising, and requires of him honourable behaviour – which is why he tries to conceal from Bathsheba the fact that Fanny Robin's coffin holds Troy's baby and why he prepares to leave the country rather than exploit Bathsheba's widowhood for his own advantage.

For all his goodnaturedness, however, Oak is not to be dismissed as a flute-playing Arcadian. He will not allow Bathsheba to patronise his affections nor exploit his skills, for he warns her more than once that he is meant for better things than that. Oak is at first fascinated with Bathsheba, painting her a beauty in the same way that Hardy had romanticised Emma, because after twenty-eight solitary years, 'his soul required a divinity . . . having for some time known the want of satisfactory form to fill an increasing void within him'.[14] But no simpleton, either, he accepts with equanimity Bathsheba's rejection of his marriage proposal. Although at first he feels his spurned love 'burning with a finer flame now that she was gone', he soon forgives her and begins to wait out her immaturity. From season to season thereafter, Gabriel witnesses her vanity, grows irritated by her careless flirtations with Boldwood, and becomes disgusted by her marriage to Troy; but these events are necessary antecedents for the shaping of a love story which emerges in the novel as Bathsheba's strengths emerge in her transformation from a self-willed brat into a self-possessed, sensible, sensitive woman and capable manager of Weatherbury Farm. If the novel is in part the tale of Bathsheba's moral education, there is a transcendent parable beyond that about two people redeemed from their loneliness by virtue of hard work and willingness to accept one another by daylight illumination of faults as well as merits. Whatever hopes Hardy may have entertained for his forthcoming marriage notwithstanding, he placed Gabriel and Bathsheba steadily on the course of realistic, practical love:

> Theirs was that substantial affection which arises (if any arises at all) when the two who are thrown together begin first by knowing the rougher sides of each other's character, and not the best till further on, the romance growing up in the interstices of a mass of hard prosaic reality. This good fellowship – camaraderie – usually occurring through similarity of pursuits, is unfortunately seldom superadded to love between the sexes, because men and women associate, not in their labours, but in their pleasures merely. Where, however, happy circumstance permits its development, the compounded feeling proves itself to be the only love which is strong as death – that love which many waters cannot quench, nor the floods drown, beside which the passion usually called by the name is evanescent as steam.[15]

Pondering the union at novel's close, rustic Joseph Poorgrass sighs, 'it might have been worse, and I feel my thanks accordingly'. Such is the pragmatic optimism of the happiest ending Hardy would ever write.

By the time Hardy met Emma at the altar on 17 September 1874, his enchantment with her had dimmed considerably owing partly to their increased contact since the engagement and partly to his having fallen 'in love' with at least two other women in the meantime. He was always to wonder how his life might have differed had he married either his refined illustrator, Helen Paterson, or Annie Thackeray, in whom he found a great deal of her father's humour. Both were genuinely educated in contrast to the superficially schooled Emma, and either would have been more intellectually compatible with Hardy than she. Their wedding day was sunny and mellow, lovely as any symbolist could hope for, but the ceremony forbode ill for the union: not one member of Hardy's family attended, even though the journey was short and all were in fine health. Of Emma's relations, only one brother and an uncle made appearance. The years would further increase hostility between the Hardys and Giffords, especially in the relationship between Jemima, who regarded her daughter-in-law as foolish and untrustworthy, and Emma, who felt that she had married beneath her social class. The honeymoon, too, was a rather disappointing affair: Hardy contracted a cold after swimming at Brighton and Emma became violently seasick during the rough channel-crossing to Dieppe. By far the most chilling honeymoon revelation occurred to the groom during the couple's stay in Paris, where he began to discover that there existed two Emmas. The pre-nuptial lover had been girlish, animated and extremely sexually permissive; the wife, on the other hand, fatigued easily, complained, liked her brandy a bit too well, and became suddenly less than sexually congenial. Fancying herself a writer, the bride overflowed her diary with long flowery passages describing the glamours of France; possibly fancying himself a condemned man, Hardy wrote absolutely nothing.

Had it not been for a handful of common interests ranging from their love for animals to their passion for gardening, the thirty-eight year marriage of Thomas and Emma Hardy might have seemed to both an interminable ordeal. And at least in the early phase of Hardy's career – before the publication of *Jude the Obscure* (1896) so enraged Emma at his double attack on marriage and religion that she accused her husband of running 'hand-in-glove with Zola'[16] – his wife assisted him invaluably by copying corrected manuscripts for publication and inscribing into notebooks passages from various readings which he thought useful to keep. It was largely to Emma's credit, in fact, that *A Laodicean* (1881) was written at all since Hardy fell seriously ill with kidney stones and a bladder inflammation just after the third instalment had been printed. Besides nursing him back to health, she acted as bedside secretary by writing out the last nine instalments as he dictated them to her. Yet despite their shared endeavours, the union remained almost entirely unromantic from about the second year on, and, if Emma's letters are to be believed, their final years of 'keeping separate' were predominated by silence so unmitigated that they rarely spoke to one another beyond the most obligatory household communication. No wonder Hardy's lifelong obsession with guilt over his wife's unexpected death in 1912:

> Why, then, latterly did we not speak,
> Did we not think of those days long dead,
> And ere your vanishing strive to seek
> That time's renewal? We might have said,
>   'In this bright spring weather
>   We'll visit together
> Those places that once we visited'.
>
>   Well, well! All's past amend,
>   Unchangeable. It must go.
> I seem but a dead man held on end
> To sink down soon . . . . O you could not know
>   That such swift fleeing
>   No soul foreseeing –
> Not even I – would undo me so![17]

The major novel following Hardy's marriage – and irreconcilable break with Jemima – represents a striking, significant digression from the simple pastoral moralism of *Far From the Madding Crowd*. *The Return of the Native* appeared in 1878 and portrays as its main character a man who has left his mother's hearth to seek his fortune in the diamond trade in Paris. Mrs Yeobright is extremely ambitious on her son's behalf and is angered when he quits the business to return to Egdon Heath in hopes of becoming a philanthropist schoolteacher. She to him:

> After all the trouble that has been taken to give you a start, and when there is nothing to do but to keep straight on towards affluence, you say you will be a poor man's schoolmaster. Your fancies will be your ruin, Clym . . . . I have always supposed you were going to push straight on, as other men do – all who deserve the name . . . .

And he to her:

> 'I cannot help it,' said Clym in a troubled tone. 'Mother, I hate the flashy business. Talk about men who deserve the name, can any man deserving the name waste his time in

that effeminate way, when he sees half the world going to ruin for want of somebody to buckle to and teach them how to breast the misery they are born to? I get up every morning and see the whole creation groaning and travailing in pain, as St. Paul says, and yet there am I, trafficking in glittering splendours with wealthy women and titled libertines, and pandering to the meanest vanities – I, who have health and strength enough for anything.[18]

The reason for Clym's depression is his consciousness that most of humanity gropes about in darkness from day to day, pitifully searching for ways to prolong their suffering – as suffering is their sole evidence of being alive. Stressed almost to breaking by this conviction, Clym is practically beside himself by the time he returns home. His face is marked with a depth of anguish which Hardy insists, in true Romantic fashion, shows that 'thought is a disease of the flesh', indirectly bearing evidence that 'ideal physical beauty is incompatible with emotional development and a full recognition of the coil of things'.[19]

But there is more to Clym's dilemma than what can be discerned in his brow or heard in his self-righteous speech. At bottom, the troubled native returns to Egdon Heath for two reasons: while many individuals recognise the grim coil of things, Clym is one of the few who feels guilty for it. Enlightened by a consciousness that has leapt ahead of its own ability to reason logically, Clym imagines himself personally accountable for man's continued misery if he does nothing to remedy it. Keith May's observation that Clym is Hardy's modern man who understands the cost of industrialisation and in whose mind the implications of Darwin have sunk in[20] is an important one because it at once yokes the native with Renaissance humanism and wrenches him away from all the old strategies with which he might have implemented those ideals in this new age in which men are threatened by reductivism. In response to his dark, late-nineteenth century vision, Clym comes home to assume his modern – perhaps post-modern – existential burden. Secondly, Clym's retreat must be regarded as an adult way of going home again, becoming his mother's child once more, and safely reintegrating within the old Wessex community. Clym is right to escape Paris and it seems healthy and wise that he should withdraw to the place where he feels loved, but his motivations indicate that whatever malady of thought afflicts him, he also suffers from heart disease. His heart convinces him that in aspiring to material prosperity, he has betrayed his upbringing and the good country folk who nurtured him. This realisation is an admirable one for a young man to make in the midst of huge monetary success, but his heart, mistranslating the message of his intellect, demands that he bear guilt for the entire human condition and that he discard his worldly vesture for sackcloth. These abnegating gestures he gladly performs for the absolution they promise, yet in another turn of the heart, he aggrandises his new lowly calling into a philosophical version of the diamond trade and thrusts himself again into the way of guilt. On every level, the native returns.

Sadly for Clym, as it will be for Tess and Jude, he cannot receive remission for sin he did not commit. More sadly still, he can never quite accept the liberation implied by that fact and becomes, like Coleridge's Ancient Mariner, an itinerant preacher of enlightenment to Laodicean crowds. While this may be a more optimistic ending than Henchard achieves, Yeobright does have ample opportunity and sufficient conscious awareness to have fared better. The initial error Clym makes reveals his confusion regarding his own identity, for in choosing to return to Mrs Yeobright he automatically reprises his role as the ungrateful child. Mrs Yeobright cherishes her son, but she also brings out the worst in him. The pair constantly bicker over his vocation and his taste in women. They snipe at each other's values and go to any length to avoid apology. She reinforces his sense of guilt; he substantiates her belief that she is to be pitied as life's official scapegoat. After his mother's death, Clym is naturally distraught, particularly over the circumstances which culminated in her fatal sunstroke. Yet the reality beyond the coincidence which causes her to turn away from his house on that sweltering afternoon is that both mother and son had had months in which to repair their rift, but – for stubbornness and pride – would not. Egdon Heath is the real mother to whom Clym should have cleaved, for it was upon her bosom that he first opened his eyes to the world and 'his estimate of life had been coloured by it' ever since. Whereas Eustacia hates the wasteland as uncouth and barbarous, the native is charmed by its scents, its oddly shaped stones and yellow furze tufts, its purple bells, and even the snakes and croppers that dart among the undergrowth. Take all the ways he loved the heath and 'you have the heart of Clym'. Clym has no quarrel with the heath and nothing there for which to atone.

Thence comes his second mistake. Since with his heart the prodigal son has come home to the wrong mother, with his intellect he settles into the wrong vocation. A sympathetic narrator assures us that his motivation is pure, that indeed

> Yeobright loved his kind. He had a conviction that the want of most men was knowledge of a sort which brings wisdom rather than affluence. He wished to raise the class at the expense of individuals rather than individuals at the expense of the class. What was more, he was ready to be the first unit sacrificed.[21]

But self-proclaimed saviours are rarely successful in real life and never in Hardy's world. Clym only succeeds in making himself look ridiculous and arrogant when he announces to Eustacia during their first formal introduction that he has come to clean away the cobwebs of superstition and hatred which cling to his countrymen; he appears all the more silly walking home from that encounter reflecting that his 'scheme had somehow become glorified' since 'a beautiful woman had been intertwined with it'. Obviously his fascination with the work and the woman has more to do with the ego-enhancement and relief from guilt they will provide for him rather than what he – through work and love – can do to elevate humanity. The ensuing scene in which Clym rushes to his room, unpacks his books and arranges them on shelves, excitedly trims his lamp, and sets his desk for study might be dear to us if we watched Jude make those preparations as a fourteen-year-old boy. In Clym's case, however, the scene is laughable – as Hardy intended it – because it is apparent that not only does he hope to win the maiden by impressing her to death, but he also climaxes his philanthrophic frenzy by sitting down like Browning's Caponsacchi and reading a book. 'Now I am ready to begin', he declares with smug determination, but no genuine action follows.

Although Hardy's metaphorical irony is too contrived to be effective, Clym's blindness – the consequence of his trying too hard to see lofty truths – does reveal to him a satisfying course of action. 'I am going to be a furze and turf cutter', he cheerfully announces to Eustacia, explaining that his sudden happiness in time of misfortune 'arises from my having at last discovered something I can do'. No mistaking the voice of Carlyle here. That 'something' is work, a salvaging industry which must occur for Clym, not in a classroom nor seated at a desk, but in the black soil of Edgon Heath. Since no occupation is more noble in Hardy's universe than that which bends labourer toward the earth, it is encouraging to find the native thus reunited in work with his true mother:

> His familiars were creeping and winged things, and they seemed to enroll him in their band. Bees hummed around his ears with an intimate air, and tugged at the heath and furze-flowers at his side in such numbers as to weigh them down to the sod. The strange amber-coloured butterflies which Egdon produced, and which were never seen elsewhere, quivered in the breath of his lips, alighted upon his bowed back, and sported with the glittering point of his hook as he flourished it up and down. Tribes of emerald-green grasshoppers leaped over his feet, falling awkwardly on their backs, heads, or hips, like unskilful acrobats, as chance might rule; or engaged themselves in noisy flirtations under the fern-fronds with silent ones of homely hue. Huge flies, ignorant of larders and wire-netting, and quite in savage state, buzzed about him without knowing that he was a man. In and out of the fern-dells snakes glided in their most brilliant blue and yellow guise, it being the season immediately following the shedding of their old skins, when their colours are brightest. Litters of young rabbits came out from their forms to sun themselves upon hillocks, the hot beams blazing through the delicate tissue of each thin-fleshed ear, and firing it to a blood-red transparency in which the veins could be seen. None of them feared him.[22]

Nor does Clym fear anything else while engaged on the heath. If his occupation is monotonous, it is soothing and a pleasure in itself. He sings. He sweats heartily. His hands grow calloused and his leathers smell of furze. He amuses his fellow labourers with stories of Parisian life. He has entered the rough society of those he came to ennoble and finds himself uplifted instead by them and their work. No self-destructive voice of the heart upbraids him here for not applying his intellect to remedy the human condition. Calming his distraught wife who thinks his new employment degrading, Clym utters the most sensible and most essentially Hardyan statement in the entire novel:

> Now, don't you suppose, my inexperienced girl, that I cannot rebel, in high Promethean fashion, against the gods and fate as well as you. I have felt more steam and smoke of that sort than you have ever heard of. But the more I see of life the more do I perceive that there is nothing particularly great in its greatest walks, and therefore nothing particularly small in mine of furze-cutting. If I feel that the greatest blessings vouchsafed to us are not very valuable, how can I feel it to be any great hardship when they are taken away?[23]

But Clym is the heath just as Catherine is Heathcliff, and just as she denies her completion in so rude a person, so Clym eventually resumes his attempt to transcend his primal nature. Mrs Yeobright's death and Eustacia's drowning revive his early conviction that he is somehow responsible for the misery of human life in general and now specifically answerable for the loss of these whom he had loved. Formerly imperceptible to anyone but himself, his burden of guilt is now formalised in an objective correlative which everyone can see: Clym is culpable for the deaths of his wife and mother, and, although the community holds him blameless, he cannot forgive himself. His heart is as self-despising as the day he left Paris, its voice now preventing his return to the comfort of fellowship and work on the heath. There will be no Romantic resolution to Clym's spiritual crisis as far as the reader can tell, for, in choosing to indulge his self-annihilative tendencies, he also elects to nullify the redemptive power of love and work. If Clym must at last assume a career as an 'itinerant open-air preacher and lecturer on morally unimpeachable subjects', Hardy implies, the reader can feel grateful that he has learned enough about heart and ego to leave alone 'creeds and systems of philosophy, finding enough and more than enough to occupy his tongue in the opinions and actions common to all good men'.[24]

The five years following publication of *The Return of the Native* in 1878 were arguably the most unsettled period in Hardy's life. His illness of 1881 had been ferociously painful, leaving him exhausted for months and regretful that the whole ordeal was wasted since he did not die and would have to 'range' again 'those grim chambers' to reach the 'all-delivering door'.[25] He and Emma found themselves discontented with London life and society during that early phase of their marriage and moved from house to house attempting to find a more satisfactory home and, I suspect, an improved relationship. Although he continued to write, producing in rapid succession *The Trumpet Major* (1880), *A Laodicean* (1881), and *Two on a Tower* (1882), Hardy's imagination floundered during the years of absence from the countryside where he was born. By his own admission he felt he had lost his way in those novels and needed to re-establish his Dorchester identity and realign himself with its traditions and values. And also by his own admission he formally, though within the private sanctum of poetry, 'abjured love' and the fool's paradise of romantic infatuation:

> No more will now rate I
> The common rare,
> The midnight drizzle dew,
> The gray hour golden,
> The wind a yearning cry,
> The faulty fair,
> Things dreamt, of comelier hue
> Than things beholden! . . .
> – I speak as one who plumbs
> Life's dim profound,
> One who at length can sound
> Clear views and certain.
> But – after love what comes?
> A scene that lours,
> A few sad vacant hours,
> And then, the Curtain.[26]

If only a few sad vacant hours were left him, Hardy yearned to spend them among Dorchester's ancient Roman walls, lush green hills and pastures, and quaint, if not positively provincial, streets. There the couple moved in 1883 and by 1885 had completed building Max Gate, their first real home, where Hardy would live and write until his death forty-three years later. And there the marriage tranquilised, at least for several years, into an achromatic, sometimes comfortable, kinship. Emma occupied herself thereafter with writing poetry, painting, gardening, and campaigning against animal cruelty, while her husband, once again able to walk narrow wooded lanes and visit sites familiar from boyhood, happily found his creativity returned undiminished by his London detour. With renewed excitement he began taking notes on the people, places, and events of the region which had in earlier years stimulated his artistic imagination.

The first fruit and supreme evidence of Hardy's restored generative capability was the 1886 publication of *The Mayor of Casterbridge*, the novel which stands squarely in the middle of his major works of fiction and depicts the most unerring vision of parity between self and community he would ever achieve. To the extent that spontaneity was dying out in Hardy's personal life, it was certainly being replaced with a sense of rootedness in his art not formerly enjoyed. This feeling of enmeshment with past and future as they merged in Dorchester's old customs and new industrialised methodology inspired the author to immortalise the time and place in his semi-fictional Wessex. Michael Henchard is the first major figure to materialise following Hardy's revival and is perhaps his most brilliant characterisation. Not only does Henchard embody the traditional values and systems of agrarian culture, but he prefigures their decline as well. This point has been made frequently, but never with more acuity than by John Holloway who insists that Henchard's example proves that 'the old order was not just a less powerful mode of life than the new, but ultimately helpless before it through inner defect.... From beginning to end Henchard's course is downward. Whenever his old way of life meets the new, it is defeated'.[27] The richness of texture Hardy achieves by interweaving ancient with modern in the novel is so gracefully accomplished that none of his characters – not even Farfrae, whose natural aptitude is sharpened by his acquaintance with chemistry and economics – fully comprehend the significance of their unique moment in history.

Stripped of its conventional narrative, however, Henchard's story is as timeless as any parable. The unfolding of the mayor's tale has less to do with his occupation of a specific juncture in time than with his own intra-psychic dilemma, for the nucleus of Henchard's character is his manifestation of the supremely moral intellect coerced into self-destruction by a supremely diseased heart. About the etiology of his perversity we can only speculate, although he admits early on to Farfrae that he is 'by nature something of a woman-hater'. Surely this remark intimates something about his upbringing, especially as conducted by women, but Hardy privileges the reader no further than that (although Elaine Showalter makes a fine case that the novel's intent is to plot the 'unmanning' of this misogynist).[28] If, therefore, the story begins when Henchard is twenty-one and the author makes no mention of his history before that moment – if indeed he knows anything of it to tell – why should anyone be interested in gleaning atextual information? The reason is that almost all of Hardy's principal characters (except for Gabriel Oak, whose childhood seems to have been a happy initiation into his family's sheep-farming business) have in some way been abandoned by their parents, and it seems unlikely that Henchard had the good fortune to have escaped this dark pattern. Mr Yeobright died while Clym was a youngster, leaving him to attain manhood with an overprotective yet dependent mother; Tess's parents abandoned their obligation to provide her a secure home and solid foundation; Sue's parents divorced; Jude's father died an alcoholic before the infant knew him, his mother drowned herself, and even Phillotson, his father substitute, discarded him for Christminster. Since these men and women have no real parental figures to guide and nurture them and no God to rely upon, and because they have personalised the abandonment to mean that they are worthless and deserving of it, they act in ways which perpetuate the rejection. I suspect that in auctioning his wife and baby, Henchard is re-enacting some scene or form of abandonment he experienced as a boy, and I frankly cannot help but pity the hurt, neglected child in him even as he cruelly draws the full circle around his own family.

There is danger, however, in carrying such sympathy too far, for it runs the risk of elevating Henchard's responses to life as being heroic merely because they are spectacular and intense. Holloway transgresses this line by asserting that despite his being a violent liar with the character of a beast, Henchard still looms above the other characters in 'psychic virtue'. Henchard's 'whole nature, good or bad', Holloway insists almost mystically, 'is centered upon a deep source of vital energy', which may ultimately fail to 'bring success, but even so, it brings greatness and in a sense goodness. . . . Henchard is able to struggle on, though defeated, because not of what he had learnt but of what he *is*. He blocks out something like the full contour of the human being.'[29] While it cannot be denied that there is great character in this 'Man of Character', it can no less be denied that many of Henchard's actions are reprehensible and surely of no more magnitude than Farfrae's unassuming acts of forgiveness simply because the former's sound and fury rages through the tale like Lear's storm. Regardless of his past or his larger-than-life stature, the Mayor of Casterbridge is morally accountable for his behaviour for the very reason that he is conscious of its bitter effect on others; yet there's the rub, for his intellect, which rationally and sensitively teaches him how to respect his fellow man, fails to convince his heart that he is anything but a scoundrel, 'an outcast, an encumberer of the ground, wanted by nobody, and despised by all'.

From the moment young Michael and Susan Henchard are seen plodding across the fields toward Weydon-Priors, he reading a ballad sheet to avoid any irksome chat, she quietly whispering now and then to her babe in arms, it is obvious that the 'deep source of vital energy' propelling the man is nothing more or less mysterious than anger. Hardy has not exposed the couple at a particular low point in their relationship, for Susan's 'hard, half-apathetic expression' shows no surprise at her husband's 'ignoring silence'; that they are in fact married, Hardy remarks from experience, 'there could be little doubt. No other than such relationship would have accounted for the atmosphere of stale familiarity which the trio carried along with them like a nimbus as they moved down the road'.[30] After he has sold his wife and daughter in a burst of rage augmented by his liberal consumption of rum, the hay-trusser finds that he has something new to be furious about. Yet try as he might to blame Susan for taking his joke seriously in her usual 'idiotic simplicity', he recognises that his shame is 'of his own making, and he ought to bear it'.

Bear it he does, but in a manner which consistently belies his anger and undermines his best intentions to obstruct it. Henchard's resolves to work hard and deny himself to atone for his sin are admirable, as are his vows not to drink nor remarry. He is as honest as any graindealer and even occasionally contributes to the poor. But these are all external constraints self-imposed to fool the community into believing what he cannot allow himself to accept: that he is a man to be respected for his scruples, to be found worthy to sit in judgement over others, to be elected as a leader. From outward appearance he is a fine, upstanding Victorian gentleman, but internally, where Hardy probes, he is a man obsessed with guilt and self-flagellation. By virtue of hard work and the performance of the duties he swore to uphold after his indefensible behaviour as a young man, Henchard has willed himself into respectability – but his heart is not engaged in the decency of his actions.

If the mayor's misery is self-induced, so is his punishment self-inflicted and merciless in its contrivance to assure him the greatest degree of pain. The woman-hater remarries Susan largely 'to castigate himself with the thorns which these restitutory acts brought in their train; among them the lowering of his dignity in public opinion by marrying so comparatively humble a woman'.[31] The former mayor underscores his social downfall by engaging himself as a journeyman hay-trusser to the new mayor. The unwelcome wedding guest thrusts himself in the way of further rejection and waives his 'privilege of self-defence' upon being turned away from the festivities. Whenever opportunity presents itself to increase his humiliation, to reaffirm his identity as a failure of the likes of Jopp and Mother Cuxsom, Henchard seizes it. When he cries in anguish that he is Cain, except that 'My punishment is *not* greater than I can bear', he is internally affirming that no conceivable chastisement is too severe for such a worthless reprobate. In his lonely convulsion we discern a familiar figure of one clenched and steeled against ire unmerited, unable to understand that it is his own heart – not Crass Casualty – to blame for his unbloomed hope.

Virginia Woolf is altogether correct in her assertion that there is no pessimism to be found in *The Mayor of Casterbridge*, and she is altogether wrong in her complaint that 'Henchard is pitted . . . against something outside himself which is opposed to men of his ambition and power . . . . He is standing up to fate, and in backing the old Mayor whose ruin has been largely his own fault, Hardy makes us feel that we are backing human nature in an unequal contest'.[32] The unequal contest is not between man and fate but between man and himself, particularly for Henchard between his guilty heart and his intellect which is unable either to control his temperamental impulses or to learn from the miserable consequences those outbursts unswervingly bring. Even the narrator, who admires Henchard's tremendous will to power, admits that 'Misery taught him nothing more than defiant endurance of it'. Had he recognised at any point in his decline that his leaps from Susan to Lucetta to Farfrae to Elizabeth-Jane were symptomatic of his longing for self-absolution, he would probably have been granted his desire in a loving relationship with any of them. Nowhere could he have found a group of people more willing to forgive and love him, but time after time his anger erupts against each of them and violates their trust while heaping increased sorrows on his own head. Or had he comprehended that his occupations as hay-trusser, businessman, mayor, magistrate, and church warden were far more than ruses to be worked at, his temperament might have steadied and his voluptuous anger abated as his respect for the work itself integrated him within the community.

I cannot believe that Henchard is predestined by nature or nurture to remain an isolate ever shadowing the periphery of a world he craves to inhabit, but it does seem self-evident that Hardy uses the mayor's explosive personality to show that in hating himself he must inevitably despise those who love him and obstruct the salvation he should achieve in work. The tremendous energy which might have ensured the survival of Henchard's most ethically fit qualities is subverted in a pact between his own wish to die and Nature's determination to reclaim its matter. In the same way that Henchard has consistently nullified every person caring for him and every action intended to redeem him, his last will nullifies his entire existence:

> That Elizabeth-Jane Farfrae be not told of my death,
> or made to grieve on account of me.
> & that I be not bury'd in consecrated ground.
> & that no sexton be asked to toll the bell.
> & that nobody is wished to see my dead body.
> & that no murners walk behind me at my funeral.
> & that no flours be planted on my grave.
> & that no man remember me.[33]

It is another of Hardy's macabre ironies that so simple a request should guarantee the accomplishment of its opposite effect, for Elizabeth-Jane and Farfrae can no more strike the memory of Henchard from their minds than can Hardy purge the family face of its genetic composition. And it is in this oppositional act that Henchard ensures the protraction of his self-hatred, long after his own death, in the memories of those who had loved him.

5

Fascination and Forgiveness

It is the incompleteness that is loved when love is sterling and true. This is what differentiates the real one from the imaginary, the practicable from the impossible, the Love who returns the kiss from the Vision that melts away.[1]

If Hardy's greatest delight in life was his writing, his deepest personal sorrow was surely the want of intimacy and mutual disclosure in a marriage which at first had offered bright anticipation. It is not surprising, then, that although Clym Yeobright and Michael Henchard fall short of salvation elementally because they never discern the right spirit in which to work, most of Hardy's characters seek – and fail to achieve – their restoration in idealised love. Predictably, love is the more badly bungled strategy of the two. Most candid people will admit to having mismanaged a romantic relationship somewhere along the line, but the problem transcends the psycho-semantic question: 'How do we truly know *what* it is we love about another person when we say "I love you"?' In Hardy's world, as I suspect in our own, narcissism, born of the self-deprecating voice of the heart, is the essence of much that passes for love: I may admire in you the image of myself as you radiantly project it back, or, if you are moneyed or famous or quite good-looking, I may love the ego-enhancement you lend me along with your arm. If I am lonely, I may love you for the momentary relief from isolation your presence gives me; if I dread caring for my own needs, I might feel affectionately toward your willingness to let me depend on you. Or perhaps my self-esteem is so impoverished that I look to your love of me for permission to love myself. These may be poor examples of genuine love, but these are the motivating desires propelling the majority of Hardy's characters to cling to one another in love's name. For instance in the early novel, *A Pair of Blue Eyes* (1873), suitors Smith and Knight compete for the attention of lovely, sophisticated Elfride. John Bayley argues, however, that each wishes 'to be in love with Elfride but not to be loved by her', so that their 'lack of ordinary competence and instinct for give and take' demonstrates 'the primacy of egoism in love.'[2] Hardy's own declaration that 'Love lives on propinquity, but dies of contact'[3] is verified not only in this instance but throughout his canon in the lives of his characters and in the impressions of his poetry. 'In all the books', Virginia Woolf comments, 'love is one of the great facts that mould human life. But it is a catastrophe; it happens suddenly and overwhelmingly, and there is little to be said about it.'[4]

Fortunately in the time since Woolf's observation, J. Hillis Miller has said much about it in his analysis of 'Distance and Desire' in Hardy's novels. The individual protagonist in Hardy's world is uniformly frustrated by his or her inability to find God or an acceptable substitute for him, and rarely does there appear a character like Gabriel Oak or Diggory Venn whose adaptability allows him to draw psychic sustenance from work and nature. Most of Hardy's men and women, writes Miller, spend their lives in a desperate search for some 'limitless joy' which will act as permanent anodyne against heartbreak and isolation:

> In a world without deity they turn toward the only thing which seems a possible substitute for it, someone who exists within the everyday social world, but who radiates a seemingly divine light upon it.... Hardy's fiction has a single theme: 'fascination.'[5]

Charmed transfixion is a vintage theme in literature from courtly love sonnets to Faulknerian gothic. Even if Hardy did not invent the theme, he lived it and his own enmeshment with Emma must be viewed in terms of Miller's theory of fascination. This variation of love, or as I cannot help but regard it, this hybrid of need, fantasy, emotion, and narcissism, is usually ignited by a distant sight of a stranger who is all the more interesting because he or she is unknown. Such was certainly the circumstance of Hardy's first unexpected meeting with Emma, and he would ever after cherish the brilliant pinpoint moment of fascination he experienced when greeted at the rectory door by 'a young lady in brown' with 'golden curls & rosy colour', even though its counterpoint in real life was the wasting away of that exhilaration.

After the lover has become consumed with fascination and has acted out the 'dance of desire', then follows the period in which the feeling of love subsides – 'the smile on your mouth was the deadest thing / Alive enough to have strength to die', as Hardy frames it in 'Neutral Tones' – and is replaced with boredom and alienation, exactly the preconditions which hastened romance in the first place. Life is bleaker than before, and dissatisfaction with self and society increases to widen the chasm separating them. The disillusionment inevitably generated by this declension of hope culminates in the adoption of a fatalistic, self-deprecating attitude, a pattern which persuades Miller to decide that 'The catastrophic experience of falling out of love is proof that in Hardy's world no person can play the role of God for another'.[6] Again it is easily possible to trace this movement in the Hardys' marriage: Emma quickly returned to a cloying, dogmatic belief in God following her pre-marital flirtation with agnosticism, and Hardy extended his ranging the philosophical cosmos to produce a tintinnabulation of voices sounding out impressions of the Immanent Will. Neither would quite forget their early mutual fascination and both would mourn the permanent return of alienation.

The cycle of *ennui*, fascination, possession, and return to boredom remained a pattern throughout Hardy's life, his successive marriages to Emma Gifford and Florence Dugdale notwithstanding. No evidence exists that his extra-marital consummations were explicitly sexual, although that attraction was necessary as a first cause. Rather, his manner of possession was subverted into friendships, working relationships, and artistic co-endeavours, especially notable his scandalous May–December infatuation with the young woman who played Tess in the Hardy Players' 1924 production of *Tess of the D'Urbervilles*. Years earlier, by virtue of his experience with Emma, Hardy had discarded any notion that a few moments of beguilement could salvage him from existential loneliness or provide him a surrogate for God, but, unlike most of his characters, he was able to accept that given and look elsewhere in the practical worlds of work and humanitarian loving-kindness for redemption on a less transcendental scale. The essential argument in Miller's study is that Hardy's canon is a 'prolonged exploration' of this theme:

> in a world without God no attempt to replace God by another person will succeed. For men who believe in God love for another human being can be an authentic religious experience. . . . Lacking this belief, Hardy sees in love only a subjective infatuation, but his characters are possessed of a longing for God or for something like a God to give order and meaning to themselves and to their world. When they fall in love they think they have found in the loved one a power of this sort. Their disillusion when they obtain possession of what they have so intensely desired is a negative religious experience. If Hardy's lovers, like the good lovers in Meredith's novels or in George Eliot's, were able to accept the fact that the persons they love are fallible human beings like themselves, then a happy and enduring love might be possible.[7]

Jocelyn Pierston learns this lesson in Hardy's next-to-last novel, *The Well-Beloved* (1892). Like Nerval in his pathetic search for *les chimères*, Pierston skims from woman to woman in an obsessive quest of the heart for 'The Beloved', an indescribable being which his intellect can barely fathom: 'Essentially she was perhaps of no tangible substance; a spirit, a dream, a frenzy, a conception, an aroma, an epitomized sex, a light of the eye, a parting of the lips. God only knew what she was; Pierston did not'.[8] Here and there he finds his Well-Beloved masquerading as a brunette or a 'pale-haired creature', sometimes tall and fine, and at other times investing the figure of a 'lithe airy being'. Pierston is adamant that he is not the fickle one; it is not due to any 'wanton game' of his instigation that as soon as possession seems imminent, she flits just out of grasp, leaving each 'emptied shape' standing 'ever after like the nest of some beautiful bird from which the inhabitant has departed and left it to fill with snow'. Heartbroken and pitying himself as 'the Wandering Jew of the love world', Pierston laments to a friend:

> To see the creature who has hitherto been perfect, divine, lose under your very gaze the divinity which has informed her, grow commonplace, turn from flame to ashes, from a

radiant vitality to a relic, is anything but a pleasure for any man, and has been nothing less than a racking spectacle to my sight. . . . I have been absolutely miserable when I have looked in a face for her I used to see there, and could see her there no more.[9]

The 'Shelleyan "one-shape-of-many-names"' seduces the 'man with the unanchored heart' across the space of three generations until, exhausted by the dance of desire, he marries an old friend and former embodiment of the Well-Beloved. Contact with a real woman whose graying hair and shrivelled face testify to her earthly fallibility marks for Pierston the death of propinquity. His illusive ideal is extinguished and he is released to concern himself with matters utilitarian and beneficial to the community. In a sense he is Hardy's Faust who recognises the redemptive value of imperfect love at five minutes till midnight.

Important for its practical implications concerning the ludicrous impracticality of ideal love, *The Well-Beloved* fails artistically because Hardy miscarries his attempt to create sufficient compassion for Pierston. At times he is pitiable, but far more often he seems obtuse and in need of a good shaking. Our sympathy tends to the other extreme when we consider the tragic consequences of Tess's search for ideal love so pure and powerful that it redeems the lover and expurgates her past. Tess's struggles with the world begin properly even before her conception. Jack and Joan Durbeyfield may be decent people, amusing in their rustic simplicity and dialectal banter, but fine parents they are certainly not. Work is a slight priority for Mr Durbeyfield partly because he is convinced that his health is ebbing and partly because he is by nature a shiftless, happy-go-lucky sort; he is generous to a fault in providing children, much less extravagant in providing *for* them. If he haunts Rolliver's Inn more frequently than his own hearth, it is purely because the refreshments there bolster his strength for the next day's toil. Amiable, ignorant, entirely dependent for wisdom on the *Compleat Fortune-Teller*, Joan is as innocently feckless as her husband. To be sure, she cooks, rocks the cradle, and scrubs clothes, but a wife's duties no less include fetching her husband from drinking himself too healthy – or at least sitting happily at his side while he does so:

This going to hunt up her shiftless husband at the inn was one of Mrs Durbeyfield's still extant enjoyments in the muck and muddle of rearing children. To discover him at Rolliver's, to sit there for an hour or two by his side and dismiss all thought and care of the children during the interval, made her happy. A sort of halo, an occidental glow came over life then. Troubles and other realities took on themselves a metaphysical impalpability, sinking to mere mental phenomena for serene contemplation, and no longer stood as pressing concretions which chafed body and soul. . . . She felt a little as she had used to feel when she sat by her now wedded husband in the same spot during his wooing, shutting her eyes to his defects of character, and regarding him only in his ideal presentation as lover.[10]

Foolish as she is, Mrs Durbeyfield instinctively measures the yardage between real and ideal and unwittingly passes the trait to her eldest daughter, along with the family face and a wealth of ancestral superstition. Luckily for the Durbeyfields they beget in Tess a child with an uncanny aptitude for evaluating their own negligent behaviour and construing from it a positive, although highly abstract and, at times, illusive, model for herself to emulate. Tess is thus an excellent mother even before she reaches young womanhood. Born with the common sense of an old woman and the 'appetite for joy' of a farm girl, she anchors her clan internally by stabilising the home environment for siblings and parents, and externally by standing as mediator between her marginal family and the somewhat more respectable Marlott community. But in divining her own moral paradigm from her parents' negative example, Tess both fancies herself accountable for the Durbeyfields' fortune and holds herself culpable for their tribulations as well.

Guilt and over-identification with responsibility are Tess's reactions both to parents who abandon her by passively delegating to her the role of family conservator and also to an apparently apathetic God who permits the transgression. Whereas Henchard cannot forgive himself for crimes committed, Tess cannot accept her own innocence. Since her heart is the 'blighted planet' in the novel, no application of intellect can persuade her that birth was not her mortal offence nor that her efforts to fabricate family security and cohesion should rightfully earn her more than the 'ache of modernism'. Wordsworth's conception of children as representing the divine unfolding of 'Nature's holy plan' strikes Tess as almost idiotic as she considers the plight of her siblings:

> All these young souls were passengers in the Durbyfield ship – entirely dependent on the judgment of the two Durbeyfield adults for their pleasures, their necessities, their health, even their existence. If the heads of the Durbeyfield household chose to sail into difficulty, disaster, starvation, disease, degradation, death, thither were these half-dozen little captives under hatches compelled to sail with them – six helpless creatures, who had never been asked if they wished for life on any terms, much less if they wished for it on such hard conditions as were involved in being in the shiftless house of Durbeyfield.[11]

Tess is as unwanted as chaff in the scheme of things, as are her father, mother, and six brothers and sisters, but unlike them, she knows it and must demonstrate her apology in acts of self-abnegation. If the sentiment seems too familiar, the reason is that this grim persona of Tess is resurrected in the grotesque caricature of *Jude*'s Little Father Time, who discharges his family obligations by hanging all the children 'because we are too menny'.

The dark pattern which Hardy observes in Tess is that her guilt and self-loathing cause her to become so tractable that she sabotages opportunities for emotional and psychological survival at every turn. How else can we explain the excessive complaisance which prevents Tess from dancing with Angel at the May Day celebration? That non-event may seem an insignificant omission, perhaps, but its contingency might well have precluded later entanglement with Alec D'Urberville. It is, furthermore, Tess's tractability coupled with pride that obliges her to attempt the darkling horse-and-wagon journey to Casterbridge rather than impose upon any number of young men eager to help a lovely maiden. I hardly need mention that the upshot of the trip is Prince's bloody death, but the more commanding implication is that in the loss of her horse Tess is granted something concrete to atone for. I do not mean that she is pleased at the conversion nor conscious of its occurrence; but if offered the choice, who would not exchange chronic anxiety and existential guilt for a a nasty gash on the arm which might bleed, even fester, but would finally heal? And Tess might have been able to objectify and resolve her guilt by working as a day-labourer until the beast was paid for – such was her plan – but Joan schemes to employ her submissive nature against her: 'We must take the ups wi' the downs, Tess . . . and never could your high blood have been found out at a more called-for moment. . . . Do ye know that there is a very rich Mrs D'Urberville living on the outskirts of The Chase, who must be our relation? You must go to her and claim kin, and ask for some help in our trouble.'[12] Grieving over the felony she has committed, the daughter dutifully, fatalistically, acquiesces.

In ninety-five out of a hundred lives, Tess's kind of passivity would incur no more harm than the cumulation of its own insensibility. But Tess's extreme tractability, motivated, as Frank Giordano quite rightly observes, by an 'inability to resist external pressure when her judgment is over powered by guilt',[13] hurls her directly in the way of Alex D'Urberville. Tess is accustomed to subverting her happiness long before Alec accepts her as a mother's sacrifice, but it is not difficult to see that his aggressive demeanour is the perfect counterpart to her tendency to passively self-destruct. By the time we witness Tess 'wandering desultorily' about the D'Urberville grounds, eating strawberries 'in a half-pleased, half-reluctant state' when Alec offers them and obeying 'like one in a dream' as he gathers blossoms and bids her tuck them into her bosom, there can be no doubt that the clever man will be next in line to turn her pliable nature and guilty conscience to his advantage. D. H. Lawrence attempts to convince us that 'Tess is passive out of self-acceptance' and that she 'knows she is herself incontrovertibly',[14] but his premise is faulty. If Tess genuinely knew herself and accepted the conditions of her being, she would never allow a series of passive non-decisions to shape her life. Tess is passive precisely because she has no conception of herself as autonomous from other people's desires. What she wants or thinks or feels must always, *always* pass by the censors of her heart, whose job it is to pare away self-indulgence, self-acceptance, self-worth, and, at times, self-control, if the result might be self-sacrifice. Ironically, although Tess does not possess a mirror large enough to reflect anything but fragments of her image, everyone sees mirrored in Tess an image of what they most long for. Society desperately needs madonnas to sanctify homes threatened by corruption, materialism, industrialism, and scientific expunction of religion, and it demands of Tess that she become a synecdoche for the 'pure woman'. She is to be mother and virgin, and she is privately to reconcile those antithetical roles without embarrassing the community. The Durbeyfields require a steady provider, as well as mother and virgin: Tess furnishes all three by working piecemeal jobs, nurturing siblings, and allowing her parents to barter her chastity as though it were a negotiable commodity. Conveniently for them, Alec views it the same way and purchases the girl's mortgage. A new horse for Jack and a few toys for the children are to him even exchange for Tess's virtue, for, Lawrence accurately writes, he sees her as 'the embodied fulfilment of his own desire: something, that is, belonging to him. She cannot, in his conception, exist apart from him nor have any being apart from his being'.[15] And, in light of Tess's commercial history, how utterly predictable it is that Angel Clare uses her as a voucher for readmission into the same community from which his scepticism and debauchery have alienated him.

By far the most outstanding irony is that the person most deeply blameable for Tess's victimisation is Tess. Others exploit her for their own egotistical gratification, but in every single instance she accepts the terms out of a tragic misapplication of negative capability. The prerogative is always hers to resist her mother's manipulation or to steadfastly refuse Alec's advances, but despite a healthy intellect which urges its own defence, Tess repeatedly defers to a heart which effaces its right to goodness. Nowhere is the motif of Tess's victimising Tess more apparent than in her 'violation', as Miller terms the act which falls somewhere between rape and seduction, by Alec. The deed itself occurs outside the text in the same way that Henchard's childhood is absent from his story, but even so a pattern has already emerged in the young woman's repertoire of responses which seems to be a reliable indicator of what likely happened during those moments. On that fog-enshrouded, moonless night – itself reflexive of eclipsed consciousness – Tess has fallen asleep on a couch of leaves just prior to Alec's return to The Chase. In a similarly dissociative state she had earlier permitted herself to be sent to Trantridge and allowed Alec the pleasure of flirting with her, and in an identical dreamlike reverie she would eventually marry Angel and murder Alec. The opiate which numbs Tess's sensibilities is not her intense desire to escape sexual encounter, but rather a reflection of the intensity of her longing to engage life as normally and libidinally as Izz, Retty, or Marian without paying a premium for it in shame. This natural artifice fails, sadly, beause she can never become so entranced that her need for punishment is obstructed by her awareness. There is little point in pretending, therefore, that Tess is anything other than a willing – if soporific – participant in her own violation. Tess's encounter with Alec is precipitated by the guilt of having enjoyed his rakish attention even a little and of owing him for his generosity toward her family. The cost of that ambivalent pleasure is that once again the maid has earned something objective for which to atone. This time the wound is localised in her belly for all Wessex to view, but unlike Hester Prynne whose moral injury produces a Pearl, Tess brings forth Sorrow. Listening to the voice of her heart she feels out of harmony with nature and man, and the pain she endures as 'a figure of Guilt intruding into the haunts of Innocence' is pain well-deserved because it is the price of atonement.

Tess's miraculous rally is an expression of a countermotif which, although too recessive to supersede her pattern of self-victimisation, demonstrates her native intelligence and instinctual desire for a peaceful, perhaps even contented, existence. The death of Sorrow literally and symbolically frees Tess from daily contemplation of her past and strengthens her ability to resist manipulation. 'Tess's passing corporeal blight', beams the narrator, 'had been her mental harvest' so that within two or three years of her wretched experience she again 'felt the pulse of hopeful life still warm within her'. At the same time that her 'unexpended youth' revives her 'invincible instinct towards self-delight', an accompanying intellectual will to survive convinces her that 'she might be happy in some nook which had no memories. To escape the past and all that appertained thereto was to annihilate it'.[16] There would be no room for foolish dreams of D'Urberville ancestry in her new life, she resolves, for in leaving home to reside at Talbothays, 'she would be the dairymaid Tess, and nothing more'. Exchanging her bonnet for a hood and sitting on a stool under a cow, milk squirting from her fist into a pail, Tess becomes Clym clad in his leathers, cutting furze on Egdon Heath. At times they are figures against nature's ground, at other moments *mise-en-scène* to the humming and clicking of insects or the organic maturing of seasons. Work is revitalising, Hardy reiterates through their example, and restores man to the earth. True work is redemptive, transcendent of the act itself. In work Clym and Tess approach that exquisite, illusive sensation of happiness unblotted by the shadow of their own selves and are pardoned old liabilities they have dragged about with them like baggage. So simple an art as milking a cow generates in Tess a serene conviction that 'she really had laid a new foundation for her future'.

It is tempting to believe that the dairymaid might have lived happily ever after in pastoral seclusion at Talbothays had Angel Clare not reappeared beyond his slight introduction at the beginning of the novel. But Tess's new foundation is more a transient positive illusion than it is a complete revision of her character, and Angel's re-entry into her life simply reawakens the guilt she has consciously undertaken to repress. Unwittingly he reminds Tess of the discrepancy between herself as a shy, chaste maiden gowned in white at the Marlott Cerealia and as she is now, an ordinary milkmaid with no rightful claim to virtue. On the surface it appears that Tess falls in love with Angel because his intelligence and goodness elevate him above any man she has ever known; indeed the examples of Jack Durbeyfield and Alec D'Urberville leave much to be desired. Yet, in fact, Tess is fascinated with Angel not for the man himself but for the power of redemption his goodness and innocence hold for her. Perhaps she cannot retrace steps in experience to recapture the girl in white, but she can adhere to an equally guileless substitute. Angel represents all that is valuable and worthy to be loved, she all that is of no account and undeserving since she has never loved herself nor been loved for herself. As Tess idolises Angel, he assumes in her mind the godlike omnipotence of a saviour, a perfect lover who will ransom her purity with his acceptance. As deeply as she despises herself is conversely how passionately she loves him. The depth of her obsession reflects how desperately she craves salvation and how fearful she is of losing it:

> Her affection for him was now the breath and life of Tess's being; it enveloped her as a photosphere, irradiated her into

forgetfulness of her past sorrows, keeping back the gloomy spectres that would persist in their attempts to touch her – doubt, fear, moodiness, care, shame. She knew that they were waiting like wolves just outside the circumscribing light, but she had long spells of power to keep them in hungry subjection there. A spiritual forgetfulness coexisted with an intellectual remembrance. She walked in brightness, but she knew that in the background those shapes of darkness were always spread.[17]

By now Tess has some inkling that the shapes of darkness are in part hobgoblins of her own diseased heart. Recognising her tendency to undermine whatever happiness comes her way and believing that Angel's love and willingness to marry her are the redeeming contingencies – rather than consummation itself – Tess attempts to sustain a 'perpetual betrothal' in which both secret and salvation are secure.

Angel holds hidden agenda for Tess, as well, for he has also escaped to the natural setting of Talbothays in hopes of effecting a spiritual rally. The youngest son of a Low Church parson, Angel is an Arnoldian figure weighted by scepticism and paralysed between the world of Cambridge and the opposing world of intellectual liberty. His diversion from religion has not been without cost; like Hardy, Angel grieves that he cannot underwrite Article Four which professes the literal resurrection of Christ, and his guilt is intensified by his father's reaction of profound shock and sadness. As a younger man he initially acted out his rebellion by studying philosophical systems antisympathetic with Biblical doctrine, and finally by living a riotous London life in which he narrowly avoided entrapment by an older woman. At last deciding that his wasteful behaviour must be channelled into useful vocation, he apprentices himself to Dairyman Crick and in true Hardyan fashion discovers solace in work and nature:

> Unexpectedly he began to like the outdoor life for its own sake, and for what it brought, apart from its bearing on his own proposed career. Considering his position he became wonderfully free from the chronic melancholy which is taking hold of the civilized races with the decline of belief in a beneficent Power. . . . He grew away from old association,

and saw something new in life and humanity. Secondarily, he made close acquaintance with phenomena which he had before known but darkly – the seasons in their moods, morning and evening, night and noon, winds in their different tempers, trees, waters, and mists, shades and silences, and the voices of inanimate things.[18]

It is as a 'fresh and virginal daughter of Nature' that the new milkmaid first attracts Angel's notice, but his sentiment portends more than Hardy's grim forecast of revelations to unfold. Angel is searching for re-entry into innocence and is fascinated with Tess for the same reason she is struck with him:

> he seemed to discern in her something that was familiar, something which carried him back into a joyous and unforeseeing past, before the necessity of taking thought had made the heavens gray. He concluded that he had beheld her before; where he could not tell.[19]

His memory lacks the clarity of hers, but each returns to the identical instant in time when both were virginal, each sees projected in the other an incarnation of a former ideal self, and each experiences afresh a desire for reunion with that perfect image. As greatly in need of salvation and self-forgiveness as Tess, Angel reciprocally transmutes her into his redeeming madonna, a 'visionary essence of woman' whom he professes to love 'for herself . . . her soul, her heart, her substance'. Utterly invested in believing Tess perfect, he trivialises whatever little confession she is so bothered about relating in part because he is full of his own self-important guilt and in part because it is in his own interest to remain ignorant to the possibility that she might be impure. 'What I cannot be, she cannot be,' Angel reassures himself, so that together – she in dreamy acquiescence and he almost arrogantly determined – they wed under false pretences in a collusion against reality.

The essential tragedy is that Tess is so tractable and Angel so rigid that their extreme polarisation prevents them from meeting on equal grounds to forgive one another and to help one another silence the voice of self-loathing which has obscured their respective pasts far more than any societal infraction. That this is within their power to do is demonstrated well – but too late. Miller's assumption that Tess 'wanders through her life like a sleepwalker, unaware of the meaning of what she is doing'[20] is not correct, really, because although she functions in a dissociative state at those crucial times when she most needs to believe her intentions and actions irreproachable, she is always hyperaware that her 'damnation slumbereth not'. Tess also knows, long before Ian Gregor intuits and verbalises it, that she is 'a true inheritor of the modern world and to receive what for Hardy is its distinctive legacy, that interior conflict which he describes as "the mutually destructive interdependence of flesh and spirit"'.[21] If she satiates flesh, Nature, or heredity, she mortifies the spirit; if she attempts to live solely according to spiritual inclinations, Nature wells up within her demanding release. This conflict at once alienates Tess from herself and the community around her and evokes the tension which quickens her character. Gathering tremendous energy as it inches through the subterrain of her heart, this bursting force erupts into Tess's consciousness not as aggression or rebellion, but as natural tractability unnaturally bending the reed upon itself.

Angel's intractability is his defence against feeling impotent in a universe which offers no evidence that one should keep faith with the Fourth Article nor with his fellow man. Tess gladly forgives her husband's past not only because she respects his 'right to be', as Lawrence proposes, but primarily because she is ready to forgive herself since his love has already begun to germinate in her the tiniest assurance of salvation. He, on the other hand, is unprepared to forgive himself and retaliates against Tess for his own inadequacy. 'O Tess, forgiveness does not apply to the case!' Angel rages in response to his wife's disclosure. 'You were one person; now you are another. My God – how can forgiveness meet such a grotesque – prestidigitation as that!' Since Tess's identity has always been a metaphor for the unlimited fulfilment of Angel's needs, she has indeed changed into a 'species of imposter; a guilty woman in the guise of an innocent one'. Formerly she was his promise of salvation, his hearthside madonna; now she is as wicked as he, if not more so since she has schemed against his good faith. If Tess can no longer embody all that is pure, she must signify in Angel's black-and-white morality all that is evil. 'God's not in his heaven; all's wrong with the world,' he murmurs, watching his bride's carriage creep out of sight toward Marlott. His quest must drag on for a redemption as inflexible as he so that it can anchor him permanently to a grace which – until the final scenes – he can only accord to himself.

As Henchard, Clym, Tess, and Angel are eclipsed largely by their self-denial of loving-kindness, so is Jude Fawley obscured by his inability to cherish his own identity and get on with life despite its injustice. Since Hardy suffered tremendous regrets that Oxford had been closed to him and that he had married a passionate Arabella who had prestidigitated into a neurasthenic Sue, it seems not implausible that the author experimented in *Jude the Obscure* (1896) with a negative scenario of what life might have resembled had he veered left instead of right at such and such a juncture on this day rather than that. If Michael Millgate's speculation is correct that *Jude* is 'the embodiment of, almost a scapegoat for, a long accumulation of personal and family distress – the poverty and violence suffered by Hardy's ancestors . . . and Hardy's own struggles for education, advancement, and sexual happiness',[22] then we can read into Hardy's statement concerning the novel affirmation that it granted him some consolation, even if that consolation took the form of elevating his distress into mythic proportion: 'The tragedy is really addressed to those into whose souls the iron of adversity has deeply entered at some time in their lives, & can hardly be congenial to self-indulgent persons of ease & affluence'.[23] But while Swinburne congratulated Hardy on his tragedy so 'equally beautiful and terrible in its pathos' and ordained him the 'most tragic of poets'[24] alive, Emma – by this time personally offended by her resemblance to Arabella and Sue, repulsed by her husband's ideology, and herself obscured from her former role as literary helpmate – furiously denounced the novel as denigrating women in general: 'He understands only the women he invents – the others not at all – & he only writes for Art, though ethics show up'.[25] Ironically, *Jude the Obscure* stands in Hardy's career and life as a novel about estrangement, as the work which permanently estranged him from novel-writing, and as the binder of future estrangement in his marriage.

The *leitmotif* which Jude shares with a number of Hardy's earlier characters is his unwanted birth and his recurrent experiences of abandonment. The Fawley's disastrous marriage produces a son as an accident of nature in contrast to a procreation of love; Aunt Drusilla bears the boy like a cross; Farmer Troutham finds him inadequate for the simplest of chores; Schoolmaster Phillotson rejects him for Christminster; Arabella desires the sexual gratification Jude can give her but has little use for the spiritual man; Sue is a self-tortured cipher who cannot determine what she wants, but unlike Arabella, disdains the corporeal man in favour of his intellect; Christminster demands only his absence. There is no Joe Gargery to Jude's Pip, no Magwitch to deliver him from fatal unnecessity. His cognitive genius, furthermore, will not permit him to remain insensible to his predicament, for Jude is born with Tess's sensibility for recognising a disturbing pattern of incongruity in the universe. At age eleven the boy is aware that his life in Marygreen is blighted not because he is being penalised for any heinous crime committed against society or his caretakers, but because he knows his existence to be an 'undemanded one'. However flawed he finds the terrestrial scheme, Jude's greater isolation from human fellowship causes him to identify with and befriend earthworms, crows, lopped-off branches of pruned trees, and the rest of nature's similarly despised creatures because, he dolefully muses, 'A magic thread of fellow-feeling united his own life with theirs. Puny and sorry as those lives were, they much resembled his own'.

In Jude's face, 'wearing the fixity of a thoughtful child who has felt the pricks of life somewhat before his time',[26] appear traces of Clym's visage, 'ruthlessly overrun' by the 'parasite, thought,'[27] and both countenances testify to Hardy's lifelong rumination upon the evolutionary necessity of thinking. Just as what is good for God's bird is bad for God's gardener, so is man's awareness of his self double-edged, informing him of his dilemma as a finite being and consigning him a crumb of freewill against it. Jude's precocious consciousness of the irony of his having been born at all is an echo of Clym's reflection that 'to be born is a palpable dilemma, and that instead of men aiming to advance in life with glory they should calculate how to retreat out of it without shame.'[28] Moreover, Jude's absorption with the fragile nature of outcasts – and with his own existence by implication – the narrator suggests, weakens his ability to thrive in the world and self-sentences him to be 'the sort of man who was born to ache a good deal before the fall of the curtain upon his unnecessary life should signify that all was well with him again'.[29]

I have argued that not a single one of Hardy's characters is preordained by fate or author to meet any particular destiny, and I am prepared to make no exception for Jude. Destructive forces internal and external ravage the immunity of each Wessex figure but none is absolutely defenseless: Tess possesses an instinctual will to survive and intuitive knowledge of right and wrong; Clym's mental constitution enables him to persevere despite adversity; even Henchard is a man who values moral integrity and decency. These characters fail, not because their strategies are defective but because the intensity behind them is not Napoleonic enough to resist breakdown by the voice of the heart. Jude's fraction of freewill is expressed in his idealism which, like most virtues, is two-faced. His ability to romanticise relationships is a survival mechanism which lifts him above the impoverished quality of associations in Marygreen but which also erodes his resilience for coping with the realities of human relationship as he learns them in Christminster.

Idealising, for example, a cursory acquaintance based on his short attendance in night school, Jude grieves that his teacher is going away to attend university. Phillotson is the sole person in Marygreen who seems to care for the youngster, and his leaving feels to Jude like yet another unprovoked abandonment. No matter that his parting words are hurried and patronising – 'Be a good boy, remember; and be kind to animals and birds, and read all you can' – for Jude detects only the tenderest, most personal sentiment. Marygreen without Phillotson is even more inhuman, more dreary and sterile than before, and in his fantasy Jude attaches to Christminster the image of a fiery-golden city of second chances, a new Jerusalem in which anyone can become wise and good like the schoolmaster. 'We are happy here!' he imagines its chimes beckoning to him across the fields. His obsession with the city grows so romantic that the very mention of its name causes him to blush like a lover hearing allusion to his mistress. At age twelve, when most boys are acting out heroic scenarios in preparation for manhood, Jude is carefully planning the steps towards a spiritual perfection which will redeem him once and for all from the loneliness of his undemanded life:

'It is a city of light,' he said to himself.
'The tree of knowledge grows there,' he added . . .
'It is a place that teachers of men spring from and go to.'

'It is what you may call a castle, manned by scholarship and religion.'
'It would just suit me.'[30]

This catechism of idealised love and relationship will be completely inverted at the end of the novel in Jude's death-bed recital from *Job*.

Scholarship and religion superficially glorify Jude's deeper quest to establish in Christminster a new identity. 'It had been the yearning of his heart,' the narrator confides, 'to find something to anchor on, to cling to – for some place which he could call admirable.' In a real sense, the admirable identity of Christminster represents to Jude the perfection of his alter ego. He despises his own image as mirrored back by Marygreen and is despised therein; he reveres the 'city of light' and expects to be transubstantiated by it from a worm into an enlightened man loved and respected for his knowledge, kindness, and generosity. His new self will be as brilliant as the windows of Christminster gleaming back the sun, as compelling to others as Christminster is to him. Predestinate for academic and religious greatness, the future bishop – archdeacon at the least – will never again want for human companionship nor feel the vitality of his existence cancelled by unnecessity. He will be educated and 'leading a pure, energetic, wise, Christian life'. In short, he will be someone else than Jude Fawley.

The only change truly effected in the downward movement of Hardy's inverted *Bildungsroman*, however, is Jude's loss of hope and his subsequent increase in alienation. If Jude's upwardly mobile ambition separates him from the society of his birth, his inability to metamorphise a new identity earns him, as it does Tess, 'the ache of modernism' rather than salvation. In Jude's lonely life is culminated all the failed strategies of all Hardy's characters before him. Heaped atop the pile is his sickening realisation that there is no higher moral order either in religion, academia, or society which values and rewards native goodness and genius such as his. 'The grind of stern reality' exposes Christminster's theologians, apologists, metaphysicians, and statesmen not as divine, benevolent mentors but as aristocrats among the philosophic élite who sneer at the efforts of men like Jude. Christminster's rejection is repeated in his disastrous relationship with Sue Bridehead. Jude has fallen in love with each sight-unseen because he is fascinated by their idealised power to change his identity. In both cases he is bitterly disappointed. His identity is irrevocably forged, he comes to believe, by circumstances which he is powerless to alter. Unwilling to live in a deromanticised world, he renounces both real and ideal selves and his desire for redemptive human love. Not without painful irony does Hardy intersperse Jude's self-administered last rites with the shouts and hurrahs of Christminster fellows cheering on the Remembrance games:

> 'Let the day perish wherein I was born, and the night in which it was said, There is a man child conceived.'
>
> ('Hurrah!')
>
> 'Let that day be darkness; let not God regard it from above, neither let the light shine upon it. Lo, let that night be solitary, let no joyful voice come therein.'
>
> ('Hurrah!')
>
> 'Why died I not from the womb? Why did I not give up the ghost when I came out of the belly? . . . For now should I have lain still and been quiet. I should have slept: then had I been at rest!'
>
> ('Hurrah!')
>
> 'There the prisoners rest together; they hear not the voice of the oppressor. . . . The small and the great are there; and the servant is free from his master. Wherefore is light given unto him that is in misery and life unto the bitter in soul?'[31]

Having discovered Nature indifferent and all sacred institutions, including human relationship, corrupt and lacking charity, Jude's ultimate response to his 'tragedy of unfulfilled aims' is a Schopenhauerean wish to unbe.

Many readers and critics have been gulled into believing that Hardy is in complete sympathy with Jude at the end of the novel and that he condones his character's suicide. Indeed, shortly after the publication of *Jude the Obscure* in 1896, Hardy admitted to his friend Clodd that he regretted having been born and 'but for the effort of dying, would rather be dead than alive'.[32] The same despairing feelings are echoed in the 'In Tenebris' poems, written concurrently with *Jude*, in which he insists that 'death will not appal / One who, past doubtings all, / Waits in unhope'.³³ Disconsolate at having lived into manhood and become aware that 'the world was a welter of futile doing', Hardy looks back to a sunny April noon and a 'winter-wild night' in his frail infancy when he could have died peacefully in his mother's embrace:

> Even then! while unweeting that vision could
>   vex or that knowledge could numb,
> That sweets to the mouth in the belly are
>   bitter, and tart, and untoward,
> Then, on some dim-coloured scene should my
>   briefly raised curtain have lowered,
> Then might the Voice that is law have said
>   'Cease!' and the ending have come.³⁴

Yet for all his yearning to unbe, there resound in Hardy the voices of Carlyle, Comte, Mill, Darwin, and Feuerbach to balance the Schopenhauer and Von Hartmann. Unlike Henchard and Jude, Hardy did not allow himself the irresponsible luxury of suicide, and by 1901 was optimistic enough to proclaim to interviewer William Archer:

> my practical philosophy is distinctly meliorist. . . . Whatever may be the inherent good or evil of life, it is certain that men make it much worse than it need be. When we have got rid of a thousand remediable ills, it will be time enough to determine whether the ill that is irremediable outweighs the good.³⁵

Jude matches perfectly Murray Krieger's description of the ethical man shocked into despair by the tragic vision that human existence is entirely futile,³⁶ and surely there are few of us who cannot empathise, as did Hardy, with his 'sickness unto death'. But the trouble with Jude is that he takes Hardy's famed 'look at the worst' and ends his vision there in a state of myopic, self-obsessed, self-induced paralysis. Gregor's assertion that 'if Jude finds in the Book of Job a text for cursing, it is also possible to find there a text for endurance'³⁷ is to be commended, and I think it not too severe, therefore, to demand more from an individual with Jude's intellect and experience than meek, disinterested resignation which generalises to others the same painful abandonment served him. Without being too harsh, might we not by the end of the book like to lean over Jude's prostrate shape and whisper into his ear a little Carlylean sermon? 'What is this that, ever since earliest years, thou hast been fretting and fuming, lamenting and self-tormenting, on account of? . . . is it not because thou art not HAPPY . . . Foolish soul! What Act of Legislature was there that thou shouldest be Happy?'[38] Quit crying! Take yourself to a real doctor – not that itinerate quack Vilbert, whom you have allowed to treat you precisely because he cannot save you – and get some real medicine! Close thy Byron *and* thy *Job*; open thy Goethe and 'Do the Duty which lies nearest thee'. Upon being turned away from Biblioll College, you resolved to invest yourself in doing 'some good thing' on behalf of human interest: are there no others suffering in Christminster? Melchester? Marygreen? Must goodness be sanctified, confined to the educated bishop? You know better than that! Use your great talent for idealisation to elevate and strengthen and worship the divine element in the common labourer next to you. And are there no more dilapidated masonries to be restored? What has become of your moment of 'true illumination' when it occurred to you that work itself is salvaging, that in the stone yard is 'a centre of effort as worthy as that dignified by the name of scholarly study within the noblest of the colleges'? All your late excuses that work makes you ill are but symptoms of 'the modern vice of unrest' and rationalisations for the real reason you remain locked inside the impossible chalk circle of your own conspiration. Save your own soul you have no star to guide you, that is true, but what a bright constellation that is if unobscured by self-willed defeat!

Eclipse is complete for Jude, however, because he cannot recover from the jarring perception that, to extract again from Krieger's interpretation of the tragic visionary, he is 'hollow at the core . . . because he has suddenly been seized from without by the hollowness of his moral universe, whose structure and meaning have until then sustained him'.[39] There are two levels of tragedy operating in Hardy's only *Bildungsroman*: the disillusionment of the idealistic, intelligent young man by circumstances outside his control, and – by far the greater calamity – his failure to employ intellect and heart in defiance of those circumscribing forces.

It would be unfair to conclude that the Wessex characters are solely responsible for their own actions, their inadequate responses to conflict and loneliness, or even their tendencies toward self-pity, for we must remember that they are essentially a contrived people almost entirely lacking preceptorial guidance. Having lived according to examples inbred over hundreds of years within their isolated, primitive, superstitious, miserably educated community, they are ill-equipped to reconcile past causes with encroaching modern effects. Granted, Hardy had no intention of writing Jamesian realism in which, amid the polite chiming of tea-cups on saucers, sophisticated ladies and gentlemen seek the counsel of their own educated hearts in opting for the right moral decision. But even if Hardy cannot be faulted for what may appear an authorial indiscretion in inventing a hero-less society, we cannot help wondering at his deliberate omission of positive, practical models. It seems to me that his purpose was to create in Wessex a microcosm of the world-as-it-was evolving into the world-that-will-be, and to achieve this he found it imperative to draw characters for whom folk-heroes had become obsolete and modern mentors had yet to emerge. In this chronological split-second between two worlds, Hardy isolates the essence of individual personalities to examine the convolutions of their hearts and intellects as they attempt to conciliate Nature with law, experience isolation, confront absurdity in the form of coincidence, search for a reclusive God, destroy or cultivate human bonds, and prepare to encounter death. What he discovers is that his characters instinctively perceive that labour and love are the vital means whereby man can attain a modicum of happiness in life. Because these rustics also represent an early stage in modern psycho-social development, however, their perceptions often occur in transitory visions which spark and evaporate like flickers of intelligence in the consciousness of a beast. That is why Henchard, Clym, Tess, and Jude understand in moments of epiphany that they are not puppets danced about on strings but rather semi-free agents with intellect, heart, and will; and it is also why the illumination does them almost no good. They are the forerunners of the imperfect, incomplete modern hero because, albeit rarely successfully, they are among the first to grapple with a world stripped to its foundation of history's power to rank, order, stabilise, and comfort.

Thus without the tutelage of Carlyle urging them to Produce! for night cometh soon enough, men like Clym and Henchard and women like Tess and Bathsheba intuit that real work is a sacred enterprise which subsumes the narrow quest for happiness, even if they are unable to reduce expectations to zero in light of that perception. And Pierston, Angel, Tess, and Jude know that idealistic passionate love which seeks self-enhancement or demands perfection of the beloved is not really love at all. These things they grasp intellectually, and at best sporadically; but their most damning failure is their incapacity to apprehend with their hearts the meaning and value of 'loving-kindness'. For Hardy, there must be acceptance of the fallible self before goodwill and down-to-earth love can be extended to others, before any love can stand 'sterling and true', and this is where most of his characters become tragic figures. Henchard is bent on self-destruction because he hates his ugly temperament; Tess is submissive and self-loathing because she feels undeserving to be loved; Jude cannot love himself enough to affirm his worth without the embrace of Christminster and Sue. Since self-affirmation and love for others are interdependent, it stands to reason that in listening to the voices of diseased hearts rather than healthier intellects these characters cast themselves at odds with self and community. Those who cannot forgive imperfection in any one or any institution must themselves suffer the loneliness attendant on lives devoid of loving-kindness.

'Pain has been, and pain is',[40] Hardy declared, and only through the practice of loving-kindness can its effects be meliorated. Work and loving-kindness establish for man stability and self-possession in the painful flux of things and are the correlates of salvation in a world evolving randomly without divine intervention. Nature, heredity, society, and tradition will always be our antagonists: rain and fire will eternally devastate crops and consume homes; Nature's indifference will always make us feel isolate; sexual instincts will continue to urge us to consummate our 'appetite for joy', while society must for its survival demand submission of individual desires; the culture into which we are born will forever define our perspectives; law will remain an unfortunate but necessary expense of community; 'hap' will undoubtedly unbloom now and again our most cherished hopes; and – until the Great Adjustment – superimposed over those immutables is the ambiguous truth that the universe operates on a course predetermined to grind out random change. Yet these oppositional forces appear almost as marginalia before the real reason 'joy lies slain' in history upon history throughout the Wessex canon. The source of tragedy in these novels is eloquently identified by Katherine Anne Porter as the discord between heart and mind which Hardy knew to be the most divisive power in the universe:

> He knew there was an element in human nature not subject to mathematical equation or the water-tight theories of dogma, and this intransigent, measureless force, divided against itself, in conflict alike with its own system of laws and the unknown laws of the universe, was the real theme of Hardy's novels. . . . Hardy's characters are full of moral conflicts and of decisions arrived at by mental processes, [yet] . . . such characters of his as are led by their emotions come to tragedy; he seems to say that following the emotions blindly leads to disaster. Romantic miscalculations of the possibilities of life, of love, of the situation; of refusing to reason their way out of their predicament; these are the causes of disaster in Hardy's novels. . . . Hardy had an observing eye, a remembering mind; he did not need the Greeks to teach him that the Furies do arrive punctually, and that neither act, nor will, nor intention will serve to deflect a man's destiny from him, once he has taken the step which decides it.[41]

I do not believe, as some contend, that Hardy's deepest sympathies are reserved for those characters who are powerless to protect themselves against fate, for I cannot concede that a single one of his characters suffers that limitation. However powerless Hardy's Wessex men and women may judge themselves, however predestined to ruin they may believe their efforts in the shadow of cosmic and instinctual entrapments, Hardy does not view them as helpless victims. Ideally, he argues through his reading of their lives, a brighter pattern of existence is possible in which man's intellect informs him of the ironies of being, the voice of his heart teaches him to cherish incompletion as he finds it in himself and others, and his mite of freewill elevates him above obscurity.

6
He Resolves to Say No More

I
When moiling seems at cease
In the vague void of night-time,
And heaven's wide roomage stormless
Between the dusk and light-time,
And fear at last is formless,
We call this allurement Peace.

II
Peace, this hid riot, Change,
This revel of quick-cued mumming,
This never truly being,
This evermore becoming,
This spinner's wheel onfleeing
Outside perception's range.[1]

The need to distill a few precious drops of essential meaning at the conclusion of a discourse reflects for most writers something more than a polite, educated nod of deference to Aristotelian rhetoric. The shaping of a proper ending which confers a sense of closure and an Oriental feeling of the roundness, the balanced complexity of the matter at hand is generally valued by stylists as a stroke of *éclat* demonstrating at once authorial ingenuity and textual validity. The problem any modern author encounters in assigning finalisms is identical to the problem Hardy faced at the conclusion of every novel, for as Ian Gregor observes, 'Endings . . . were always a source of difficulty for Hardy, because they implied unity where he sought plurality, they expressed finality where he sought continuity'.[2] While some themes may lend themselves to parochial summarisation, the study of Hardy's voices is not – happily, in my opinion – among them. Hardy recognised more astutely than any other Victorian novelist that all endings are fictions because however alluring resolution may seem, the 'spinner's wheel onfleeing' continually unravels change upon change in pursuit of variation and impermanence. This recognition was hardly a comfort to a man who yearned to be 'freed the fret of thinking' about it, and yet multiplicity, continuity, instability, and unfathomability comprise the philosophical quintessence of Hardy's art and characterise the design of his own peculiar inscape. Such plurality does not comfortably translate into any synoptic discussion, but the frightening spectre of irresolution notwithstanding, this chapter of fictional finalisms will examine Hardy's sense of his own ending and the final voice which emerges from his poetry to enfold the polyphony preceding it.

On the eve of Hardy's sixty-third birthday, journalist Henry Nevinson departed from his interview at Max Gate with the impression that the author had not long to live:

> Face a peculiar grey-white like an invalid's or one soon to die; with many scattered red marks under the skin, and much wrinkled – sad wrinkles, thoughtful and pathetic, but none of power or rage or active courage. Eyes bluish grey and growing a little white with age. . . . Head nearly bald on the top. . . . The whole face giving a look of soft bonelessness, like an ageing woman's.[3]

Naturally Hardy was stung by the brutal overdramatisation of his physical description, but, as a man who had felt used up by age twelve, he could hardly contest Nevinson's insinuation that at sixty-three he was indeed at the threshold of death. When old age finally overtook Hardy some twenty years later, it settled congenially about his shoulders like a familiar cloak. His bitterest ragings largely past, he could afford to become the gracious, quietly charming, spiritual father of the modern lineage of English poets. Even if he was never to be ordained England's Poet Laureate, he had become universally known as 'the Grand Old Man of English Letters' and was to accept among other honours a Litt. D. from Cambridge in 1913 and an honorary Doctor of Letters from Oxford in 1920. The numbers of literary figures who came to sit adoringly at his feet – among them Siegfried Sassoon, Walter De La Mare, J. M. Barrie, Robert

Graves, John Galsworthy, and T. E. Lawrence – were astounding to a man who had so obstinately refused to play Mentor to anyone's Telemachus. Yet, Irving Howe insists, they came not only to imbibe the distinguished serenity of an older writer but because he represented

> a purity of spirit which was inherently precious, and all the more precious during the contaminated post-war years; he seemed like a remembrance, at once fragile and magnificent, of an England gone forever; he was a man to venerate precisely because he remained untouched by the febrile sophistication of the twenties. Hardy had begun his intellectual life as a disciple of agnosticism, and now he seemed like the very embodiment of traditional verities and styles.[4]

If the younger Hardy had fumed against evolution's blunder which produced in man consciousness of his impending death, the elder Hardy seemed comfortably reconciled to Nature's imperative. After all, he reflected on his eighty-sixth birthday, 'He Never Expected Much'[5] from life, and the world had kept faith with its promise of 'neutral-tinted haps and such'. Their bargain had been fair, he conceded from his vantage of equipoise between life and death, for his acceptance of the circumstance had allowed him to 'stem such strain and ache / As each year might assign'.

I have no trouble believing that, despite his ambition, Hardy expected little return on his tentative investment in life, but I do not find it conceivable that a man who lived always expecting death in every cough or ache did so with no apprehension toward its arrival. The idea of his own ending puzzled and distressed Hardy since the thing behind his head was plural in possibility yet singular in fact; moreover, that fact was one completely inaccessible to human divination. Beginnings, as well as endings, are fictions and there is general consensus that the author fabricated to some degree the account of his infancy and boyhood in *The Life of Thomas Hardy*. But since he could not posthumously rematerialise to explore the fictions of his own death, he attempted through poetry to create a sensibility capable of postmortem augury. Rebecca West's rather catty observation that 'Mr Hardy has persuaded himself that a macabre subject is a poem in itself: that, if there be enough of death and the tomb in one's theme, it needs no translation into art'[6] is frivolous and misleading since every one of his mortality-related verses – there are at least 150 of them in his published collections – must be considered crucially important, if not always artistically gratifying, because they represent Hardy's experimental excavations into the multiple possibilities of his own end and after-end.

And because Hardy could not vouchsafe that the lowest creature was qualitatively dissimilar to the noblest human, it mattered little whether he died vicariously as a man, woman, or beast. In one humorous instance he muses whether his passing will affect the household any differently than did the decease of Florence's dog, Wessex: Will he be thought of wistfully 'At the creep of evenfall, / Or when the sky-birds call / As they fly?' Will he be sought as companion when 'the hour for walking chimes, / On that grassy path that climbs / Up the hill?'[7] Certainly, these are among the pleasures for which Hardy wished to be remembered. Or perhaps, as 'Shelley's Skylark',[8] he will live his meek life, fall one day to be reclaimed by earthy loam, and reappear throbbing in a 'myrtle's green' or sleeping in 'the coming hue / Of a grape on the slopes of yon inland scene'. At present, he reflects in 'A Singer Asleep',[9] he can visit Swinburne's tomb on the Isle of Wight and return at twilight to his secure study at Max Gate, but eventually he must lie alongside his friend here

> beneath the waking constellations,
> Where the waves peal their everlasting strains,
> And their dull subterrene reverberations
> Shake him when storms make mountains of their plains.

If Swinburne's phantom may draw up from the grave to revisit those whom he had loved, so might Hardy's; yet open as he is in poetry to the existence of spirits, he could find no daylight evidence to support their reality. The worst possible contingency, Hardy speculates in 'The To-be-Forgotten',[10] is to die a second death when, 'with the living, memory of us numbs, / And blank oblivion comes!' In the meantime he and all other cosmic integers are consigned to wait out the end:

> A star looks down at me,
> And says, 'Here I and you
> Stand, each in our degree:
> What do you mean to do, –
>   Mean to do?'
> I say: 'For all I know,
> Wait, and let Time go by,
> Till my change come.' – 'Just so,'
> The star says: 'So mean I: –
>   So mean I.'[11]

While Hardy pays lipservice to the relaxed attitude that his death is not to be regretted or mourned, for, 'Beneath the sunny tree / I lie uncaring, slumbering peacefully',[12] his nonchalance is belied by the fact that each final poem in his last four volumes of verse is intended as an epitaph should he die before compiling another. As the finale of *Moments of Vision* (1917), 'Afterwards' casts, as it has been noted, a pleasantly nostalgic glow upon the scenes of ordinary agrarian life in Dorset which Hardy wanted to be remembered as having treasured, and would have been a lovely fiction with which to end his career at age seventy-nine. In fact while Hardy was preparing *Moments of Vision* for publication, he was concurrently involved in the process of setting in order his personal effects and attempting to update his memoirs in what Michael Millgate calls a 'pre-emptive strike in the shape of an official biography'.[13] The unexpected development which rather spoiled the timing of his self-eulogising was that he did not die. While I am not proposing that Hardy begrudged his own longevity, I do find it significant that the collection of poems which followed five years later begins and ends on a markedly less romanticised, less cordial note. A severe bout with influenza, possibly complicated by a recurrence of bladder inflammation, confined Hardy to bed the entire month of January 1922. Lying ill and unable to do much else, he brooded for hours on end over the apology to his forthcoming work, deciding that he might as well have a go at expressing in prose his indignation at having been maligned over the years by individuals and institutions eager to discredit his art as the snivelling of a pessimistic apostate. Concerned that he not appear too 'cantankerous' but feeling no need at eighty-two to solicit anyone's approval, Hardy sent *Late Lyrics and Earlier* (1922) to press with the lengthy, excoriating preface intact. Quite unlike anything Hardy had previously written for public disclosure, this apology attacks the 'dark madness' of the present time which countermands individuality in the artistic 'exploration of reality' and imperils civilisation with its ignorant optimism. Censorship of his kind of 'obstinate questionings' and 'blank misgivings', he warns irately, 'tends to a paralysed intellectual stalemate'.[14] And yet the concluding poem in *Late Lyrics* hints that Hardy was himself feeling that an image of spiritual paralysis might be a more fitting epitaph for him than the kindly 'Afterwards'. At what was surely this time his life's end, he takes a critical 'Surview'[15] of his demeanour over the past eight decades:

> A cry from the green-grained sticks of the fire
>   Made me gaze where it seemed to be;
> 'Twas my own voice talking therefrom to me
> On how I had walked when my sun was higher –
>   My heart in its arrogancy.

When in the chill of old age the poet retires to warm himself by the fire of his life's achievements, he discovers that unseasoned wood has made for a meagre flame. Since there is no God with auditory capability, it is Hardy's voice which reprimands his egoism from the burning bush:

> '*You held not to whatsoever was true,*'
>   Said my own voice talking to me:
> '*Whatsoever was just you were slack to see;*
> *Kept not things lovely and pure in view,*'
>   Said my own voice talking to me.
>
> '*You slighted her that endureth all,*'
>   Said my own voice talking to me;
> '*Vaunteth not, trusteth hopefully;*
> *That suffereth long and is kind withal,*'
>   Said my own voice talking to me.
>
> '*You taught not that which you set about,*'
>   Said my own voice talking to me;
> '*That the greatest of things is charity. . . .* '

Judging himself against Pauline creeds which he has professed as his own and attempted to teach in fiction and verse, Hardy is disconsolate over the conviction that he has failed to hold dear only those things which are true and pure, to remain compassionate under the strain of longsuffering, and above all, to practise loving-kindness. Had he realised his vanity when his sun was higher, there might have been time enough for *pentimento*. As it stands, however:

> the sticks burnt low, and the fire went out,
> And my voice ceased talking to me.

It becomes apparent in these end-poems that Hardy is preparing not only for death but for a cessation even more final than death: he is at last getting ready to be silent. 'Why do I go on doing these things?' he queries at the close of *Human Shows* (1925), 'Why not cease?'[16] Unmistakable is the tenor of exhaustion as he ponders whether the vitality of Florence, the young wife with whom at seventy-three he has found a marriage of true melancholic minds, keeps him embroiled 'in this world of welterings and unease'. Perhaps he indulgently reminds himself of Tennyson's Tithonus wed to the dawn and fears that though 'the woods decay and fall . . . Me only cruel immortality / Consumes'.[17] Certainly this is another possible fictional ending; but the point is that Hardy has reached the time when he is ready to 'hush this dinning gear' and to escape the polyphonic clattering of voices he has sent into articulation over the past sixty years.

I cannot help but believe, however, that we should have missed the seasoning of Thomas Hardy had he died in 1917 or 1922 or 1925. The poem which ultimately stands as his last word about himself is one which at once transports him backward to the silent, detached watchfulness of his childhood and projects him into the future as mute observer of apocalyptic revelation. Published at the close of *Winter Words* eight months after his death in 1928, 'He Resolves to Say No More'[18] reflects Hardy's clenched determination to keep further 'impressions' and 'obstinate questionings' to himself:

> O my soul, keep the rest unknown!
> It is too like the sound of a moan

He Resolves to Say No More

When the charnel-eyed
Pale Horse has nighed:
Yea, none shall gather what I hide!

Why load men's minds with more to bear
That bear already ails to spare?
From now alway
Till my last day
What I discern I will not say.

Let Time roll backward if it will;
(Magians who drive the midnight quill
With brain aglow
Can see it so.)
What I have learnt no man shall know.

And if my vision range beyond
The blinkered sight of soul in bond,
– By truth made free –
I'll let all be,
And show to no man what I see.

Hardy had trifled with this theme as early as 1901 in 'Mute Opinion', a poem in which the speaker returns from the grave with news that Truth is not audible in the noisy clamouring of 'pulpit, press, and song', but in the silent suspicioning of 'A large-eyed few and dumb'. But 'He Resolves to Say No More' is no flirtation with silence, for here, as nowhere else among Hardy's other 946 poems, an authoritative voice solemnly and stentorially denies the public further access to his imaginings. Whether the Pale Horse bears good tidings or bad is actually of secondary importance in this poem, and in any case I cannot imagine Hardy withholding new revelations divulged him by death's proximity; what really matters here is that what has already been written must now be sufficient unto itself. Little survives of what Hardy thought or wrote after October 1927,[19] and although Florence refused to accept the poem as her husband's last communication with the readers he variously loved and hated, his silence seems to me a *dénouement* perfectly befitting his lifelong preoccupation with voice.

In contrast to the bitter invective posted at the beginning of *Late Lyrics*, the introductory remarks to *Winter Words* are succinct and yield the impression that with this 'last appearance on the literary stage', the author has said all he intends to say, regardless of whether he should die by morning or live to be 100. While it is inevitable that 'the same perennial inscription' of pessimism 'will be set on the following pages', Hardy writes, 'I also repeat what I have often stated . . . that no harmonious philosophy is attempted in these pages – or in any bygone pages of mine, for that matter'.[20] This denunciation is by now perhaps too familiar, but in the context of Hardy's winter ruminating it seems more a new wineskin than an old one. What I mean is this: Hardy's final articulation – silence – is the binding together of all previous voices into a single plurality which insistent literary critics must examine not as a *gestalt* nor as separate ideas, but as the perpetually evolving perplexities of both. His resolution is a fine strategy, then, for achieving what no amount of vociferation could hope: as if to concur with Anton Tchekhov that 'it is not the business of novelists to solve such questions as those of God, pessimism, and so on',[21] Hardy employs silence as his way of leaving the ending open, the possibilities innumerable.

In his examination of episodic silence in Hardy's narratives, Wayne C. Anderson concludes that the canon is 'fundamentally a rhetoric of silence' in which all major characters are obliged to become readers of the mute text of experience. Elizabeth-Jane, for instance, must divine from the 'silent and elliptical' relationship between Lucetta and Farfrae that the two are in love; Mrs Yeobright turns away from Clym's closed door as Egdon Heath 'thrills silently in the sun', indifferent to her suffering and her imminent death; and 'Nature is "ruled" by silence when Alec seduces Tess, merely reiterating itself, unconcerned with Tess's catastrophe'.[22] Anderson argues that because of these silences Hardy's characters are required to exercise freedom and responsibility in their actions:

> Hardy's suggestion is that in a world of silences we are called to read. In a world where God is silent, we must build hypotheses by which to live; in a world where nature is silent, we must create our own order and meaning; in a world where people around us are silent, we must struggle to establish love and relationship.[23]

Responsibility for answering Hardy's mute questionings is shifted from interrogator through interlocutory Wessex men and women to us as readers; plainly, Hardy's ultimate refusal to speak must be read as his final text. Silence is by nature a protean medium of expression, and yet as Herman Melville observes in *Pierre*, 'All profound things, and emotions of things are preceded and attended by Silence'.[24] Some silences reflect ineffable communion while others are to be taken pejoratively; silence may be nihilistic when erected as a barrier between self and community, or sinister when read as a gaping blank dug out by censorship. And, of course, there is God's silence which denotes to men like Browning's Johannes Agricola or Porphyria's lover a sort of 'unconditional positive regard', but signifies to others that God is absent or apathetic, dead or non-existent. Whether disclosing paramount meaning or utter nescience, silence is an impediment to its own intepretation since each would-be exegete approaches it from the individual texts of his peculiar philosophy, experience, and expectation. No less confounding is the silence of Hardy's winter text; yet if we are willing to sacrifice the integrity of its plurality for a moment, the possibilities may be collapsed into two thematic conjectures. It is at this point that any thorough exploration of Hardy's work or life is obliged to deal with the issue of his pessimism. Although Hardy never admitted to holding a grim outlook on the human condition, he did find it unconscionable to ignore in art the woeful contingencies of real life; and although he insisted that his art was not to be misconstrued as mimetic of reality, he granted in a letter to essayist John Addington Symonds in 1889 that:

> The tragical conditions of life imperfectly denoted in *The Return of the Native* & some other stories of mine I am less & less able to keep out of my work. I often begin a story with the intention of making it brighter & gayer than usual; but the question of conscience soon comes in; & it does not seem right, even in novels, to wilfully belie one's own views. All comedy, is tragedy, if you only look deep enough into it. A question which used to trouble me was whether we ought to write sad stories, considering how much sadness there is the world already. But of late I have come to the conclusion that, the first step towards cure of, or even relief from, any disease

being to understand it, the study of tragedy in fiction may possibly here & there be the means of showing how to escape the worst forms of it, at least, in real life.[25]

Hence, the first way in which to interpret Hardy's resolve that 'none shall gather what I hide' is to consider it an introversion into pessimism.

If Hardy vehemently renounced the label of pessimist, it may seem that he did so at the expense of protesting too much. His personal writings are punctuated with self-consciously witty quips and barbed retorts defending the philosophical position while holding it at arm's length:

> Pessimism (or rather what is called such) is, in brief, playing the sure game. You cannot lose at it; you may gain. It is the only view of life in which you can never be disappointed. Having reckoned what to do in the worst possible circumstances, when better arise, as they may, life becomes child's play.[26]

> Why people make the mistake of supposing pessimists, or what are called such, incurably melancholy, I do not know. The very fact of their having touched bottom gives them a substantial cheerfulness in the consciousness that they have nothing to lose. . . . [27]

> 'Pessimism' – as the optimists nickname what is really only a reasoned view of effects & probable causes, deduced from facts unflinchingly observed – leads to a mental quietude that tends rather upwards than downwards, I consider. As for professional optimists, one is always sceptical about them: they wear too much the strained look of the smile on a skull. . . . [28]

> As to pessimism. My motto is, first correctly diagnose the complaint – in this case human ills – and ascertain the cause; then set about finding a remedy if one exists. The motto or practice of the optimists is: Blind the eyes to the real malady, and use empirical panaceas to suppress the symptoms.[29]

In his general preface to the Wessex Edition of his novels and poems (1912), Hardy offers what at first may appear to be his most circumspect evaluation of pessimism and other speculative philosophies:

> That these impressions [Hardy's novels and poems] have been condemned as 'pessimistic' – as if that were a very wicked adjective – shows a curious muddle-mindedness. It might be obvious that there is a higher characteristic of philosophy than pessimism, or than meliorism, or even than the optimism of these critics – which is truth. Existence is either ordered in a certain way, or it is not so ordered, the conjectures which harmonize best with experience are removed above all comparison with other conjectures which do not so harmonize. So that to say that one view is worse that other views without proving it erroneous implies the possibility of a false view being better or more expedient than a true view; and no pragmatic proppings can make that *idolum specus* stand on its feet, for it postulates a prescience denied to humanity.[30]

But the problem here is that Hardy undermines his own defence by challenging his adversaries to prove his impressions true or false according to a higher truth which cannot be deciphered through pragmatic reasoning or preternatural divination. The debate is reduced to a quibble over semiotics, and Hardy's extremely defensible position emerges as untenable as any other philosophy. If Hardy inclined toward solipsism before settling into silence, the echo of that early predilection is certainly audible in this passage.

Perhaps the reason Hardy failed to establish a watertight case against pessimism is that his desperate trust in meliorism was undercut by a deeper conviction that such confidence was historically unwarranted. By the early twenties he had become discouraged, fearful that his endeavour to rationalise religion had miscarried despite his repeated plea that 'all the churches in Europe should frankly admit the utter failure of theology, & put their heads together to form a new religion which should have at least some faint connection with morality'.[31] That the Church remained the only establishment 'of sufficient dignity and footing, with such strength of old association, such scope for transmutability, such architectural spell', capable of cleaving together England's 'shreds of morality', Hardy had no doubt, but its stubborn adherence to 'preternatural assumptions' prevented 'the gathering of many millions of waiting agnostics into its fold'.[32] Hardy had no quarrel with a more practical brand of Christianity in which the teachings of Christ are accepted as excellent moral instruction, but neither had he patience with creeds which offered false hopes of eternal life in exchange for obedience. Already alarmed that civilisation had irrevocably exiled to the Elgin Room of the British Museum all the salvaging qualities of pagan deities and had exalted in their stead a self-defeating reverence for the impractical, the unattainable, and the impossible, Hardy recognised his concerns substantiated in the mid-twenties when the new *Prayer Book* appeared with a liturgy entirely unrevised with respect to rationalistic thought. 'From that time', Hardy conceded dispiritedly, '[he] lost all expectation of seeing the Church representative of modern thinking minds.'[33]

However much the inefficacy of religion had gloomed Hardy's spirits, it was the Great War of 1914 which threatened to mete a death blow to his restrained optimism. Inflamed by his perception that men's minds were 'moving backwards rather than on', Hardy fumed in 1922 that

> Whether owing to the barbarizing of taste in the younger minds by the dark madness of the late war, the unabashed cultivation of selfishness in all classes, the plethoric growth of knowledge simultaneously with the stunting of wisdom, 'a degrading thirst after outrageous stimulation' (to quote Wordsworth again), or from any other cause, we seem threatened with a new dark Age.[34]

Hardy's earlier war poems, specifically those which treated the Boer conflict, had emphasised the grief of civilians bereft of loved ones, the lonely suffering of soldiers dying under 'foreign constellations', and the absurdity of barbaric old credos which glorified bloodshed; but the tone of Hardy's second round of war verse is considerably darker, argues Harold Orel, because the Great War put an end to his belief that international camaraderie would set the foundation for peace:

> Hardy foresaw, even in the first months of war, that ancient friendships, shared experiences, a common love of learning,

would be forgotten amidst the tumult and the shouting. . . . Somehow it all seemed so repetitive of earlier lunacies, so useless in what it sought to accomplish. . . . Hardy had now become convinced that internationalism, however potent its promise, would not come to pass in his lifetime; and the realisation that it would not came close to breaking his heart.[35]

Orel's postulations seem all the more valid when read against the enormous measure of disparity between Hardy's perspective on the problem of war at the beginning of the twentieth century and his radically modified view in 1914. To William Archer, Hardy cheerfully proclaimed in 1901:

> Oh yes, war is doomed. It is doomed by the gradual growth of the introspective faculty in mankind – of their power of putting themselves in another's place, and taking a point of view that is not their own. In another aspect, this may be called the growth of a sense of humour. Not to-day, not tomorrow, but in the fulness of time, war will come to an end, not for moral reasons, but because of its absurdity.[36]

But in the days just following England's declaration of war against Germany, a subdued Hardy recorded in third person his sorrow and his resignation over the absurd fact that war is not doomed by its absurdity:

> It was seldom he had felt so heavy at heart as in seeing this old view of the gradual bettering of human nature, as expressed in these verses of 1901 ['The Sick Battle God'], completely shattered by the events of 1914 and onwards. War, he had supposed, had grown too coldly scientific to kindle again for long all the ardent romance which had characterized it down to Napoleonic times, when the most intense battles were over in a day, and the most exciting tactics and strategy led to the death of comparatively few combatants. Hence nobody was more amazed than he at the German incursion into Belgium, and the contemplation of it led him to despair of the world's history thenceforward. . . .[37]

It may be added here that the war destroyed all Hardy's belief in the gradual ennoblement of man, a belief he had held for many years. . . . He said he would probably not have ended *The Dynasts* as he did end it if he could have forseen what was going to happen within a few years. Moreover, the war gave the *coup de grace* to any conception he may have nourished of a fundamental ultimate Wisdom at the back of things.[38]

Even the signing of the Armistice on 11 November 1918 failed to resurrect Hardy's great expectations, Orel concludes, because his 'final reading of the movement of history' precluded any possibility that ' "the Great Calm" of the Armistice was permanent'.[39] The end of dreams such as those imagined by the Spirit of the Pities is near, Hardy prophesies in a late sonnet, for

> We are getting to the end of visioning
> The impossible within this universe,
> Such as that better whiles may follow worse,
> And that our race may mend by reasoning.
>
> We know that even as larks in cages sing
> Unthoughtful of deliverance from the curse
> That holds them lifelong in a latticed hearse,
> We ply spasmodically our pleasuring.[40]

What is it that incites man century upon century to annihilate those things he holds most dear? Ironically, it is the irrationality of evolution's only rational offspring:

> And that when nations set them to lay waste
> Their neighbours' heritage by foot and horse,
> And hack their pleasant plains in festering seams,
> They may again – not warely, or from taste,
> But tickled mad by some demonic force, –
> Yes. We are getting to the end of dreams![41]

And equally as incongruous, it is a consequence of humanity's betrayal by religion. In his scorching quatrain, 'Christmas: 1924',[42] Hardy berates the Church for its culpability in neglecting to prevent war:

He Resolves to Say No More 161

'Peace upon earth!' was said. We sing it,
And pay a million priests to bring it.
After two thousand years of mass
We've got as far as poison-gas.

Contemplating the occasion of his eightieth birthday, Hardy judged that his disappointment in society, religion, and even science had left him little to celebrate, since even though 'my life . . . covers a period of more material advance in the world than any of the same length can have done in other centuries, I do not find that real civilisation has advanced equally. People are not more humane . . . than they were in the year of my birth. Disinterested kindness is less.'[43] Some may accept Orel's conclusion that 'Thomas Hardy, who so violently and so often reacted against charges that he was a pessimist in his art, finally became one in his study at Max Gate'.[44] Others may choose to align more moderately with Millgate in his assertion that Hardy's pessimism was confined within the parameters of abstract reasoning:

> Fundamentally pessimistic about the human condition, in the sense that he believed birth and coming to consciousness to be a kind of original doom, Hardy could nevertheless respond with compassion to human (and animal) suffering and bring a reformist zeal to bear upon evils perceived as social and hence as potentially susceptible to amelioration or even eradication. He could also remain perpetually alert to the possibility, however faint, of some 'blessed hope' of which the most diligent search had thus far left him 'unaware.' Abstractly, theoretically, generally he could see only an incomprehensible and probably meaningless universe; concretely, practically, specifically he cared deeply about the human condition, perceived value in individual lives, supported humanitarian causes, and thought that things could and indeed did get better.[45]

In either case, Tchekhov's maxim for beginning novelists seems uncannily appropriate to Hardy: 'Everything that has no direct relation to the story must be ruthlessly thrown away. If in the first chapter you say that a gun hung on the wall, in the second or third chapter it must without fail be discharged'.[46] At the very least, we must conclude, Hardy fires the weapon which hangs implicitly over each of his works.

Yet many critics, both Victorian and modern, have erred in their refusal to read Hardy as anything other than a lingering screen of gunsmoke. While it is true that the author seemed to go out of his way to bring the tragic element of any situation into glaring relief, he also demanded that each work be considered a fragment of the great mass of 'impressions' which comprise the whole of experience. From this perspective, his silence must also be read as a reiteration of all that he has already said, pessimistic and optimistic, neither of which is voided by the inclusion of the other. In spite of his declaration that a civilisation which fiendishly applies its intellect to scientific munition-making is not worth the saving, Hardy could still counter in 1918, 'However, as a meliorist (not a pessimist as they say) I think better of the world'.[47] He conceded in 1922 that perhaps Comte was right that progress advances not in a straight line but in a 'looped orbit', so that what appears now to be an 'ominous moving backward' is in truth a 'drawing back for a spring'. To this end Hardy continued as late as 1926 to encourage the new generation of Church reformers to 'make a bold stand' against supernatural doctrine and other primitive ideas in the liturgy. If a forceful body of young dissidents were to launch 'a sort of New Oxford Movement', he insisted, 'they would have a tremendous backing from the thoughtful laity, and might overcome the retrogressive section of the clergy'.[48] In 'The Graveyard of Dead Creeds',[49] collected in *Human Shows* in 1925, Hardy argues with all his former hopefulness that what are presently no more than weed-begirded sepulchres of 'deceased Catholicons' and other 'old wastes of thought' may in time be metamorphosed into useful precepts purged of obscure dogma:

> When in a breath-while, lo, their spectres rose
> Like wakened winds that autumn summons up: –
> 'Out of us cometh an heir, that shall disclose
> New promise!' cried they. 'And the caustic cup
> We ignorantly upheld to men, be filled
> With draughts more pure than those we ever distilled,
> That shall make tolerable to sentient seers
> The melancholy marching of the years.'

Borrowing against Comte's positive reassessment of negative events, Hardy manages to revive his conviction that religion would eventually be able to respond intelligently and redemptively to the practical needs of every man and woman. When that ignorance has been eclipsed and the 'thick darkness' which has heretofore enveloped man is accordingly removed, claims the poem immediately following 'Graveyard', an illumined age will emerge to supplant the old one blackened by dead creeds. Neither the Great War nor the dereliction of religion signified for Hardy that civilisation had deteriorated, as in Ezra Pound's estimation, into 'an old bitch gone in the teeth'.[50] From some unseen space, a voice calls out to man in familiar and comforting scriptural vernacular:

> 'Men have not heard, men have not seen,
> Since the beginning of the world
> What earth and heaven mean;
> But now their curtains shall be furled,
>
> 'And they shall see what is, ere long,
> Not through a glass, but face to face;
> And Right shall disestablish Wrong:
> The Great Adjustment is taking place.'[51]

The voice does not disclose whether the terms of the Great Adjustment will be goodwill among men on earth or a Von Hartmann-like obliteration of time, space, matter, and energy, but Hardy's optimism in raising the question implies a continued faith in man's intelligent stewardship of his talents against that day.

Visiting Max Gate in 1923, T. E. Lawrence could find nothing melancholic about Hardy's manner or appearance. Describing his pilgrimage to 'the most honorable stopping place I've ever found', Lawrence wrote in a letter to Robert Graves:

> There is an unbelievable dignity and ripeness about Hardy: he is waiting so tranquilly for death, without a desire or ambition left in his spirit, as far as I can feel it: and yet he entertains so many illusions, and hopes for the world, things which I, in my disillusioned middle-age, feel to be illusory. They used to call this man a pessimist. While really he is full of fancy expectations. . . . It is strange to pass from the noise

and thoughtlessness of sergeants' company into a peace so secure that in it not even Mrs Hardy's tea-cups rattle on the tray: and from a barrack of hollow senseless bustle to the cheerful calm of T. H. thinking aloud about life to two or three of us. If I were in his place I would never wish to die.[52]

What Lawrence remarks as 'fancy expectations' were in Hardy's mind the thinly audible carolings of a darkling thrush aged inestimably by disillusionment and grief since its first ecstatic perch atop 'the Century's corpse outleant'. And the 'cheerful calm' which Lawrence notes in Hardy's reflections about life seems to be his affirmation that the frail creature sings yet of 'Some blessed hope, whereof he knew / And I was unaware'.[53]

Among Hardy's last journal entries is a fragmented commentary regarding 'A Philosophical Fantasy',[54] published in the *Fortnightly Review* in January 1927, in which the author explains that he wanted to begin the new year with a poem which hints that 'still a ray of hope is shown for the future of mankind'.[55] The familiar premise is that an earthling attracts God's attention long enough to ask the question which has long troubled mortal philosophers:

> 'Tis this *unfulfilled intention*,
> O Causer, I would mention: –
> Will you, in condescension
> This evening, ere we've parted
> Say why you felt fainthearted,
> And let your aim be thwarted,
> Its glory be diminished,
> Its concept stand unfinished?

God replies good-naturedly that no offence was ever intended man – that, in fact, man himself was never intended except 'As something Time hath rendered / Out of substance I engendered' – by the kind of aimless, unmotivated treatment which man despises as unethical and unjust because, frankly,

> To me 'tis malleable matter
> For treatment scientific
> More than sensitive and specific –
> Stuff without moral features,

> Which I've no sense of ever,
> Or of ethical endeavour,
> Or of justice to Earth's creatures,
> Or how Right from wrong to sever.

The old Edenic scenario about life in a perfect garden, continues God dispassionately, is simply a story mankind has invented to make itself feel elect, if dispossessed. There was never a man such as Adam because there has never existed a God resembling the one in humanity's collective imagination. So God reiterates:

> 'To return from wordy wandering
> To the question we are pondering;
> Though, viewing the world in *my* mode,
> I fail to see it in *thy* mode,
> As 'unfulfilled intention',
> Which is past my comprehension
> Being unconscious in my doings
> So largely, (whence thy rueings). . . . '

But God will not be pinned to one course of action any more than Hardy would commit himself to a single 'impression'. I do not comprehend what is meant by 'woes that shatter', God concludes, but it is possible that I may learn:

> Aye, to human tribes nor kindlessness
> Nor love I've given, but mindlessness,
> Which state, though far from ending,
> May nevertheless be mending.

Hardy's earlier disparaging mood not discounted, the ending of *The Dynasts* stands.

Hardy's position at the end of his life is not unlike that of Job when he realises that no response he makes to his suffering will prevail upon God to end it. The advice of friends, the wailing of his own lamentation, and even God's intermittent oration are all voices which permeate Job's misery and unify the dramatic composition of his dilemma, but which fail to deliver him from it or provide succour in the midst of it. After enduring the most agonising and unmerited torment, the trials of which have taken forty chapters to recount, Job abruptly changes his strategy in a resolution to say no more:

> Then Job answered Jehovah,
>   and said,
> Behold, I am of small account;
>   what shall I answer thee?
> I lay my hand upon my mouth.
> Once have I spoken, and I
>   will not answer;
> Yea, twice, but I will proceed
>   no further.[56]

In his *Answer to Job*, C. G. Jung maintains that Job's retreat into silence reveals his sudden comprehension that God is not a moral personality with whom he can reason, but rather 'an antinomy – a totality of inner opposites – and this is the indispensable condition for his tremendous dynamism, his omniscience and omnipotence'.[57] God is so at odds with himself, so unconscious of his antinomy, discovers Job, that he is at once man's consummate evil persecutor and his perfect advocate. Jung argues that the innocent man's only guilt is 'his incurable optimism in believing that he can appeal to divine justice', and that his sole consolation arises from his realisation that the part of God intent upon crushing him is entirely unaware of the pain it inflicts. Job's silence, in fact, shows that he 'revoke[s] his demand for justice' and will remain loyal and submissive to that aspect of God which, although incognisant of it, represents good. Hardy's Prime Mover and Immanent Will, I submit, are no less unconscious antinomies than Job's Yaweh, and Hardy, as did Job, understands that man's consciousness elevates him to a position morally superior to the Power which created him. If Hardy would inform God's emerging percipience, he might do so by silently reiterating, as also did Job, his faith in immanent goodness.

Jung's analysis implies that the virtue found in Job's ordeal is that he learns to accept the absurdity of existence and to rebuild his life on the new sensibility that even if God is inaccessible and unjust, man is responsible to and for himself. I. A. Richards, the influential Cambridge critic of the 1920s who, like Matthew Arnold, argued that poetry possesses the power to replace defunct religion as a 'perfectly possible means of overcoming chaos', admires Hardy for his courageous acceptance of the 'neutralization of nature' and the impossibility of knowing for certain anything about the existence of God. Hardy's response to the traumatic disorganisation of the times, insists Richards, is a commendable one because it confronts man with the exigency of living according to reasonable and moral principles regardless of whatever unknown disposition awaits him beyond the veil:

> He is the poet who has most steadily refused to be comforted. The comfort of forgetfulness, the comfort of beliefs, he has put these away. Hence his singular preoccupation with death; because it is in the contemplation of death that the necessity for human attitudes, in the face of an indifferent universe, to become self-supporting is felt most poignantly.[58]

What Richards finds most hopeful about Hardy is his Job-like endurance in the face of transcendent loss and his unwillingness to bend to any orthodox opinion that the pleasure of living must be diminished by the probability that life itself is terminal. Even in Hardy's most optimistic voicings wherein the Immanent Will is shown to be slowly arousing to mindfulness, never is there an intimation that man's soul or consciousness extends its vitality beyond death. 'To-day', Hardy reflects in a brief journal note, 'has length, breadth, thickness, colour, smell, voice. As soon as it becomes yesterday it is a thin layer among many layers, without substance, colour, or articulate sound.' [59]

Since today is the only life mankind is assured of experiencing, now is the moment for intelligent, humane action and articulation. Hardy expounds this axiom repeatedly in his novels and deplores in his poetry civilisation's mass refusal to heed it. He is not dismayed so much by mankind's 'meanness, . . . ill-teachings, . . . false preachings, . . . banalities, . . .' or even 'immoralities', he admits in 'Thoughts at Midnight',[60] as he is

> by your madnesses
> Capping cool badnesses,
> Acting like puppets
> Under Time's buffets;
> In superstitions

> And ambitions
> Moved by no wisdom,
> Far-sight, or system,
> Led by sheer senselessness
> And presciencelessness
> Into unreason
> And hideous self-treason.

Now, before humanity is consumed by Jude's self-destructiveness or Napoleon's egoistic ambitiousness, is the time to gather intellect, heart, and will into a realistically sanguine voice which endorses Feuerbach's reassurance that 'It does not follow that goodness, justice, wisdom, are chimaeras because the existence of God is a chimaera',[61] and incorporates Darwin's optimistic deduction that:

> A man who has no assured and ever present belief in the existence of a personal God or of a future existence with retribution and reward, can have for his rule of life, as far as I can see, only to follow those impulses and instincts which are the strongest or which seem to him the best ones. A dog acts in this manner, but he does so blindly. A man, on the other hand looks forward and backwards, and compares his various feelings, desires, and recollections. He then finds, in accordance with the verdict of all the wisest men that the highest satisfaction is derived from following certain impulses, namely the social instincts. If he acts for the good of others, he will receive the approbation of his fellow men and gain the love of those with whom he lives; and this latter gain undoubtedly is the highest pleasure on this earth. His reason may occasionally tell him to act in opposition to the opinion of others, whose approbation he will then not receive; but he will still have the solid satisfaction of knowing that he has followed his innermost guide or conscience.[62]

J. Hillis Miller proposes that one essential law regarding the study of Hardy is that 'what you have in the present as an actual physical presence you do not really have'.[63] You neither truly possess it nor understand it nor properly value it until that object or person is removed in corporeality and returns in memory as an 'avenging ghost'. This kind of retrospective comprehension, I think, is something of what Hardy meant when he asserted that 'No man's poetry can be truly judged till its last line is written. What is the last line? The death of the poet'.[64] In one respect Hardy was surely consoling himself that despite present censure, he might be understood, perhaps even appreciated, posthumously; however, in a larger sense his statement implies that the poet's death is to be interpreted just as we would decipher any other line of his poetry, except that this final verse must be read as a silence which comprises his entire canon. Since Hardy had no artistic compulsion toward closure, he could resolve to say no more and leave his last line, his avenging shade, to resonate with possibilities hopeful and gloomy. If he left *Winter Words* in need of revision, then all the better to defend it from any authoritative seal set upon it by 'licensed tasters'. At the end of his life and at the end of his art, Hardy makes a strategic withdrawal into silence not in order to take back his many 'impressions', but to return them to us as a round collective which we can finally possess and understand.

By late October 1927, Florence Hardy had assumed her husband's business of crafting his biography as he chose for posterity to view it. Her spare notes thereafter reveal a rather unfamiliar Hardy who in his last days regressed easily into childhood memories, spied strangers standing about where there were none, costumed himself in black mourning for several days in remembrance of the fifteenth anniversary of Emma's death, dictated bitter epitaphs for his most hated critics,[65] and, for the first time in his life, grew disinterested in the music of church bells on the crossing breeze. One natural propensity which the approach of death did not alter, however, was the old man's intractable committment to non-committment. In the few hours before his death on the evening of 11 January 1928, Hardy, having just become bedridden the previous day, asked his wife to read aloud portions of two poems. The first was 'Rabbi Ben Ezra', Browning's dual statement of faith in the soul's immortality and attack on Edward FitzGerald's subscription to hedonism in the *Rubáiyát of Omar Khayyám*; the other was a stanza from the *Rubáiyát* itself:

> Oh Thou, who Man of Baser Earth didst make,
> And ev'n with Paradise devise the Snake,
> For all the Sin wherewith the Face of Man
> Is blackened – Man's forgiveness give – and take!⁶⁶

Hardy died, as he had lived, in the centreground of the hymnal, *in medias res*, and he chose to do so not because that was a most comfortable spot nor a position of ideological safety, but because he gathered from the confrontation of opposites the courage he needed to 'exact a full look at the worst' and the energy he required to make the best of what he discerned there. His voices, if I may invoke Bakhtin's meta-linguistic terminology one last time, are variform 'utterances' which build upon the values intoned in one another to create a handful of fictions concerning God's nature and man's response to his abstruse behaviour.

The reason Hardy could not write to suit the popular Victorian intelligence was that most men and women of the time desired a straighter answer, preferably one which reinforced their belief in a catholic God and braced their faith in material progress. Religion was for them a talisman which they protected for the protection it in turn guaranteed them against mischance and purblind Doomsters. The only counsel Hardy could offer them in good conscience was to 'Take of Life what it grants, without question! . . . Enjoy, suffer, wait: spread the table here freely. . . . And, satisfied, placid, unfretting, watch Time away beamingly!'⁶⁷ Few were content to accept that life is as ephemeral for man as it is for moths, for they insisted upon the reassurance of a happier ending to make them feel invulnerable to Time. Frank Kermode's observation that the truest ending of any fiction is one which allows us to experience 'the freedom of a discordant reality',⁶⁸ even if that perspective is a disturbing vision of chaos and absurdity, describes well the ending of Hardy's polyphonic catechism. In his ending and pre-eminently in his art, Hardy implores his fellow man to confront this troublesome discord by probing its meanings, attending to its voices, observing its manifest intentions, and doggedly refusing to shut it out of consciousness when its dissonance becomes unbearable. This plumbing of external confusion is by no means a nihilistic indulgence, he argues repeatedly, because it motivates us to determine internal co-ordinates of orderliness and composure and self-reliance and enlightenment. In all likelihood, God will not resume intercourse with man, the Prime Mover will slumber on in rote creativity, war will escalate, and the Church will never convert to rationalism; yet salvation is not contingent upon any of these superficial – albeit grievous – circumstances. In Hardy's temporal world, redemption is gained through an introspective progression toward self-discovery and self-forgiveness, and it is necessarily the result of that self-acceptance transformed into action by the compassionate exercise of freewill. If a man denies his brotherhood, extorts sympathy or profiteers grace, despises his own identity or seeks easy absolution in another's, he has unequivocally damned himself to a fate which has nothing to do with purblind Doomsters; if a man binds himself to the daily renewal of this practical religion, he may suffer random misfortune, persecution, or even condemnation as 'the letter killeth' in its blind application of justice, but his salvation – that 'chief fact with regard to him' – endures to the end.

Notes and References

INTRODUCTION

1. Thomas Carlyle, *On Heroes, Hero-Worship, and the Heroic in History*, vol. V of *The Works of Thomas Carlyle* (New York: Charles Scribner's Sons, 1841), pp. 2–3.
2. Thomas Hardy,'The Occultation', in *Variorum Edition of The Complete Poems of Thomas Hardy*, edited by James Gibson (London: Macmillan, 1979; New York: Macmillan, 1979), p. 463.
3. Thomas Hardy, *The Collected Letters of Thomas Hardy*, edited by Richard Little Purdy and Michael Millgate (Oxford: Clarendon Press, 1980), II, p. 143.
4. Hardy, 'Christmas in the Elgin Room', in *Poems*, p. 928.
5. Hardy, *Collected Letters*, III, p. 5.
6. Michael Millgate, *Thomas Hardy: A Biography* (Oxford: Oxford University Press; New York: Random House, 1982), p. 220.
7. Florence Emily Hardy, *The Life of Thomas Hardy* (London: Macmillan; New York: St Martin's Press, 1962), pp. 332.
8. F. Hardy, *Life*, p. 375.
9. T. S. Eliot, *After Strange Gods: A Primer of Modern Heresy* (New York: Harcourt, Brace, 1934), p. 59.
10. F. Hardy, *Life*, p. 284–5.
11. William Makepeace Thackeray, 'The Roundabout Papers No. 8', in *Cornhill Magazine*, vol. 2 (London: Smith & Elder, 1860), p. 504.
12. Herman Melville, *Redburn* (New York: Doubleday, 1957), p. 178.
13. Millgate, *Thomas Hardy*, p. 35.
14. Frank O'Connor, *The Mirror in the Roadway* (New York: Knopf, 1956), p. 15.
15. Charles Kingsley, *Yeast* (London: Macmillan, 1891), p. 32.
16. John Holloway, 'Hardy's Major Fiction', in *From Jane Austen to Joseph Conrad: Essays Collected in Memory of James T. Hillhouse*, edited by Robert C. Rathburn and Martin Steinman Jr (Minneapolis: University of Minnesota Press; London: Oxford University Press, 1958), p. 235.
17. F. Hardy, *Life*, p. 14.
18. Thomas Hardy, 'A Necessitarian's Epitaph', in *Poems*, p. 889.
19. Thomas Hardy, *Jude the Obscure*, edited by Norman Page (London and New York: W. W. Norton, 1969), p. 15.
20. Ibid., p. 17.
21. Ibid.

Notes and References 173

22. F. Hardy, *Life*, p. 15.
23. Ibid., p. 48.
24. Wayne C. Booth, Introduction to *Problems of Dostoevsky's Poetics*, by M M. Bakhtin, translated and edited by Caryl Emerson (Minneapolis: University of Minnesota Press, 1984), p. xxi.
25. Thomas Hardy, *Thomas Hardy's Personal Writings*, edited by Harold Orel (London: Macmillan; Kansas: University of Kansas Press, 1966), p. 5.
26. M. M. Bakhtin, *Rabelais and His World*, translated by Helene Iswolsky (Cambridge, Mass. and London: Massachussetts Institute of Technology Press, 1968), p. 9.
27. M. M. Bakhtin, *The Dialogic Imagination*, translated by Caryl Emerson and Michael Holquist (Austin: University of Texas Press, 1900), p. 425.
28. Hans Vaihinger, *The Philosophy of As If*, translated by C. K. Ogden (London, 1924), pp. 12–13.
29. F. W. Nietzsche, *Beyond Good and Evil*, translated by Helen Zimmern (London: Macmillan, 1907), pp. 8–9.

1. THE COMPLAINING DOOR

1. Florence Emily Hardy, *The Life of Thomas Hardy* (London: Macmillan; New York: St Martin's Press, 1962), p. 224.
2. Thomas Hardy, 'General Preface to the Novels and Poems', in *Tess of the D'Urbervilles* (London and New York: Harper & Bros, 1920), p. xii.
3. F. Hardy, *Life*, pp. 342–3.
4. Thomas Hardy, *The Collected Letters of Thomas Hardy*, edited by Richard Little Purdy and Michael Millgate (Oxford: Clarendon Press, 1980), IV, p. 26.
5. Hardy, *Collected Letters*, IV, p. 287.
6. Algernon Charles Swinburne, 'Hymn of Man', in *The Poems of Algernon Charles Swinburne* (London and New York: Harper & Bros, 1904), II, pp. 96–108.
7. George Meredith, 'Dirge in the Woods', in *The Poems of George Meredith*, edited by Phyllis B. Bartlett (New Haven and London: Yale University Press, 1978), I, pp. 427–8.
8. Thomas Hardy, 'A Sign-Seeker', in *Variorum Edition of The Complete Poems of Thomas Hardy*, edited by James Gibson (London: Macmillan, 1979; New York, Macmillan, 1979), p. 49–50.
9. Robert Browning, 'Pippa Passes', in *The Poetical Works of Robert Browning*, vol. 2 (London: Smith Elder & Co., 1884), p. 238.
10. Hardy, 'Before Life and After', in *Poems*, p. 277.
11. Hardy, 'The Aërolite', in *Poems*, p. 769.
12. Hardy, *Collected Letters*, III, pp. 157–8.
13. Hardy, 'The Oxen', in *Poems*, p. 468.
14. Hardy, 'The Impercipient', in *Poems*, pp. 67–8.

15. Swinburne, 'Laus Veneris', in *Poems*, I, p. 16.
16. Hardy, 'In Tenebris I', in *Poems*, p. 167.
17. F. Hardy, *Life*, p. 332–3.
18. George Eliot, *Adam Bede*, edited by Stephen Gill (Harmondsworth and New York: Penguin, 1980), pp. 224–5.
19. Hardy, 'In Time of "The Breaking of Nations"', in *Poems*, p. 543.
20. F. Hardy, *Life*, p. 410.
21. David Hume, *David Hume: The Philosophical Works*, vol. I, edited by Thomas Hull Green and Thomas Hodge Grose (London: Scientia Verlag, Aalen, 1964), p. 495.
22. Hardy, 'God's Funeral', in *Poems*, p. 326–9.
23. Ludwig Feuerbach, *The Essence of Christianity*, translated by George Eliot, edited by Karl Barth (London and New York: Harper & Row, 1957), p. 107.
24. Feuerbach, *The Essence of Christianity*, p. 281.
25. Hardy, 'The Problem', in *Poems*, p. 120.
26. John Stuart Mill, 'On Liberty', in *On Liberty and Other Essays*, edited by Emery E. Neff (New York: Macmillan, 1926), p. 59.
27. Hardy, 'A Plaint to Man', in *Poems*, pp. 325–6.
28. Swinburne, 'Hymn of Man', *Poems*, vol. 2, pp. 96–108.
29. Mill, 'On Liberty', p. 61.
30. Hardy, 'Unkept Good Fridays', in *Poems*, pp. 842–3.
31. Hardy, *Collected Letters*, I, p. 136.
32. F. Hardy, *Life*, p. 224.
33. James Thomson, 'The City of Dreadful Night', in *Poems of James Thomson*, edited by Gordon Hall Gerould (New York: Henry Holt, 1927), pp. 167–9.
34. Swinburne, 'Hymn of Man', *Poems*, vol. 2, p. 108.
35. Feuerbach, *The Essence of Christianity*, p. xiv.

2. NATURE, DARWIN AND THE PATTERN IN THE CARPET

1. Florence Emily Hardy, *The Life of Thomas Hardy* (London: Macmillan; New York: St Martin's Press, 1962), p. 153. There appears to be no connection between Hardy's use of the image of the pattern in the carpet and Henry James' employment of the same metaphor in his fable, 'The Figure in the Carpet'. As far as can be determined from existing documents, Hardy's remarks are confined to a private journal entry written in 1882, a source obviously inaccessible to James writing his story in 1895.
2. G. Bernard Shaw, *Back to Methuselah* (Harmondsworth and New York: Penguin, 1987), p. 32.
3. Alfred, Lord Tennyson, *In Memoriam*, in *The Works of Alfred, Lord Tennyson*, edited by William J. Rolfe (Boston: Dana Estes, 1985), IV, p. 59.
4. John Ruskin, *Modern Painters*, vol. III of *The Complete Works of John*

Notes and References 175

Ruskin, edited by Alexander Wedderburn, (London: George Allen, 1904), pp. 321–2; quote in Ruskin from Ephesians, 2:12.
5. Charles Darwin, *The Autobiography of Charles Darwin*, edited by Nora Barlow (London: W. W. Norton; New York: Harcourt, Brace, 1959), pp. 87.
6. Thomas Hardy, 'The Temporary the All,' in *Variorum Edition of The Complete Poems of Thomas Hardy*, edited by James Gibson (London: Macmillan, 1979; New York: Macmillan, 1979), p. 7.
7. Joseph W. Beach, *The Concept of Nature in Nineteenth-Century English Poetry* (New York: Macmillan, 1936), p. 521.
8. Hardy, 'Nature's Questioning', in *Poems*, pp. 66–7.
9. Thomas Hardy, *The Collected Letters of Thomas Hardy*, edited by Richard Little Purdy and Michael Millgate (Oxford: Clarendon Press, 1980), III, p. 113.
10. Simone de Beauvoir, *The Ethics of Ambiguity*, translated by Bernard Frechtman (New York: Philosophical Library, 1948), p. 7.
11. Hardy, 'The Bullfinches', in *Poems*, pp. 122–3.
12. Darwin, *Autobiography*, pp. 75–7. Darwin's father strongly objected to his son's volunteering as naturalist aboard the *Beagle* and forbade him to accept the offer unless 'you can find a man of common sense, who advises you to go'. Josiah Wedgwood, Darwin's uncle and son of the famous potter, was just such a man, and persuaded Dr Robert to give consent. Wedgwood drove his nephew to Shrewsbury, thirty miles away, to meet with Captain Fitz-Roy, Commander of the *Beagle*, but the initial interview did not portend well. The Captain was a man of morose temper, Darwin mused, and was 'an ardent disciple of Lavater, and was convinced that he could judge a man's character by the outline of his features; and he doubted whether anyone with my nose could possess sufficient energy and determination for the voyage. But I think he was afterwards well-satisfied that my nose had spoken falsely.' Darwin would later reflect on the role that coincidence had played in his life: 'The voyage of the *Beagle* has been by far the most important event in my life and has determined my whole career; yet it depended on so small a circumstance as my uncle offering to drive me 30 miles to Shrewsbury, which few uncles would have done, and on such a trifle as the shape of my nose.'
13. Darwin, *Autobiography*, pp. 92–3.
14. Ibid., p. 93.
15. Ibid., p. 162.
16. Ibid., p. 139.
17. Ibid., p. 94.
18. F. Hardy, *Life*, p. 337.
19. Ibid.
20. Ernest A. Baker, *The History of the English Novel* (London: Witherby, 1938), IX, p. 26.
21. Ibid., p. 19.
22. Thomas Hardy, *The Dynasts* (London: Macmillan, 1923), p. 7.

23. F. Hardy, *Life*, p. 149.
24. Ibid., p. 218.
25. Hardy, 'The Blinded Bird', in *Poems*, p. 446.
26. Hardy, 'Hap', in *Poems*, p. 9.
27. Dorothy Van Ghent, *The English Novel: Form and Function* (New York: Macmillan; London: Holt, Rinehart & Winston, 1923), p. 205.
28. Thomas Hardy, *Tess of the D'Urbervilles*, edited by Scott Elledge (London and New York: W. W. Norton, 1979), p. 85.
29. Irving Howe, *Thomas Hardy* (New York: Macmillan; London: Weidenfeld & Nicolson, 1967), p. 130.
30. Van Ghent, *The English Novel*, pp. 198–9.
31. Hardy, 'New Year's Eve', in *Poems*, pp. 277–8.
32. Albert J. Guerard, *Thomas Hardy: The Novels and Stories* (Cambridge, Mass.: Harvard University Press; London: Oxford University Press, 1949), p. 91.
33. Ibid.
34. Thomas Hardy, *The Return of the Native*, edited by James Gindin (London and New York: W. W. Norton, 1969), p. 4.
35. Nathan A. Scott, 'The Literary Imagination and the Victorian Crisis of Faith: The Example of Thomas Hardy', *Journal of Religion*, 40 (October 1960), p. 278.
36. D. H. Lawrence, *Selected Literary Criticism*, edited by Anthony Beal (New York: Viking Press, 1964), p. 168.
37. F. R. Leavis, *New Bearings in English Poetry: A Study of the Contemporary Situation* (London: Chatto & Windus, 1932), p. 18.
38. Harold Orel, *The Final Years of Thomas Hardy, 1912–1928* (Lawrence: University of Kansas Press, 1976), p. 83.
39. Thomas Carlyle, *Sartor Resartus* (London: Service & Paton; New York: G. P. Putnam's Sons, 1897), p. 62.
40. Hardy, 'Before and After Summer', in *Poems*, pp. 333–4.
41. Hardy, 'The Year's Awakening', in *Poems*, p. 335.
42. Hardy, *Tess*, p. 109.
43. Hardy, 'Proud Songsters', in *Poems*, pp. 835–6.
44. Tom Paulin, *Thomas Hardy; The Poetry of Perception* (London: Macmillan, 1975), p. 63.
45. Thomas Hardy, *The Woodlanders*, edited by James Gibson (Harmondsworth and New York: Penguin, 1982), p. 93.
46. Charles Darwin, *The Origin of Species and The Descent of Man* (New York: Random House, 1974), p. 373.
47. Ibid., p. 374.
48. John Stuart Mill, *Autobiography* (London: Longmans, Green, Reader & Dyer, 1873), p. 152.
49. F. Hardy, *Life*, p. 213.
50. Hardy, 'Let Me Enjoy', in *Poems*, p. 238.
51. Hardy, 'Afterwards', in *Poems*, p. 553.
52. Hardy, 'To Outer Nature', in *Poems*, p. 61.

3. 'THE GREAT ADJUSTMENT': EVOLUTIONARY MELIORISM IN *THE DYNASTS*

1. Florence Emily Hardy, *The Life of Thomas Hardy* (London: Macmillan; New York: St Martin's Press, 1962), p. 319.
2. Ibid., p. 296.
3. Ibid., p. 376.
4. Ibid.
5. G. K. Chesteron, 'Great Victorian Novelists', in *The Victorian Age in Literature* (London: William & Norgate; New York: Holt, 1913), p. 144.
6. Carl Van Doren, 'Anatole France and Thomas Hardy', *Century Magazine*, ns, 87 (1925), p. 422.
7. Thomas Hardy, 'Fragment', in *Variorum Edition of The Complete Poems of Thomas Hardy*, edited by James Gibson (London: Macmillan, 1979; New York: Macmillan, 1979), pp. 513–14.
8. T. H. Huxley, 'Evolution and Ethics', in *Touchstone for Ethics, 1893–1943*, by T. H. and Julian Huxley (London: Harper & Bros, 1947), p. 91–2.
9. Hardy, 'God's Education', in *Poems*, pp. 278–9.
10. F. Hardy, *Life*, pp. 334–5.
11. Thomas Hardy, *The Collected Letters of Thomas Hardy*, edited by Richard Little Purdy and Michael Millgate (Oxford: Clarendon Press, 1980), V, p. 50.
12. F. Hardy, *Life*, p. 148.
13. Ibid., p. 334.
14. J. O. Bailey, *Thomas Hardy and the Cosmic Mind* (Chapel Hill: University of North Carolina Press, 1956), p. 14.
15. Thomas Mann, 'Presenting Schopenhauer', in *Schopenhauer: His Philosophical Achievement*, edited by Michael Fox (Brighton: Harvester Press, 1980), p. 6.
16. Arthur Schopenhauer, *The World as Will and Idea*, translated by R. B. Haldane and J. Kemp (London: Kegan Paul, Trench, Trubner, 1906), I, p. 141.
17. Ibid., p. 238.
18. Mann, 'Presenting Schopenhauer', p. 7.
19. Pierre d'Exideuil, *The Human Pair in the Work of Thomas Hardy*, translated by Felix W. Crosse (Port Washington, New York: Kennikat Press, 1970), p. 209.
20. Schopenhauer, *The World as Will and Idea*, I, p. 356.
21. Eduard Von Hartmann, *Philosophy of the Unconscious*, translated by William Chatterton Coupland (London: Kegan Paul, Trench & Trubner, 1893), III, p. 125.
22. Ibid., p. 127.
23. Hardy, *Collected Letters*, III, p. 298.
24. Hardy, 'Agnostoi Theoi', in *Poems*, pp. 186–7.
25. J. Hillis Miller, *The Disappearance of God* (Cambridge, Mass.: Har-

vard University Press; London: Oxford University Press, 1963), p. 2.
26. Ibid., p. 268.
27. Ibid., p. 14.
28. Hardy, 'The Sleep-Worker', in *Poems*, pp, 121–2.
29. F. Hardy, *Life*, p. 220.
30. Hardy, 'At Waking', in *Poems*, p. 224.
31. Hardy, 'God-Forgotten', in *Poems*, pp. 123–4.
32. F. Hardy, *Life*, p. 148.
33. T. E. Lawrence, *Letters of T. E. Lawrence*, edited by David Garnett (New York: Doubleday, Doran, 1939), pp. 429–30.
34. Thomas Hardy, *The Dynasts* (London: Macmillan, 1923), pp. viii–ix.
35. Hardy, 'Thoughts from Sophocles', in *Poems*, p. 936.
36. Hardy, *Collected Letters*, III, pp. 153–4.
37. F. Hardy, *Life*, p. 177.
38. Hardy, *The Dynasts* p. 6.
39. Ibid., p. 124.
40. Ibid , p. 137.
41. Ibid., p. 201.
42. Ibid., p. 520.
43. Ibid., p. 521.
44. Ibid., p. 520.
45. Schopenhauer, *The World as Will and Idea*, I, p. 237–8.
46. Hardy, *The Dynasts*, p. 1.
47. Ibid., p. 6.
48. Ibid., p. 76.
49. Ibid., pp. 99–100.
50. Von Hartmann, *Philosophy of the Unconscious*, II, pp. 246–7.
51. Hardy, *The Dynasts*, p. 118.
52. Hardy, *Collected Letters*, III, p. 255.
53. Ibid., V, p. 153.
54. Hardy, 'He Wonders About Himself', in *Poems*, p. 510.
55. Hardy, *The Dynasts*, p. 179.
56. Ibid., p. 363.
57. Ibid., pp. 519–20.
58. Ibid., p. 521.
59. Ibid., p. 322.
60. Ibid., p. 119.
61. F. Hardy, *Life*, p. 315.
62. Harold Orel, *Thomas Hardy's Epic Drama: A Study of The Dynasts* (New York: Greenwood Press, 1969), pp., 70–1.
63. Hardy, *The Dynasts*, p. 306.
64. Ibid., p. 517–18.
65. Ibid., p. 525.
66. Bailey, *Thomas Hardy and the Cosmic Mind*, pp. 167–8.
67. F. Hardy, *Life*, p. 172.
68. Lionel Stevenson, 'Thomas Hardy', in *Darwin Among the Poets* (Chicago: University of Chicago Press; London: Oxford University Press, 1932), p. 296.

Notes and References 179

69. Thomas Hardy, 'Xenophanes, the Monist of Colophon', in *Poems*, pp. 728–30.
70. F. Hardy, *Life*, p. 320.
71. Edmund Blunden, *Thomas Hardy* (London: Macmillan, 1941), p. 229.
72. Richard Dawkins, *The Selfish Gene* (London and New York: Oxford University Press, 1978), p. 63. (Dawkins, *The Blind Watchmaker* (London: W. W. Norton, 1986)).
73. F. Hardy, *Life*, p. 155.

4. FREEDOM, FAILURE AND FATE: READING THE WEB OF WESSEX

1. Thomas Hardy, 'He Fears His Good Fortune', in *Variorum Edition of The Complete Poems of Thomas Hardy*, edited by James Gibson (London: Macmillan, 1979; New York: Macmillan, 1979), pp. 509–10.
2. Hardy, 'Heredity', in *Poems*, p. 434.
3. J. Hillis Miller, *Thomas Hardy: Distance and Desire* (Cambridge, Mass.: Harvard University Press, 1970), p. xi.
4. David Daiches, *Poetry and the Modern World: A Study of Poetry in England Between 1900 and 1939* (Chicago: University of Chicago Press, 1940), p. 19.
5. Florence Emily Hardy, *The Life of Thomas Hardy* (London: Macmillan; New York: St Martin's Press, 1962), p. 229.
6. Frederick R. Karl, 'The Mayor of Casterbridge: A New Fiction Defined', *Modern Fiction Studies*, 6 (Autumn 1960), p. 202.
7. Albert J. Guerard, *Thomas Hardy: The Novels and Stories* (Cambridge, Mass.: Harvard University Press; London: Oxford University Press, 1949), p. 83.
8. Thomas Hardy, *Tess of the D'Urbervilles*, edited by Scott Elledge (London and New York: W. W. Norton, 1979), pp. 178–9.
9. Miller, *Thomas Hardy: Distance and Desire*, p. 21.
10. Ludwig Feuerbach, *The Essence of Christianity*, translated by George Eliot, edited by Karl Barth (London and New York: Harper & Row, 1957), p. 195.
11. Thomas Carlyle, *Past and Present* (London: Chapman & Hall, 1897), p. 196.
12. Thomas Hardy, *Far From the Madding Crowd* (Harmondsworth and New York: Penguin, 1983), p. 164.
13. Ibid., p. 163.
14. Ibid., pp. 171–2.
15. Ibid., p. 439.
16. Emma Hardy, *Some Recollections* (Oxford: Oxford University Press, 1979), p. xii.
17. Hardy, 'The Going', in *Poems*, p. 339.

18. Thomas Hardy, *The Return of the Native*, edited by James Gindin (London and New York: W. W. Norton, 1969), p. 138.
19. Ibid., p. 109.
20. Keith M. May, *Out of the Maelstrom: Psychology and the Novel in the Twentieth Century* (London: Paul Elek, 1977), p. 3.
21. Hardy, *The Return of the Native*, p. 135.
22. Ibid., p. 197.
23. Ibid. pp. 199–200.
24. Ibid. p. 315.
25. Hardy, 'A Wasted Illness', in *Poems*, p. 152.
26. Hardy, 'He Abjures Love', in *Poems*, pp. 236–7.
27. John Holloway, *The Chartered Mirror: Literary and Critical Essays* (London: Routledge & Kegan Paul, 1960), pp. 96–7.
28. Elaine Showalter, 'The Unmanning of the Mayor of Casterbridge' in *Critical Approaches to the Fiction of Thomas Hardy*, edited by Dale Kramer (London: Macmillan Press, 1979), pp. 99–115.
29. Holloway, *The Chartered Mirror*, p. 97.
30. Thomas Hardy, *The Mayor of Casterbridge*, edited by James K. Robinson (London and New York: W. W. Norton, 1977), p. 4.
31. Ibid., p. 64.
32. Virginia Woolf, *The Second Common Reader* (New York: Harcourt & Brace, 1932), p. 231.
33. Hardy, *The Mayor of Casterbridge*, p. 254.

5. FASCINATION AND FORGIVENESS

1. Florence Emily Hardy, *The Life of Thomas Hardy* (London: Macmillan; New York: St Martin's Press, 1962), p. 239.
2. John Bayley, *An Essay on Hardy* (Cambridge: Cambridge University Press, 1978), pp. 141, 158.
3. F. Hardy, *Life*, p. 220.
4. Virginia Woolf, *The Second Common Reader* (New York: Harcourt & Brace, 1932), p. 228.
5. J. Hillis Miller, *Thomas Hardy: Distance and Desire* (Cambridge, Mass.: Harvard University Press, 1970), p. 114.
6. Ibid., p. 120.
7. Ibid., p. 183.
8. Thomas Hardy, *The Well-Beloved*, edited by Tom Hetherington (Oxford: Oxford University Press, 1986), p. 16.
9. Ibid., p. 40.
10. Thomas Hardy, *Tess of the D'Urbervilles*, edited by Scott Elledge (London and New York: W. W. Norton, 1979), p. 18.
11. Ibid., p. 19.
12. Ibid. p. 29.
13. Frank R. Giordano, Jr, *'I'd Have My Life Unbe': Thomas Hardy's Self-Destructive Characters* (Alabama: University of Alabama Press, 1984), p. 165.

14. D. H. Lawrence, *Selected Literary Criticism*, edited by Anthony Beal (New York: Viking Press, 1964), p. 192.
15. Ibid.
16. Hardy, *Tess of the D'Urbervilles*, p. 84.
17. Ibid., p. 164.
18. Ibid., pp. 100–1.
19. Ibid. p. 102.
20. J. Hillis Miller, *Fiction and Repetition* (Cambridge, Mass.: Harvard University Press, 1982), p. 141.
21. Ian Gregor, *The Great Web: The Form of Hardy's Major Fiction* (London: Faber & Faber, 1974), p. 183.
22. Michael Millgate, *Thomas Hardy: A Biography* (New York: Random House; Oxford: Oxford University Press, 1982), pp. 350–1.
23. Thomas Hardy, *The Collected Letters of Thomas Hardy*, edited by Richard Little Purdy and Michael Millgate (Oxford: Clarendon Press, 1980), II, p. 94.
24. Algernon Charles Swinburne, *The Swinburne Letters*, vol. 6, edited by Cecil Y. Lang (New Haven, Conn.: Yale University Press, 1962), p. 91.
25. Quoted from Millgate, *Thomas Hardy*, p. 356. His notes indicate that it was from Emma Lavinia Hardy in a letter to Mary Hawais on 13 November, probably in 1894. The MS is owned by the University of British Columbia.
26. Thomas Hardy, *Jude the Obscure*, edited by Norman Page (London and New York: W. W. Norton, 1969), p. 11.
27. Thomas Hardy, *The Return of the Native*, edited by James Gindin (London and New York: W. W. Norton, 1969), p. 109.
28. Hardy, *The Return of the Native*, p. 295.
29. Hardy, *Jude the Obscure*, p. 15.
30. Ibid., p. 23.
31. Ibid., p. 320.
32. Quoted from Millgate, *Thomas Hardy*, p. 411. He obtained it from the diary of Edward Clodd. The entry date was 3 February 1896. The MS is in the private collection of Mr Alan Clodd.
33. Thomas Hardy, 'In Tenebris I', in *Variorum Edition of The Complete Poems of Thomas Hardy*, edited by James Gibson (London: Macmillan, 1979; New York: Macmillan, 1979), p. 167.
34. Hardy, 'In Tenebris III', in *Poems*, p. 169.
35. William Archer, *Real Conversations* (London: William Heinemann, 1904), p. 45.
36. Murray Krieger, *The Tragic Vision* (New York: Holt, Rinehart & Winston, 1969), p. 14.
37. Gregor, *The Great Web*, p. 232.
38. Thomas Carlyle, *Sartor Resartus* (London: Service & Paton; New York, G. P. Putnam's Sons, 1897), p. 182.
39. Krieger, *The Tragic Vision*, p. 15.
40. F. Hardy, *Life*, p. 315.
41. Katherine Anne Porter, 'Notes on a Criticism of Thomas Hardy', *Southern Review*, 6 (Summer 1940), pp. 159–60.

6. HE RESOLVES TO SAY NO MORE

1. Thomas Hardy, 'According to the Mighty Working', in *Variorum Edition of The Complete Poems of Thomas Hardy*, edited by James Gibson (London: Macmillan, 1979; New York: Macmillan, 1979), p. 571.
2. Ian Gregor, *The Great Web: The Form of Hardy's Major Fiction* (London: Faber & Faber, 1974), p. 230.
3. Henry W. Nevinson, *Changes and Chances* (New York: Harcourt Brace, 1923), pp. 307–8.
4. Irving Howe, *Thomas Hardy* (New York: Macmillan; London: Weidenfeld & Nicolson, 1967), p. 189.
5. Hardy, 'He Never Expected Much', in *Poems*, p. 886.
6. Quoted in Victoria Glendinning, *Rebecca West; A Life* (London: Weidenfeld & Nicolson, 1987), p. 142.
7. Hardy, 'Dead "Wessex" the Dog to the Household', in *Poems*, pp. 915–16.
8. Hardy, 'Shelley's Skylark', in *Poems*, p. 101.
9. Hardy, 'A Singer Asleep', in *Poems*, p. 323–5.
10. Hardy, 'The To-Be-Forgotten', in *Poems*, pp. 144–5.
11. Hardy, 'Waiting Both', in *Poems*, p. 701.
12. Hardy, 'Regret Not Me', in *Poems*, p. 388.
13. Michael Millgate, *Thomas Hardy: A Biography* (New York: Random House; Oxford: Oxford University Press, 1982), p. 517.
14. Hardy, 'Apology' to *Late Lyrics and Earlier*, in *Poems*, p. 557.
15. Hardy, 'Surview', in *Poems*, p. 698.
16. Hardy, 'Why Do I?' in *Poems*, p. 831.
17. Alfred, Lord Tennyson, 'Tithonus', in *The Works of Alfred, Lord Tennyson*, edited by William J. Rolfe (Boston: Dana Estes, 1985), II, p. 189.
18. Hardy, 'He Resolves to Say No More', in *Poems*, pp. 929–30.
19. It is quite possible that only those letters, notes and documents personally selected by Hardy to represent him posthumously have survived for examination. If the recollections of Mr Bertie Norman Stephens, Hardy's gardener at the time of his death, are credible, enormous quantities of personal papers were destroyed by Florence several days after her husband's funeral:

> Within a week or so of Hardy's death there was a grand clearance of his clothes, and masses of letters and other papers from his study. I was given the task of burning his clothes and bundles of newspapers on a bonfire in the garden. Mrs Hardy stood by the whole time and watched, presumably to ensure that nothing escaped the flames. . . . Mrs Hardy herself burnt, on another bonfire, baskets full of the letters and private papers that I had carried down from the study to the garden under her supervision and watchful eye. She would not let me burn these, but insisted upon doing it herself, and after all the papers

had been destroyed, she raked the ashes to be sure that not a single scrap or word remained. It was a devil of a clear out.

Bertie Norman Stephens, 'Thomas Hardy in His Garden', as told to J. Stephens Cox (Dorset: Toucan Press, 1963), pp. 15–16.
20. Hardy, 'Introductory Note' to *Winter Words in Various Moods and Metres*, in *Poems*, p. 834.
21. Anton Tchekhov, *Anton Tchekhov: Literary and Theatrical Reminiscences*, translated and edited by S. S. Koteliansky (New York: Benjamin Blom; London: Routledge & Kegan Paul, 1965), p. 14.
22. Wayne C. Anderson, 'The Rhetoric of Silence in Hardy's Fiction', *Studies in the Novel*, 17, 1 (Spring 1985), p. 61.
23. Ibid., pp. 61–2.
24. Herman Melville, *Pierre or The Ambiguities* (New York: New American Library, 1979), p. 237.
25. Thomas Hardy, *The Collected Letters of Thomas Hardy*, edited by Richard Little Purdy and Michael Millgate (Oxford: Clarendon Press, 1980), I, p. 1910.
26. Florence Emily Hardy, *The Life of Thomas Hardy* (London: Macmillan; New York: St Martin's Press, 1962), pp. 311.
27. Hardy, *Collected Letters*, III, p. 187.
28. Ibid., p. 308.
29. F. Hardy, *Life*, p. 383.
30. Thomas Hardy, 'General Preface to the Novels and Poems', in *Tess of the D'Urbervilles* (London and New York: Harper & Bros, 1920), p. xii.
31. Hardy, *Collected Letters*, V, p. 43.
32. Hardy, 'Apology', to *Late Lyrics and Earlier*, in *Poems*, p. 561.
33. F. Hardy, *Life*, p. 415.
34. Hardy, 'Apology', to *Late Lyrics and Earlier*, in *Poems*, p. 560.
35. Harold Orel, *The Final Years of Thomas Hardy, 1912–1928* (Lawrence: University of Kansas Press; London: Macmillan, 1976), pp. 132–3.
36. William Archer, *Real Conversations* (London: William Heinemann, 1904), pp. 45–7.
37. F. Hardy, *Life*, pp. 365–6.
38. Ibid., p. 368.
39. Orel, *The Final Years*, p. 134.
40. Hardy, 'We Are Getting To The End', in *Poems*, p. 929.
41. Ibid.
42. Hardy, 'Christmas: 1924', in *Poems*, p. 914.
43. F. Hardy *Life* p. 405–6.
44. Orel, *The Final Years*, p. 122.
45. Michael Millgate, *Thomas Hardy: A Biography* (Oxford: Oxford University Press; New York: Random House, 1982), p. 410–11.
46. Tchekhov, *Literary and Theatrical Reminiscences*, p. 23.
47. F. Hardy, *Life*, p. 387.
48. Ibid., p. 431.
49. Hardy, 'The Graveyard of Dead Creeds', in *Poems*, pp. 724–5.
50. Ezra Pound, *Selected Poems* (London: Faber & Faber, 1975), p. 101.

51. Hardy, 'There Seemed a Strangeness', in *Poems*, pp. 725–6.
52. T. E. Lawrence, *The Letters of T. E. Lawrence*, edited by David Garnett (New York: Doubleday & Doran, 1939), pp. 429–30.
53. Hardy, 'The Darkling Thrush', in *Poems*, p. 150.
54. Hardy, 'A Philosophical Fantasy', in *Poems*, pp. 893–97.
55. F. Hardy, *Life*, p. 436.
56. Job 40:3–5, *The Holy Bible*, American Standard Version (Camden, N.J.: Thomas Nelson & Sons, 1929), p. 555.
57. C. G. Jung, *Answer to Job*, translated by R. F. C. Hull (Princeton: Princeton University Press, 1973), p. 7.
58. I. A. Richards, 'I. A. Richards', in *The Great Critics: An Anthology of Literary Criticism*, edited by James Harry Smith and Edd Winfield Parks (New York: Norton & Norton, 1932)), p. 761.
59. F. Hardy, *Life*, p. 285.
60. Hardy, 'Thoughts At Midnight', in *Poems*, p. 836.
61. Ludwig Feuerbach, *The Essence of Christianity*, translated by George Eliot, edited by Karl Barth (London and New York: Harper & Row, 1957), p. 21.
62. Charles Darwin, *The Autobiography of Charles Darwin*, edited by Nora Barlow (London: W. W. Norton; New York: Harcourt, Brace, 1959), pp. 94–5.
63. J. Hillis Miller, 'Topography and Tropography in Thomas Hardy's "In Front of the Landscape"', in *Identity of the Literary Text*, edited by Mario J. Valdez and Owen Miller (London: University of Toronto Press, 1985), p. 77.
64. F. Hardy, *Life*, p. 303.
65. The following epitaphs are not included in *Winter Words*, Hardy's final volume of verse published posthumously in 1928, but the original manuscripts are held in the Dorset County Museum. Accompanying the manuscripts is a note from 'F. E. Hardy', establishing these poems as 'Last lines dicated [sic] by T. H., referring to George Moore and G. K. Chesterton'. They have been reprinted in *Poems*, p. 954.

Epitaph for G. K. Chesteron

Here lies nipped in this narrow cyst
The literary contortionist
Who prove and never turn a hair
That Darwin's theories were a snare
He'd hold as true with tongue in jowl,
That Nature's geocentric rule
 . . . true and right
And if one with him could not see
He'd shout his choice word 'Blasphemy'.

Epitaph for George Moore

On one who thought no other could write such English as himself

'No mortal man beneath the sky
Can write such English as can I

>They say it holds no thought my own
>What then such beauty (perfection) is not known.'

>Heap dustbins on him:
>They'll not meet
>The apex of his self-conceit.

66. Edward Fitzgerald, 'Rubáiyát of Omar Khayyam', in *The Variorum and Definitive Edition of the Poetical and Prose Writings of Edward Fitzgerald*, edited by George Bentham (New York: Phaeton Press, 1967), I, p. 28.
67. Hardy, 'Night in the Old Home', in *Poems*, pp. 269–70.
68. Frank Kermode, *The Sense of an Ending* (London and New York: Oxford University Press, 1967), p. 179.

Index

Adam Bede (Eliot), 23n18
Alton Locke (Kingsley), 6
Anderson, Wayne C., 154
Answer to Job (Jung), 166
Apologia pro Vita Sua (Newman), 10
Archer, William, 141, 159
Arnold, Matthew, 3, 27, 30, 54, 68, 69, 70, 166
Autobiography (John Stuart Mill), 53
Autobiography of Charles Darwin, The, 38n13, 38–9n14, 168n2

Bailey, J.O., 61, 92
Barker, Ernest, 40
Bakhtin, Mikhail, 11–13, 15, 40, 77, 170
Barrie, Sir J(ames) M(atthew), 147
Bayley, John, 123
Beach, Joseph Warren, 34, 49
Beckett, Samuel Barclay, 103
Beerbohm, (Sir Henry) Max(imilian), 93
Bergson, Henri, 21–2
Blake, William, 27
Blind Watchmaker, The (Dawkins), 94
Blunden, Edmund Charles, 94
Book of Common Prayer, The, 33
Book of Job, The, 139, 140, 141, 142, 166
Booth, Wayne, 11
Bridges, Robert, 5
Brontë, Emily Jane, 68
Browning, Robert, 2, 42, 68, 69, 70, 112, 155, 169
Burke, Edmund, 1, 6

Camus, Albert, 43

Carlyle, Thomas, 1–2, 5–6, 49, 51, 68, 104, 113, 141–2, 144
chance (coincidence), 14, 33–4, 39, 40, 44–5, 47, 48, 53, 65, 87, 99–103, 119, 144, 170–1
Chesterton, G(ilbert) K(eith), 56, 184n65
Christianity, 3, 20–1, 26–7, 30, 56, 77, 139, 158
Christian Year, The (Keble), 33
Church, 3, 10, 12, 19–21, 26–7, 30, 105, 140, 157–8, 160–2, 171
City of Dreadful Night, The (Thomson), 27
Clodd, Edward, 60, 140
Clough, Arthur Hugh, 68
Coleridge, Samuel Taylor, 13, 22, 30, 75
Comte, Auguste, 22–3, 60, 141, 162, 163
Conrad, Joseph (Teodor Josef Konrad Korzeniowski), 100
consciousness (man's evolved), 6, 19, 41–7, 49, 53, 57–68, 70, 73, 85–7, 89–90, 94, 97, 110, 130, 137, 148, 161, 166–7
Creative Evolution, (Bergson), 21–2

Daiches, David, 99
Darwin, Charles Robert, 30–1, 32, 33–4, 36–40, 52–3, 57, 60, 61, 64–7, 94, 97, 100, 102, 110, 141, 168, 175n12
Darwinism, *see* evolution
Das Leben Jesu (Strauss), 30
Dawkins, Richard, 94
de Beauvoir, Simone, 36, 48
de la Mare, Walter (John), 147
Democritus, 22

Index

de Quincey, Thomas, 68
d'Exideuil, Pierre, 64
Dickens, Charles (John Huffham), 7, 102, 104
'Dirge in Woods' (Meredith), 17
Distance and Desire (Miller), 123, 125n7

Ecclesiastical Politie, Of the Laws of (Hooker), 33
Eliot, George (Mary Ann Evans), 23–4, 100, 125
Eliot, T(homas) S(tearns), 4, 5, 32
Empedocles, 31
Epicurus, 22
Essays and Reviews (Jowett), 33
Essence of Christianity, The (Feuerbach), 24, 28n35, 103n10, 168n61
Ethics of Ambiguity, The (de Beauvoir), 36
evolution, 1, 21, 29, 31–44, 47–9, 50–4, 57–9, 64–5, 77, 85, 94, 100, 102, 110, 144, 148
Evolution and Ethics (Huxley), 58
evolutionary meliorism, 57–60, 64–5, 67, 70–3, 77, 89–94, 160; *see also* meliorism

fate, 13, 42, 44–7, 87, 93, 102, 119, 120, 129, 138, 145, 170–1
Faulkner, William Harrison, 123
Feuerbach, Ludwig, 24, 28, 103, 104, 141, 168
Fitzgerald, Edward, 169–70
freewill, 44, 86–7, 89, 92, 138, 143, 145, 171
Freud, Sigmund, 63, 66

Galsworthy, John, 77, 86, 148
Gaskell, (Mrs) Elizabeth (Cleghorn), 6
Giordano, Frank, 129
God, 1, 5, 10, 12–14, 15–28, 29–35, 37–40, 42, 46, 54, 56–7, 59, 67–73, 88, 93, 97, 103, 117, 124–5, 127, 135, 137, 143, 151, 154–5, 164–8, 170–1; *see also* God (synonyms), Nature, Will (Hardy)
God (synonyms): Creative Intelligence, 29; Creator, 52–3, 59; drowsed knitter, 57; Eternal Urger, 39, 88; First Cause, 38, 56–7, 94; Immanent Will, *see* Will (Hardy); Necessity, 39, 87; Prime Mover, 5, 46, 54, 67–8, 166, 171; rapt Determiner, 54; Sleep-Worker, 70, 73; Supreme Mover, 5; Ultimate Cause, 57–8; Will, *see* Will (Hardy)
Goethe, Johann Wolfgang von, 6, 62
Gosse, Sir Edmund William, 5, 29–30
Graves, Robert von Ranke, 147–8, 163
Gregor, Ian, 135, 141, 146
Guerard, Albert J., 47, 100–1

Hardy, Emma Lavinia Gifford, 104–5, 106, 107–9, 115–16, 123–4, 136, 169
Hardy, Florence Emily Dugdale, 124, 152, 153, 169, 182–3n19, 184n65; *see also The Life of Thomas Hardy*
Hardy, Jemima Hand, 9, 108
Hardy, Thomas
  FICTION: *The Dynasts*, 39, 41, 60–2, 64–5, 67, 73–94, 102, 160, 165; *Far from the Madding Crowd*, 104–7, 109; *Jude the Obscure*, 10, 108, 136–42; *A Laodicean*, 3–4, 108, 115; *The Mayor of Casterbridge*, 116–121; *A Pair of Blue Eyes*, 47, 123; *The Return of the Native*, 109–14, 155; *Tess of the D'Urbervilles*, 14, 50, 71, 101–2, 124, 126–36; *The Trumpet Major*, 75, 115; *Two on a Tower*, 115; *Under the Greenwood Tree*, 12; *The Well-Beloved*, 125–6; *Wessex Edition of Novels and Poems* (Preface

Hardy, Thomas – *continued*
  to), 156–7; *The Woodlanders*, 36,
  51–2n45
  POETRY: *Human Shows*, 153, 162:
  'The Graveyard of Dead
  Creeds', 163–4; 'There
  Seemed a Strangeness',
  163n51; 'Waiting Both',
  150n11; 'Why Do I?', 152n16;
  'Xenophanes, the Monist of
  Colophon', 93; *Late Lyrics and
  Earlier*, 151, 153: 'According to
  the Mighty Working', 146n1;
  'Surview', 151–2; *Moments of
  Vision*, 150: 'Afterwards', 54,
  151; 'A Backward Spring', 50;
  'The Blinded Bird', 42–3;
  'Fragment', 57; 'He Fears His
  Good Fortune', 96n1;
  'Heredity', 97–8; 'He Wonders
  About Himself', 87; 'In Time
  of "The Breaking of
  Nations" ', 23; 'The
  Occultation', 3n2; 'The Oxen',
  19–20; *Poems of the Past and
  Present*, 67: 'Agnostoi Theoi',
  67–8; 'The Bullfinches', 36–7;
  'The Darkling Thrush', 49,
  164n53; 'God-Forgotten', 71–3;
  'In Tenebris I', 141n33; 'In
  Tenebris II', 13; 'In Tenebris
  III', 141n34; 'Mute Opinion',
  153; 'The Problem', 24n25;
  'Shelley's Skylark', 149; 'The
  Sick Battle God', 159; 'The
  Sleep-Worker', 70; 'The To-
  Be-Forgotten', 149; *Time's
  Laughingstocks*: 'At Waking',
  71; 'Before Life and After',
  19n11; 'God's Education', 59;
  'He Abjures Love', 115n26;
  'Let Me Enjoy', 53n50; 'New
  Year's Eve', 46; 'Night in the
  Old Home', 170n67; *Satires of
  Circumstance:* 'Before and
  after Summer', 50; 'God's
  Funeral', 5, 24, 26; 'The
  Going', 109n17; 'A Plaint to
  Man', 25; 'Regret Not Me',
  150n12; 'A Singer Asleep',
  149; 'The Year's Awakening',
  50; *Uncollected Poems and
  Fragments* (James Gibson):
  'Epitaph for G.K.Chesterton',
  184n65; 'Epitaph for George
  Moore', 184–5n65; 'Thoughts
  from Sophocles', 77–8; *Wessex
  Poems*, 74: 'Hap', 43–4; 'The
  Impercipient', 20–1; 'Nature's
  Questioning', 34–6, 37;
  'Neutral Tones', 124; 'To
  Outer Nature', 54–5n52; 'A
  Sign-Seeker', 17–19; 'The
  Temporary the All', 33–4;
  Winter Words, 152–4, 169:
  'Christmas: 1924', 160–1;
  'Christmas in the Elgin
  Room', 3n4; 'Dead "Wessex"
  the Dog to the Household',
  149n7; 'He Never Expected
  Much', 148; 'He Resolves to
  Say No More', 152–3; 'A
  Necessitarian's Epitaph', 9n8;
  'A Philosophical Fantasy',
  164–5; 'Proud Songsters',
  50–1; 'Thoughts at Midnight',
  167–8; 'Unkept Good
  Fridays', 27; 'We Are Getting
  to the End', 160n40, 160n41
Hardy, Thomas II (father), 9
Hardy, Thomas Masterman, 74
'Hardy's Major Fiction'
  (Holloway), 8–9
The Hero as Divinity (Carlyle), 2
Holloway, John, 8–9, 116, 117–18
Hooker, Sir Joseph, 39
Hopkins, Gerard Manley, 68
Horace, 32
Howe, Irving, 45, 148
Hume, David, 23–4, 60
Huxley, T(homas) H(enry), 3, 58,
  60
'Hymn of Man' (Swinburne), 17n6,
  26n28, 27n34

In Memoriam (Tennyson), 31–2

James, Henry, 143, 174n1

Index

Job, 165–7
Jowett, Benjamin, 33
Jung, Carl Gustav, 166

Kant, Immanuel, 62, 87
Karl, Frederick, 100
Keble, John, 30, 33
Kermode, Frank, 170
Kingsley, Charles, 6, 8
Krieger, Murray, 141, 142

'Laus Veneris' (Swinburne), 20
Lawrence, D(avid) H(erbert), 48–9, 83, 100, 129–30, 135
Lawrence, T(homas) E(dward), 74, 148, 163–4
Leavis, F(rank) R(aymond), 49
Lewes, George Henry, 22
Life of Thomas Hardy, The (Florence Hardy): Art, 100n5; Church, 21n17, 158n33, 162n48; consciousness (man's), 42n23, 42n24; creeds and theories, 4n7, 95n73; *The Dynasts*, 60n10, 73n32, 77n37, 94n70, 159–60n38; God, 15n1, 21n17, 39n18, 56n1, 56n2, 56n3, 56n4; The Golden Rule, 27n32; history, 92n67; Immanent Will, 60n10, 61n12, 61n13; impressionings, 4n8, 23n20; love, 71n29, 122n1, 123n3; meliorism, 162n47, 164n55; Nature, 29n1; Necessity, 39n19; Newman, 10n23; pain, 144n40; pessimism 156n26, 156n29, 159n37, 159–60n38, 161n43; poetry, 5n10, 169n64
love, 104, 106–7, 112, 120, 122–7, 132–5, 139–40, 144, 154
loving-kindness, 25, 58–9, 90, 92, 94, 124, 136, 144, 152
Lyell, Sir Charles, 29–30, 34

Mann, Thomas, 62–4
Mary Barton (Gaskell), 6
May, Keith, 110
meliorism, 60, 64, 67, 71, 141, 162; *see also* evolutionary meliorism, optimism
Melville, Herman, 2, 7, 155
Meredith, George, 16–17, 40–1, 43, 125
Mill, John Stuart, 3, 6, 24–5, 26, 53, 60, 141
Miller, J(oseph) Hillis, 68–70, 98, 102, 123–5, 130, 134–5, 168
Millgate, Michael, 3–4, 8, 136, 150, 161
Modern Painters III (Ruskin), 33n4
Moore, George, 184–5n65

'National Apostasy' (Keble), 30
Natural Theology (Paley), 37
Nature, 10, 29, 31–55, 57, 65–6, 70, 90, 120, 128, 134–5, 140, 143–4, 154; *see also* God, Will (Hardy)
Nerval, Gerard de, 125
Nevinson, Henry, 147
Newman, John Henry, 10, 30, 33
Nietzsche, Friedrich Wilhelm, 13, 25–6

O'Connor, Frank (Michael Francis O'Donovan), 8
Oliver Twist (Dickens), 7
On Liberty (Mill), 25
optimism, 5, 32, 48–54, 67, 141, 156, 158, 162–8; *see also* meliorism
Orel, Harold, 49, 90, 158–9, 160, 161
Origin of Species, On the (Darwin), 33, 38–9, 52–3, 61, 64
Ovid, 32

Paley, William, 29, 34, 37
Pater, Walter Horatio, 3
Paterson, Helen, 107
Paulin, Tom, 51
pessimism, 45, 99, 119, 150, 154, 155–62, 163
Philosophy of the Unconscious (Von Hartmann), 61–2, 65–7, 85
Pierre (Melville), 155
Pilgrim's Progress (Bunyan), 33
'Pippa Passes' (Browning), 3, 18

Porter, Katherine Anne, 145
Pound, Ezra Weston Loomis, 163
Principles of Geology (Lyell), 29
Problems of Dostoevsky's Poetics (Bakhtin), 11

'Rabbi Ben Ezra' (Browning), 169
religion, 2, 5, 12, 23, 28, 29, 97, 103, 104, 133, 139, 158, 161, 163, 167, 170–1
Richards, I(vor) A(rmstrong), 166–7
Rubáiyát of Omar Khayyám, The (Fitzgerald), 169–70
Ruskin, John, 27, 33

St Augustine, 87
Saleeby, Caleb, 60
Sassoon, Siegfried, 147
Schopenhauer, Arthur, 60–5, 67, 82–3, 84, 89, 141
Scott, Nathan A., 48
Selfish Gene, The (Dawkins), 94n72
Shakespeare, William, 33
Shaw, (George) Bernard, 31
Shelley, Percy Bysshe, 22, 49, 126
Showalter, Elaine, 117
Sidney, Sir Philip, 14
Smith, Adam, 6
Some Recollections (Emma Hardy), 108n16
Sophocles, 84
Spencer, Herbert, 60
Spinoza, Benedict, 22
Stephens, Bertie Norman, 182–3n19
Stevenson, Lionel, 93
Strauss, David Friedrich, 30

Swinburne, Algernon Charles, 3, 16–17, 20, 26–7, 58, 136, 149
Symonds, John Addington, 155

Tchekhov, Anton, 154, 161
Tennyson, Alfred, Lord Tennyson, 2, 31–2, 152
Thackeray, Annie, 107
Thackeray, William Makepeace, 7, 100, 104
Thomson, James, 27
'Tithonus' (Tennyson), 152n17
Trollope, Anthony, 104

Vaihinger, Hans, 13
Van Doren, Carl, 56
Van Ghent, Dorothy, 44–5
Von Hartmann, Eduard, 60–2, 65–7, 70, 85–6, 92, 141

Walkley, A.B., 93
West, Dame Rebecca, 148–9
Will (Hardy), 5, 41, 54, 58–61, 67, 70, 73, 75–6, 78–81, 83–94, 166, 171; *see also* God, Nature
Will (Schopenhauer), 61–5, 82–3, 84, 89
Will (Von Hartmann), 61, 65–7, 70, 85–6
Woolf, Virginia, 119, 123
Wordsworth, William, 33, 49, 128
work, 104, 106–7, 112–13, 119, 120, 122, 123, 131–4, 142, 144
World as Will and Idea, The (Schopenhauer), 61–7, 82–3
Wright, Edward, 60, 61

Zola, Emile, 99, 102, 108